WHITE HOUSE E-MAIL

The Top Secret Computer Messages the Reagan/Bush White House Tried to Destroy

EDITED BY TOM BLANTON

A National Security Archive Documents Reader

THE NEW PRESS   NEW YORK

LIBRARY OF CONGRESS CATALOGING-IN-PUBLICATION DATA

White House E-Mail:
    the top secret computer messages the Reagan-Bush White House
    tried to destroy/edited by Tom Blanton.
        p.   cm.
    "A National Security Archive documents reader."
    Includes bibliographical references.
ISBN 1-56584-276-6 (pbk.)
        1. United States—Politics and government—1981–1989—Sources.
        2. United States—Politics and government—1989–1993—Sources.
        3. Reagan, Ronald. 4. Bush, George, 1924– . 5. Electronic mail systems—
    United States. 6. Presidents—United States—Staff—Archives.
    I. Blanton, Thomas S.
E876.W48 1995
973.927'0922—dc20 95-16167 CIP

Published in the United States by The New Press, New York
Distributed by W. W. Norton & Company, Inc., New York

ESTABLISHED IN 1990 AS A MAJOR ALTERNATIVE TO THE LARGE, COMMERCIAL PUBLISHING HOUSES,
THE NEW PRESS IS THE FIRST FULL-SCALE NONPROFIT AMERICAN BOOK PUBLISHER
OUTSIDE OF THE UNIVERSITY PRESSES.

THE PRESS IS OPERATED EDITORIALLY IN THE PUBLIC INTEREST, RATHER THAN FOR PRIVATE GAIN;
IT IS COMMITTED TO PUBLISHING IN INNOVATIVE WAYS WORKS OF EDUCATIONAL,
CULTURAL, AND COMMUNITY VALUE THAT, DESPITE THEIR INTELLECTUAL MERITS,
MIGHT NOT NORMALLY BE COMMERCIALLY VIABLE.

THE NEW PRESS'S EDITORIAL OFFICES ARE LOCATED AT THE CITY UNIVERSITY OF NEW YORK.

Book design by HALL SMYTH and GORDON WHITESIDE Production management by KIM WAYMER
Printed in the United States of America

95 96 97 98 9 8 7 6 5 4 3 2 1

Other books from the National Security Archive:
THE CUBAN MISSILE CRISIS, 1962 · THE IRAN-CONTRA SCANDAL
SOUTH AFRICA AND THE UNITED STATES

CONTENTS

INTRODUCTION

What exactly is so sensitive about the White House electronic mail that three presidents tried to keep citizens from seeing the contents of this book?

> ✗ Ronald Reagan tried to erase the White House e-mail computer backup tapes during his last week in office, in January 1989.

> ✗ George Bush signed a secret deal with the Archivist of the United States just before midnight on his last day in office, in January 1993 — an attempt to put the White House e-mail under seal and take it with him to Texas.

> ✗ Bill Clinton reversed forty years of legal precedent in March 1994 by defining the National Security Council out of existence as an "agency" of the U.S. government, in an attempt to put the White House e-mail beyond the reach of the Freedom of Information Act.

For the past six years, these three presidents have poured taxpayers' money into a legal battle against public access to the White House e-mail. They claimed, first, that the White House e-mail does not "rise to the level" of regular government documents protected by the federal records laws, and, second, that even if the e-mail were records, you couldn't see them. In other words, presidents could order electronic shredding parties with impunity. If they had had their way, neither this book nor the 5,907 computer tapes and disk drives on which it is based would exist today.

But we caught them, and, by and large, we stopped them. By "we" I mean my own organization, the National Security Archive, its founder and former director, Scott Armstrong, our allies in the historical and library communities, and some superb public interest lawyers. How we won, and what's still at stake in the courts, is outlined in the rest of this introduction.

Up front, however, I want to suggest an answer to the question of exactly what was so sensitive about the White House e-mail. In the several hundred e-mail messages in this book (and the additional several hundred on the computer disk inside the back cover), you will read candid conversations by computer in which no participant ever suspected that any of their words would see the light of day. You will peruse shrewd descriptions of White House staff, high-ranking government officials, domestic lobbyists, foreign allies, and members of Congress, among other targets. Through the e-mail peephole, you will view the substantive and occasionally slimy details of policy-making at the highest levels.

Publication of this e-mail will, no doubt, cause acute embarrassment for some. The authors were not writing for a public audience or even "for the file," the way so many government documents are created. As a result, there's an urgency, an immediacy, and a level of candor very rarely displayed in public records. These e-mail notes speak in common language the way people talk to each other, with few filters and no editing. In fact, there's hardly even any correcting of spelling errors; the White House e-mail system apparently contained no spell-check program. Here you will find a torrent of computerized words more akin to direct speech than any documents other than transcripts of taped conversations.

Obviously, publishing this e-mail raises a significant concern about personal privacy. This book tries to address this concern by focusing on policy instead of prurience, and even where we found gossip, emphasizing the e-mail messages that illuminated daily life at the office instead of officials' personal lives. We believe that effective privacy protections are both necessary for and complementary to sufficient open government processes. As plaintiffs, we did not challenge a single one of the government's privacy claims. In fact, this book even omits a few names the government did release.

Power—and the (mis)use of it—is the real issue in the White House e-mail case. Presidents Reagan, Bush, and Clinton wanted to control the information generated on their internal computer systems precisely because of its candor. Fundamentally, power in the public arena derives from control over the debate, the ability to define the terms and frame the parameters. Yet the White House e-mail reveals stories the powerful would rather not become public—secret deals with foreign dictators and domestic lobbyists, manipulations of the press and public opinion, internal jousting for position and prestige, covert operations and arbitrary censorship, to name but a few.

This is not the full story of how things really work at the highest reaches of U.S. national security decision-making. It is just a part that has never been told before.

HOW WE KNOW ABOUT THE WHITE HOUSE E-MAIL

The White House e-mail system might still be secret today but for the Iran-contra scandal. It's hard to remember the extraordinary dimensions of that crisis, but back in November 1986, the White House staff was running scared. Headlines shouted accusations about secret deals with the Ayatollah, off-the-books covert operations in Central America and the Middle East, lies from all the president's men. After six years of rule, the Republicans had lost the U.S. Senate, and the president's approval rating was in the middle of the steepest one-month decline in the history of public opinion polls. Someone's head would roll; and it was only a matter of days before a bloodbath.

The national security adviser to the president had a pretty good idea his days were numbered. On the particular weekend of November 22-24, 1986, a team of Justice Department lawyers were camped out in one of his subordinate's offices, next door to the White House at the Old Executive Office Building, leafing through the paper trail, trying to cobble together an explanation for the controversial covert operations that would get the president out of trouble while having the added advantage of maybe being true. Just around the corner from the lawyers, the subordinate, National Security Council staffer Oliver North, busily stuffed handfuls of memos and printouts into a shredder; and when the lawyers left for lunch, and again at the end of the day, North went to his computer for some electronic shredding in his e-mail account. Over at the White House, the national security adviser, John Poindexter, did the same.

The White House had started its first e-mail system in 1982, as a prototype that linked electronically various cabinet departments; but a fully operational system—including all the National Security Council staff—began only in April 1985. In 1985 and 1986, e-mail had become North and Poindexter's favorite means of communication, allowing them a back-channel called "Private Blank Check" that avoided the central bureaucracy at the White House. Their colleague, and former national security adviser, Robert "Bud" McFarlane, kept e-mailing from his home terminal even after leaving the White House. By late 1986, the rest of the Executive Office of the President also went operational with e-mail; and by the end of the Reagan presidency in January 1989, more than seven million digital e-mail messages resided in the various White House systems.

As two of the most prolific e-mailers in the entire U.S. government, North and Poindexter had a lot to hide. During that weekend in November 1986, Oliver North punched the *delete* button to eliminate 750 out of 758 electronic mail messages saved in his "user area" of the White House system memory; and he believed that they were gone for good. John Poindexter deleted 5,012 out of 5,062 e-mail messages in his own user area. Poindexter knew that the military personnel in the White House Communications Agency (WHCA) who staffed the computer systems backed up the system memory every night on computer tapes in case of a crash, and took a complete backup "snapshot" of the system every Saturday. But Poindexter also knew that the tapes were recycled after two weeks, overwritten with the newest version of the data on the system. He would blip out his messages, and a few weeks later even the backup versions would be blipped automatically as well.

A handful of career public servants saved what Poindexter and North deleted. On Friday, November 28, 1986, only three days after Poindexter and North departed the White House, Lt. Col. Patrick M. McGovern, the commander of the military unit managing the computer systems, told his staff to set aside the backup tapes made the previous two Saturdays, just in case. With the backup created on Saturday, November 29, McGovern's order meant that three complete sets of the tapes now existed. And a comparison of the November 15 and November 22 versions against the November 29 tapes could show exactly which messages North and Poindexter had deleted.

The investigators soon came calling. An FBI agent later testified that Brenda Reger, the NSC's freedom of information officer, was the first to demonstrate the e-mail system for the outsiders, in early December. By February 1987, FBI agents working for Iran-contra independent counsel Lawrence Walsh were commissioning wholesale dumpings of data from the backup tapes, for long lists of e-mail users. Simultaneously, a young researcher named Kenneth Kreig, who previously worked at the White House and knew about the system, had retrieved a four-foot stack of e-mail printouts for the Tower Commission inquiry into Iran-contra, causing a wholesale last-minute rewrite of the commission's report.

The report of the Tower Commission, released on February 26, 1987, marked the public debut of the White House e-mail system. An instant best-seller, the report printed verbatim hundreds of the deleted North and Poindexter e-mail messages, touting them as "conversations by computer...a first-hand, contemporaneous account of events." Edmund Muskie, a commission member and former secretary of state, called the e-mail "a real mother lode." Brent Scowcroft, also a member of the commission, said the e-mail "proved that Ollie wasn't a loose cannon, but that he communicated extensively with [his superiors] at every step."

In retrospect, the Tower report was the high point of government openness on Iran-contra and the White House e-mail. Critics in and out of the Reagan administration accused the commission of damaging national security by releasing too many secrets. By the time Congress had its special committees up and running with hearings on Iran-contra during the summer of 1987, the White House had cut back investigators' access to the e-mail. In fact, Congress's experts did not get the results of their special search program for the e-mail tapes until the week after the final Congressional report was published, in November 1987.

THE BATTLE TO SAVE THE WHITE HOUSE E-MAIL

In January 1989, a freelance consultant to the National Security Archive named Eddie Becker made a routine, curious inquiry about the records of the outgoing Reagan White House staff. Eddie had worked on the Archive's high-profile Iran-contra project, so he knew about the e-mail system; and as a self-taught computer whiz, he was particularly interested in how the government intended to save the e-mail tapes for the long haul. To Eddie's great surprise, officials at the National Archives & Records Administration (NARA) told him that they did not consider the White House e-mail to qualify as "records" worthy of preservation. They told him that the e-mail related to Iran-contra was all set aside for the ongoing legal cases, but the other e-mail tapes and hard drives from the Reagan White House were scheduled for "disposal" the night before George Bush's inauguration.

The news set off a frenzy in our offices. The Archive's founder and then-director, Scott Armstrong, was a veteran of the Senate Watergate committee staff and the *Washington Post;* the parallels were not hard for any of the rest of us to grasp, either. Here was a potential "gap" consisting not of eighteen-and-a-half minutes, as on the Nixon tapes, but of years, involving millions of messages. We immediately set up a meeting, on Wednesday, January 18, with the responsible official at NARA—John Fawcett of the Office of Presidential Libraries; but Fawcett, while diplomatic, was less than helpful. He demonstrated his own office e-mail for us, compared the messages to telephone message slips, and offered no assurance that he or the White House would even reconsider.

Less than thirty hours were left before the destruction deadline. Standing in the hallway outside Fawcett's office, Scott decided the only recourse left was a lawsuit asking for a temporary restraining order to stop the destruction. Working the phones, we quickly found legal support from our colleagues at the Center for National Security Studies, whose director, Morton Halperin, volunteered CNSS attorney Kate Martin. Eddie Becker and I repaired to Kate's office for what turned out to be an all-nighter, pulling together every piece of information ever published about the White House e-mail system, researching the requirements of the federal records preservation laws, drafting legal papers and affidavits, and, as our ultimate insurance policy, designing a series of Freedom of Information Act requests for the entire corpus of e-mail tapes. Even if a computer-illiterate judge ruled the records laws did not apply to e-mail, even if a stickler-for-legalisms judge ruled we did not have "standing" to sue, surely no judge would countenance the government destroying information a FOIA requester asked for specifically. Eddie delivered the FOIA requests and the legal papers, on his bike, the next morning, Thursday, January 19.

The judge on call that day at U.S. District Court, the late Barrington D. Parker, called the hearing to order at 5:15 P.M. Civil Action No. 89-142, *Scott Armstrong, et al v. Ronald Reagan et al* featured Kate Martin at the plaintiffs' table, and for the defense, to our surprise, the acting attorney general of the United States, John Bolton. Here is the heat of the action:

KATE MARTIN: Your Honor, I think our position is that it's a very simple case. We are only asking that the Court order that there be no destruction pending a judicial determination of whether or not the tapes are covered by the [records] acts. I don't believe the government can show any damage from the entry of such an injunction, and we are here because they have refused to assure us that they were not going to destroy the tapes....

JOHN BOLTON: Your Honor, the outgoing staff members of the White House, who will be leaving tomorrow, are doing what anyone does when they leave one job to go to another. They are taking the pictures off their walls. They are cleaning out their desks and they are eliminating—

THE COURT: They are not seeking a restraining order against taking pictures off the wall.

JOHN BOLTON: I understand that, Your Honor, but what is going on here is not some sinister conspiracy. What is going on here is the normal termination of one staff to give room for the other staff to come in....

THE COURT: That may be true, but what is happening to the material that's the subject of this litigation?

JOHN BOLTON: It is being prepared for deletion.

THE COURT: What?

JOHN BOLTON: It is being prepared for deletion.... When the new people come into the White House at noon tomorrow, they need to have access to the system and they need to be able to do whatever they are going to do with it. And it would impair that ability, that is to say the ability of the new president of the United States, on his first day in office, to get his administration up and running. It would be as if the halls of the White House were filled with furniture from the outgoing administration. It's important for an orderly transition, which is vitally important to the notion as a whole, that we be allowed to go ahead and complete what is nothing more than normal housecleaning...

KATE MARTIN: Briefly, Your Honor... what they can do is dump the information that is now on the computer on an electronic, magnetic tape, which is a procedure that they've been following every night in any event, and that they then preserve that electronic tape that then frees up the computer memory for the new administration....

THE COURT: I think that the plaintiffs have made a threshold showing sufficient cause. The world is not going to cave in if I grant a temporary restraining order. This case is assigned to Judge Richey, and Judge Richey, I'm sure, will do what is consistent with the law and that which is right. I shouldn't say that which is right, but that which is consistent with the law.

Later that night, the government called. Lawyers from the National Security Council and the Justice Department accused us of harassment. They said the court order had effectively frozen the whole system, that the White House staff could not enter a single new keystroke because it might overwrite one protected by the order. Margaret Thatcher was waiting for a reply to her congratulatory message to the new president, but the system was tied up. VIPs were backed up at the White House gates, unable to be cleared in because the e-mail system was down. So as not to be seen as merely obstructionist, we agreed to let them use the system again as long as they backed up everything onto a master set of tapes, and also saved all the existing backup tapes.

For the entire duration of the Bush administration, from January 1989 to January 1993, we traipsed back and forth to U.S. District Court, with a sidetrip to the U.S. Court of Appeals, although the government never came up with an argument for e-mail destruction beyond the one John Bolton so lamely offered to Judge Parker: "It would be as if the halls of the White House were filled with furniture from the outgoing administration." On our side, attorneys Katherine Meyer of Public Citizen Litigation Group, and then Michael Tankersley, also of Public Citizen, took up the cause. On the government's side, the lawyers filled up three, four, five rows of the courtroom at every hearing. The blow-by-blow can be found in the bibliography and acknowledgments at the back of this book and in the chronology on the enclosed disk. Suffice it to say, U.S. District Judge Charles R. Richey was quite familiar with computer backup systems, often invoked his own personal computer experience, and did what was right and consistent with the law. When George Bush lost the 1992 election, Judge Richey granted our motion to include the Bush White House e-mail tapes in the case. And in January 1993, Judge Richey ruled that e-mail had to be treated like all other government records—covered by the laws, appraised by archivists, and preserved for posterity where appropriate.

Apparently, the Bush White House staff panicked at this point. Out of arrogance or disdain, they had made no plans to save the tapes, and they dreaded the idea of the new Clinton staff being able to sift through the system. So on Inauguration Eve January 19, 1993, they staged a midnight ride to round up the computer tapes and put them beyond the law. On White House orders, a task force of NARA employees hurriedly rented vans, raced to the Old Executive Office Building, hand-scribbled makeshift inventories, and worked through the night to load 4,852 computer tapes into cardboard boxes and haul them away. A subsequent memo from this group complained that due to haste and the lack of bubble-wrap, a number of disk drives were simply stacked in boxes with no padding. The whole process violated NARA's own procedures for taking custody of electronic information.

Several weeks later, through discovery, we found out that the midnight ride was a sideshow to the main event: a secret deal between President Bush and the Archivist of the United States, Don W. Wilson. Signed in the last few hours before Bill Clinton's inauguration, the agreement purported to give President Bush control over all the computer tapes, ignoring the Presidential Records Act of 1978, which precludes such a claim. Judge Richey's January 1993 ruling already held that Wilson had abdicated his duties as archivist by approving the original decision to destroy the Reagan White House e-mail. Under fire for the secret deal and for management problems during his tenure at NARA, Wilson then resigned as archivist and accepted a new job as head of the George Bush Presidential Library to be built at Texas A&M University.

The incoming Clinton administration could have opted for openness. Instead, Clinton-appointed officials marched into federal appeals court in the spring of 1993 to support not only the Bush and Reagan arguments for destruction of the e-mail, but also the now-infamous Bush-Wilson agreement. The *Washington Post* paraphrased top Clinton aide George Stephanopoulos as saying, "like Bush's White House, the Clinton White House does not want a succeeding, potentially unfriendly administration pawing over its computer memos." But the appeals court was about as receptive to these claims as Judge Richey had been. In August 1993, a unanimous appeals panel (chaired by future Clinton White House counsel Abner Mikva) ruled that the White House e-mail qualified as records, was covered by the records laws, and had to be preserved. Faced with an unbroken string of resounding legal defeats, the Clinton administration finally gave up the preservation argument and decided not to appeal to the Supreme Court.

WHAT'S LEFT IN THE LAWSUIT
The appeals court decided that the records laws applied to e-mail, but they sent the case back to Judge Richey on the question of "which law?". Most units in the White House came under the Federal Records Act (FRA), meaning that they created "agency" records and were

subject to the Freedom of Information Act as well. Other units (such as the White House counsel's office) came under the Presidential Records Act, not the FRA or FOIA, because they "solely" advised and assisted the president, performing no agency functions.

Ever since its creation in 1947, the National Security Council did both agency and presidential work. That changed, at least rhetorically, in March 1994, when President Clinton reversed the policy of all nine presidents who have chaired the National Security Council and declared that the NSC was not an agency of the federal government under the Freedom of Information Act and other federal records laws but purely presidential in its functions. If this policy had been in place back in 1989, the Reagan White House would have gotten away with destroying the White House e-mail, because presidential decisions on presidential records are not reviewable by the courts.

Readers of the copious NSC e-mail in this book will quickly recognize the expedient nature of this argument. Judge Richey certainly did: In February 1995 he rejected the Clinton arguments as "arbitrary and capricious... contrary to history, past practice and the law." The Clinton administration appealed, and the litigation continues. It might never have been necessary if the National Archives & Records Administration had simply done its job under the law, holding even the White House accountable. Perhaps that's the final lesson of the White House e-mail case: We need a reinvented National Archives, a vigorous information watchdog. Otherwise, NARA will be relegated to the role of the nation's attic; and there, among the cobwebs, will roam the ghost of government accountability.

WHAT WAS SAVED BY THE WHITE HOUSE E-MAIL LAWSUIT

 1,055 computer tapes from the Reagan White House of which 800 were open reel magnetic tapes

4,852 computer tapes from the Bush White House of which 4,409 were cartridge tapes

 135 computer hard drives from the Bush National Security Council staff

THE MAKING OF THIS BOOK

The e-mail in this book is public today for three reasons: (1) to justify destroying the electronic versions of the e-mail, the government claimed it had printed out every important message, so we asked for all these printed copies; (2) the printed copies were such a small fraction of the total e-mail on the backup tapes that we asked for a sampling of the electronic versions, just for the highest-ranking White House national security officials; (3) the Clinton National Security Council staff felt so guilty about declaring themselves not an agency that they created a "voluntary" openness system that declassified almost all of the printed and electronic e-mail messages we requested.

The main problem was *too much* e-mail. White House Communications Agency staff estimated that printing out just the first 163 tapes from the Reagan White House would produce as much as five million pages of e-mail. Our original Freedom of Information requests covered everything on the tapes up through January 1989, because we needed legal standing to fight to preserve everything. Clearly, the government did not have the resources to review each of the millions of messages (almost all of them assumed to be classified) residing on these tapes from the National Security Council computers. So we worked out a compromise.

First, we asked just for e-mail that had been handed over to investigators. In addition to the Tower and Congressional releases, we had learned from depositions that the whole time the government had been arguing that e-mail weren't records, their own officials had been using the tapes looking for evidence in various proceedings. For example, the Justice Department had the e-mail tapes searched as part of their prosecution of the Panamanian strongman, Manuel Noriega. When President Bush nominated Robert Gates to be director of the Central Intelligence Agency in 1991, White House staff searched the e-mail for Gates' Iran-contra connections. And when former Secretary of Defense Caspar Weinberger was indicted on Iran-contra charges in October 1992, his lawyers served a subpoena for e-mail related to his case. Some 2,000 White House e-mail messages, mostly Iran-contra related and much of it almost illegible, have trickled out of the government over the years in this fashion.

But we wanted to go beyond Iran-contra to look at other major national security issues of the 1980s, such as relations with the Soviet Union, the development of the Strategic Defense

Initiative ("Star Wars") responses to terrorist incidents, relations with Saddam Hussein and other world leaders. To do so, we narrowed our Freedom of Information Act request for the electronic versions of the e-mail to a core sample of only 2,500 documents. For a fair sample, we demanded an index, a listing of e-mail messages residing in the user areas of several dozen top White House officials during the period 1982-1989. We asked for the listing in electronic form, but the government refused because of the possibility of "leakage" of classified data. The result was two boxes of printouts totaling 42,000 individual listings of TO and FROM, date and time, and SUBJECT. After scanning the listings into a database, we picked 2,500 that looked most interesting, based on who wrote them, who received them, when they were sent, and what the subject line said (or didn't say).

This book and disk actually contain our selection of the 500 most illustrative, substantive, and interesting of the more than 4,000 e-mail messages we have pried loose from the White House to date. The universe from which we selected these ranged from late 1982, when the system was just a prototype and most NSC staff were not logged on, through April 1985 when the system became fully operational and scores of NSC staffers started cranking out e-mail messages, through January 1989 when the Reagan administration left office.

We do not yet have any of the e-mail from the Bush administration, partly because the FOIA does not apply to presidential records until five years after a president leaves office, that is, January 20, 1998, and the presidential versus agency issue is still in litigation. Similarly, it may be the year 2002 or later before we get any of President Clinton's White House e-mail.

The bulk of the e-mail included here is from 1985 to 1987, for a fairly straightforward reason: On February 26, 1987, the Tower Commission released its report on the Iran-contra scandal, in which nearly a third of the report consisted of references to, or reprints of, e-mail notes exchanged between McFarlane, Poindexter, and North. NSC staff were quick to notice that their e-mail might not be so secure after all, and NSC higher-ups also got on the case. In January 1988, National Security Adviser Colin L. Powell had his executive secretary, Paul Schott Stevens, warn the NSC users of the e-mail system (at the time an IBM product called PROFS, or Professional Office System) as follows:

```
From: NSPSS    -CPUA                    Date and time    01/21/88 15:34:13
To: ALL PROFS USERS

NOTE FROM: Paul S. Stevens
SUBJECT: PROFS Notes

When PROFS was first inistituted at the NSC it was intended as a means of
quick communication among the staff (a substitute for the telephone). PROFS
notes to Colin Powell and John Negroponte have increased of late, both in
volume and in length. To the fullest extent possible, please limit PROFS notes
to two screens; if the message is unavoidably long or complex, a typed memo
put in the system will be preferable except under circumstances where time
truly is of the essence. Your cooperation is appreciated.
```

The drop-off in e-mail candor after the Tower Commission report raises a larger issue, posed most bitterly by former NSC staffer Peter Rodman (in "Memos to Cover Your Trail," the *Washington Post*, 2 July 1993). Rodman despaired that "early disclosure corrupts record keeping." He warned that "fear of premature disclosure only increases the tendency of top officials to hold the most important discussions without note takers. One result is a diminished historical record."

Quick to refute Rodman was former U.S. Navy historian Ronald H. Spector, professor at George Washington University ("Historians Can Handle Data," the *Washington Post*, 16 July 1993). Spector wrote that Rodman's argument "sound[ed] plausible," but just wasn't so. Spector cited his personal experience and the reality that historians deal with daily:

The truth is that with the explosion of communications means over the past three or four decades, officials are leaving a larger and not a smaller documentary trail. We have far better records about Lyndon Johnson's decision for war in Vietnam than we do about William McKinley's decision for war with Spain in 1898. Of course, there are many potential problems with the completeness and veracity of historical records. These problems are not new and did not begin with Iran-contra. There are two solutions to these problems. To have government officials decide what aspects of the past the public should know about, as in Orwell's *1984*, or to open government records to public scrutiny, even with the knowledge that those records may be incomplete or distorted.

Despite the risks of disclosure, the U.S. government is creating vastly more documentation and exponentially more e-mail every day. Instead of the paperless office, computers have made possible the almost infinite duplication and proliferation of paper records. Large bureaucracies require records for the same reason that a whispered comment beginning at one side of a room comes out completely differently on the other side.

Peter Rodman will hate this book, not only because he is in it. But his argument fails precisely because the government has at its disposal an elaborate legal framework to protect the privacy of internal government deliberations. For example, the fifth exemption to the Freedom of Information Act specifically protects pre-decisional deliberative records; and presidential records are not available to the public until five years (for unclassified items) or twelve years (for classified documents) after the president leaves office. The idea is to allow officials to speak their minds without fear of retribution, to encourage candor. Unfortunately, this otherwise valid purpose often serves to inhibit public debate, cover up bureaucratic mistakes, and reduce accountability. Most of the weight of the federal bureaucracy comes down on the nondisclosure side of this balance, so it's entirely fair for this book to place a small weight on the openness side of the scale.

It is true that this book may decrease whatever candor is still exercised on the White House e-mail system. But that is the cost of public scrutiny, of accountability. The CIA now says that it assesses its potential covert actions and other programs by this criteria: Will we be proud of this when (not if) it shows up on the front page of the *New York Times?* That's not such a bad standard for any e-mail user to keep in mind.

HOW TO READ E-MAIL

This book and the accompanying disk contain scanned images of actual White House e-mail messages created during the 1980s and subsequently officially declassified by the U.S. government. Nothing has been altered in the language; no errors or misspellings (of which there are many) have been corrected. For purposes of clarity and legibility in the book, however, the printed version does take three significant shortcuts:

1. The book presents messages from sequences of e-mail in traditional top-to-bottom chronological order, for ease of reading. This separates previously attached messages which, in the originals, are found in reverse chronological order as part of the forwarding process. The final locations of the messages on the mainframe computer memory are cut as are most of the classification codes and declassification notices.
2. The sender, recipient, and date of each e-mail have been highlighted with circles and underscores.
3. The book presents a few of the more lengthy e-mail messages in excerpted form, with missing sections indicated by a thin black box outline in place of ellipses.

Most of the e-mail here was classified in late 1994 and 1995, after the declassifiers acquired a new printer. The e-mail released from 1987-1993, is often barely legible, but the book does include some of those because of their substantive value. The additional 260 e-mail messages on the disk are included in full, as scanned, with their original sequencing plus the associated classification codes and the like. Where the scanner could not pick up a character from an illegible original, the reader will find question marks or an explanation of how much material is illegible. The originals for both the book and the disk are on file and available for public use at the National Security Archive in Washington, D.C.

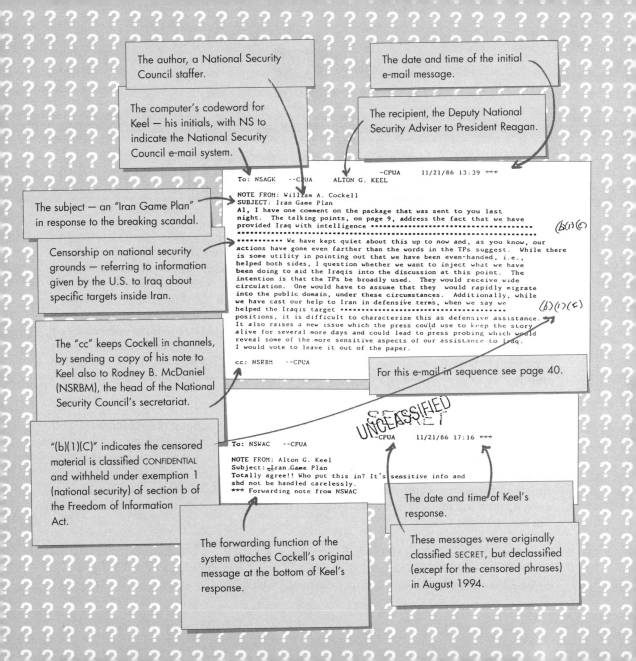

The author, a National Security Council staffer.

The computer's codeword for Keel — his initials, with NS to indicate the National Security Council e-mail system.

The date and time of the initial e-mail message.

The recipient, the Deputy National Security Adviser to President Reagan.

The subject — an "Iran Game Plan" in response to the breaking scandal.

Censorship on national security grounds — referring to information given by the U.S. to Iraq about specific targets inside Iran.

The "cc" keeps Cockell in channels, by sending a copy of his note to Keel also to Rodney B. McDaniel (NSRBM), the head of the National Security Council's secretariat.

"(b)(1)(C)" indicates the censored material is classified CONFIDENTIAL and withheld under exemption 1 (national security) of section b of the Freedom of Information Act.

The forwarding function of the system attaches Cockell's original message at the bottom of Keel's response.

The date and time of Keel's response.

These messages were originally classified SECRET, but declassified (except for the censored phrases) in August 1994.

For this e-mail in sequence see page 40.

```
To: NSAGK    --CPUA      ALTON G. KEEL          -CPUA    11/21/86 13:39 ***

NOTE FROM: William A. Cockell
SUBJECT: Iran Game Plan
Al, I have one comment on the package that was sent to you last
night.  The talking points, on page 9, address the fact that we have
provided Iraq with intelligence ••••••••••••••••••••••••••••••••••     (b)(1)(C)
••••••••••• We have kept quiet about this up to now and, as you know, our
actions have gone even farther than the words in the TPs suggest.  While there
is some utility in pointing out that we have been even-handed, i.e.,
helped both sides, I question whether we want to inject what we have
been doing to aid the Iraqis into the discussion at this point.  The
intention is that the TPs be broadly used.  They would receive wide
circulation.  One would have to assume that they  would rapidly migrate
into the public domain, under these circumstances.  Additionally, while
we have cast our help to Iran in defensive terms, when we say we
helped the Iraqis target ••••••••••••••••••••••••••••••••••••          (b)(1)(C)
positions, it is difficult to characterize this as defensive assistance.
It also raises a new issue which the press could use to keep the story
alive for several more days and could lead to press probing which would
reveal some of the more sensitive aspects of our assistance to Iraq.
I would vote to leave it out of the paper.

cc: NSRBM    --CPUA
```

UNCLASSIFIED

```
To: NSWAC    --CPUA                              -CPUA    11/21/86 17:16 ***

NOTE FROM: Alton G. Keel
Subject: Iran Game Plan
Totally agree!! Who put this in? It's sensitive info and
shd not be handled carelessly.
*** Forwarding note from NSWAC
```

WHO'S WHO

There is no evidence in the multiple file drawers of legal papers, depositions, and declassified documents from the White House e-mail lawsuit that either PRESIDENT RONALD REAGAN or VICE-PRESIDENT GEORGE BUSH ever personally punched out an e-mail message on the White House system during the period from 1982-89 covered by this book. The President and Vice-President may well have seen e-mail, either printed-out in their briefing books, or on-screen over the shoulders of their assistants, but this book cannot render either Reagan or Bush as electronic voices, only as looming presences — central gravitational forces around which almost all the e-mail revolves. Similarly, some important lists of White House user ID's are still censored, so we don't know if chiefs of staff JAMES BAKER (1981-84), DONALD T. REGAN (1985-87), or HOWARD BAKER (1987-89) used their own e-mail accounts, or just had assistants and secretaries do it for them.

Where we do have evidence — gigabytes of evidence — is among the national security officialdom at the White House, so the Who's Who of the White House e-mail begins and ends at the National Security Council. The NSC staff seems to have been the earliest unit in the White House to go digital with a comprehensive e-mail system, driven by the need for secure communication of highly classified information, and the need to keep up with the massive electronic output of the Pentagon, State Department, and intelligence agencies.

One of the earliest White House e-mail we have is a draft cable written by NSC staff for WILLIAM "JUDGE" CLARK (National Security Adviser to President Reagan, 1982-83) to send to Vice-President Bush via a "privacy channel." Clark had served as chief of staff when

Reagan was governor of California, and on the California Supreme Court. His first post under President Reagan was as Deputy Secretary of State, but when Reagan's first National Security Adviser, Richard Allen, resigned under fire for accepting gratuities from Japanese sources, Clark moved to the White House. During Clark's short tenure (he became Secretary of the Interior in 1983), he presided over the beginnings of the NSC's intensive computerization, centralizing the electronic information flow from national security sources in the Crisis Management Center and the Situation Room, and installing the first e-mail system.

Clark's successor, ROBERT C. "BUD" MCFARLANE, became a prolific e-mailer, keeping a terminal at home even after leaving the NSC. The son of a Democratic Congressman from Texas, McFarlane graduated from the U.S. Naval Academy and served 24 years in the Marine Corps, retiring in 1979 as a Lieutenant Colonel. During this time he served as a Military Assistant to Henry Kissinger and Brent Scowcroft on the Nixon and Ford NSC staff. After a stint as a professional staff member on the Senate Committee on Armed Services, he became Counselor at the State Department, before following Clark to the NSC as his deputy. McFarlane served as National Security Adviser from October 1983 to December 1985. In May 1986, he led the infamous secret mission to Tehran. Three months after the Iran-contra scandal broke, in February 1987, he attempted suicide. In 1988, he pleaded guilty to four misdemeanor counts of withholding information from Congress. Most recently, he has written an autobiography entitled SPECIAL TRUST, with Zofia Smardz.

McFarlane's successor, JOHN M. POINDEXTER (1985-86), raised e-mail to an art form, writing and receiving thousands of messages during his NSC tenure. First in his class at the U.S. Naval Academy and a Ph.D. in physics from CalTech, Poindexter rose to the rank of Vice Admiral. He had served as executive assistant to the Chief of Naval Operations, commander of the missile cruiser *USS England* and Destroyer Squadron 31, and as a personal staff member to three Secretaries of the Navy. He joined the NSC in June 1981 as Military Assistant to Richard Allen and stayed on under William Clark. When Robert McFarlane took over in October 1983, he made Poindexter the Deputy National Security Adviser. After turning down command of the U.S. Sixth Fleet to stay at the White House, Poindexter became National Security Adviser to President Reagan on McFarlane's resignation in December 1985. Poindexter resigned as the Iran-contra scandal broke in

November 1986. After leaving government, he was indicted in April 1988, along with Oliver North, Richard Secord, and Albert Hakim on Iran-contra-related charges. In April 1990, he was tried and convicted on six felony counts and then sentenced to a six-month jail term, which he subsequently appealed. Ultimately, prosecutors were forced to drop the charges because of overlaps with testimony given to Congress under grants of immunity.

One of the most experienced insiders in Washington, FRANK C. CARLUCCI, III, succeeded Poindexter as National Security Adviser to President Reagan in the wake of the Iran-contra scandal, in December 1986. A native of Scranton, Pennsylvania, and a Princeton graduate, career Foreign Service Officer Carlucci had served in South Africa, Zaire, Zanzibar, and Brazil prior to stints at the Office of Economic Opportunity, Office of Management and Budget, and the Department of Health, Education and Welfare. In 1975-78, he was U.S. Ambassador to Portugal, then became Deputy Director of CIA under Stansfield Turner in the Carter administration, and in 1981, became Deputy Secretary of Defense under Caspar Weinberger in the Reagan administration. Immediately prior to coming to the White House, Carlucci headed the private-sector firm, Sears World Trade. When Weinberger resigned as the Secretary of Defense in the fall of 1987, Carlucci replaced him at the Pentagon.

Carlucci's deputy, COLIN L. POWELL, then became President Reagan's sixth and last National Security Adviser. A career Army officer (through ROTC, not West Point) and the son of Jamaican immigrants to the South Bronx, Powell had served in Korea and Vietnam, and in the early 1970s was a White House Fellow at OMB under Carlucci. Powell went on to command the 2nd Brigade, 101st Airborne Division and the V Corps, U.S. Army, in Germany. He became familiar with the White House staff while serving as Senior Military Assistant to Secretary of Defense Caspar Weinberger for three years (1983 to 1986). He joined the NSC in early 1987, as Carlucci's deputy. After the Reagan administration, Powell served as Chairman of the Joint Chiefs of Staff under Presidents Bush and Clinton from 1989 to 1993, when he retired from the Army as a four-star General.

The other authors and recipients of e-mail in this book all reported to Clark, McFarlane, Poindexter, Carlucci, and Powell. Biographical information on each of them appears in the Who's Who file on the enclosed disk.

CHAPTER 1

DANCING WITH DICTATORS

The White House electronic mail system arrived in the early 1980s as the intended anti-dote to chronic telephone tag. No longer would piles of telephone slips build into mounds on the desks of senior staffers busy with the latest crisis around the globe. No longer would the return calls from that busy staff generate only more message slips, in an almost endless cycle of unrequited reaching out. Instead, e-mail allowed everyone to read the full text of their messages at their convenience, while sitting at their desks, tapping on their computer terminals, and responding immediately whenever they chose. The system encouraged "conversations by computer," as one presidential blue-ribbon commission described them.

However, these were no ordinary conversations. This was candid chatter at the top of the power pyramid, among the highest-level White House staff charged with managing our country's most sensitive national security affairs. Reading their e-mail puts us virtually at their desks, with a perspective no outsider has ever had before. These are not memos written for the file or to cover a bureaucratic rear; instead, the White House e-mail features seat-of-the-pants judgments and instant responses to world-shaking issues, in tones that are often highly emotional, sometimes vicious, sometimes jocular, but almost always using the colloquial language with which these powerful officials speak to each other in private, but never in public. Never, that is, until this book.

Among these extraordinary computer messages, perhaps the most explosive are those dealing with "friendly" foreign dictators. Franklin Delano Roosevelt is said to have observed about the Nicaraguan dictator Anastasio Somoza: "He's an S.O.B., but he's our S.O.B."

Taking care of "our S.O.B.s," particularly the ones fleeing popular democratic uprisings or those who are one jump in front of the law, generated a lot of e-mail on the White House system in the 1980s—e-mail the White House staff never expected to see the light of day.

Leading this chapter are the inside e-mail details on the secret support the Reagan-Bush White House lent to two dictators, Manuel Antonio Noriega of Panama and Saddam Hussein of Iraq, against whom the Bush administration would later go to war and spill American blood (not to mention Panamanian and Iraqi). In Noriega's case, the e-mail notes let us into the secret debate within the highest levels of the U.S. government after media revelations of Noriega's murdering, thieving, and drug-running ways; only to be followed by a quid pro quo deal consummated between Noriega and Oliver North—to fix up Noriega's image in return for his help in waging war in Nicaragua. In Saddam's case, the e-mail notes detail the high-level debate about the U.S. "tilt" toward Iraq to prevent an Iranian victory in the 1980–88 war between those countries, followed by extensive intelligence sharing, which helps explain why Saddam did not expect the forceful U.S. response to his subsequent invasion of Kuwait.

Somewhat more levity is found in the e-mail messages around the departure from the Philippines in February 1986 of Ferdinand Marcos, who earned the nickname "the Flying Dutchman" because no country would take him. Likewise, U.S. efforts to relocate Haitian dictator Jean Claude "Baby Doc" Duvalier make for fascinating reading, especially regarding the various real-estate deals proposed to finance his retirement in France (where he remains today).

The finale takes place closer to home, as an object lesson in how powerful people can corrupt the criminal justice system to their own ends. Through the intervention of White House staff—with every jot and tittle laid out in the e-mail—a Honduran general, José Bueso Rosa, does his time at "Club Fed," a minimum security prison, even though he was convicted on felony charges of conspiracy to assassinate the president of Honduras and pay for the hit with profits from a major cocaine shipment. Otherwise, the NSC staff fear the Honduran will "spill the beans" about their covert operations in Central America; so, from President Reagan down to action officer Oliver North, they just say "yes."

On June 12, 1986, the front page of the *New York Times* announced the findings by investigative reporter Seymour Hersh that Panamanian dictator (and longtime U.S. intelligence asset) Manuel Antonio Noriega had participated in drug deals and gunrunning, as well as the murders of his political opponents. The next day, NSC Latin America staffer Raymond Burghardt reports to his boss John Poindexter what happened in the secret interagency discussion of Hersh's story, including the recommendation from the U.S. ambassador to Panama that the United States publicly deny the charges. Chaired by the assistant secretary of state for inter-American affairs, Elliott Abrams, the group decides not to avoid working with Noriega, but to avoid "the image of working with Noriega." The deleted section was apparently taken out at the behest of the CIA, since it gives details of the basis of the CIA's planned presentation to Congress on its intelligence about Noriega.

Page 1 of 1
/86 19:23

```
FROM: NSRBM  --CPUA    TO: NSDRF  --CPUA         06/13/86 19:23:21
To: NSJMP  --CPUA    JOHN M. POINDEXTER NSDRF  --CPUA    DONALD FORTIER
NOTE FROM: ROD B. MCDANIEL
Subject: Panama
*** Forwarding note from NSRFB  --CPUA    06/13/86 18:05 ***
To: NSRBM  --CPUA    JOHN M. POINDEXTER NSWRP  --CPUA    JOHN M. POINDEXTER
NOTE FROM: Raymond Burghardt
SUBJECT: Panama
Elliott chaired an interagency meeting this afternoon to discuss Panama: our
press line, what we say in congressional hearings, and where our policy
stands. Like most meetings on Panama, this discussion only reinforced our
sense of policy dilemmas. The system there is thoroughly rotten, it works
against our interests; but we have a major stake there and it is very
difficult to effect political change. One item for discussion was Ambassador
Davis' recommendation that we publicly deny Hersh's charges against Noriega;
the foreign minister has threatened that otherwise our relationship (intel.
cooperation etc.) will be affected. The meeting decided: That we cannot say
there is no evidence to support Hersh's charges; that would be untrue and
defense of Noriega would undermine our Central American policy. That at
congressional hearings next week (beginning on Monday with House Narcotics
Committee) CIA will give a factual presentation, ........................
...................................................................
...................................................................
.................... State will draw up a list of very specific
items which we will insist require action (e.g. names of companies we want
shut down). Davis, Galvin ...... will make staged approaches to Noriega,
Delvalle and other actors there to make clear that things are on the wrong
track and their action is needed to prevent worse problems. The approach has
to avoid the image of "working with" Noriega. CIA and Defense will take a
careful look at the PDF to identify some leadership alternatives (e.g. ......
.................. if Noriega and Diaz Herrera (Noriega's Cuban-aligned
deputy and rival) are removed, what are the alternatives. Finally, when Abrams
is summoned for hearings, he will seek to educate Congress on the complexity
of the situation; yes, itsrotten, but we cannot solve the Panamanians' problem
and any precipitate action could make things worse.
cc nsepd
```

WHITE HOUSE E-MAIL

This sets the stage for an extraordinary exchange between the NSC and Noriega. After the *New York Times* story, other press coverage of Noriega's criminal activities sprouts like mushrooms after rain. Noriega needs public relations help, so who does he call?—the White House. On August 23, 1986, Oliver North writes his boss, Adm. John Poindexter: "You will recall that over the years Manuel Noriega in Panama and I have developed a fairly good relationship." North describes an overture from Noriega: "In exchange for a promise from us to 'help clean up his (Noriega's) image' and a commitment to lift our ban on FMS [Foreign Military Sales] to the Panamanian Defense [Force, he would] undertake to 'take care of' the Sandinista leadership for us."

```
TO: NSJMP    ,  --CPUA

*** Reply to note of 05/08/86 10:54
NOTE FROM: OLIVER NORTH
Subject: Iran
```

```
       NICARAGUA:You will recall that over the years Manuel Noriega in Pana
a and I have developed a fairly good relationship. It was Noriega who had
old me that Panama wd be willing to accept Barcos - a plan that got fouled up
y a bungled approach to DelValle. Last night Noriega called and asked if I wd
eet w/ a man he trusts - a respected Cuban American - the president of a
ollege in Florida. He flew in this morning and he outlined Noriega's
roposal: In exchange for a promise from us to "help clean up his (Noriega's)
mage" and a commitment to lift our ban on FMS sales to the Panamanian Defense
```

```
                     ...d undertake to "take care of" the Sandinista leadership for
us. I told the messenger that such actions were forbidden by our law and he
countered that Noriega had numerous assets in place in Nicaragua that could
accomplish many things that wd be essential and that after all, Noriega had
helped us w/ the operation last year that resulted in the EPS arsenal
explosion and fire in Managua and that w/o many more of these kinds of
actions, a contra victory was out of the question. I thanked the emissary for
his message and told him that we wd get back to him. The emissary told me
that I should go directly to Noriega if there were any msgs back, that his
instructions were limited to delivering the msy to me. I have checked w/ our
████ friends who ran the Managua Op and they now inform me (but had not at the
time) that they did indeed use a Panamanian civilian ordnance expert as the
means of access to the storgage facility. Interesting. My sense is that this
is a potentially very useful avenue, but one which wd have to be very
carefully handled. A meeting w/ Noriega could not be held on his turf - the
potential for recording the meeting is too great (you will recall that he was
head of intelligence for the PDF before becoming CG). My last mtg w/ Noriega
was in June on a boat on the Potomac. Noriega travels frequently to Europe this
time of year and a meeting could be arranged to coincide w/ one of my
other trips. My sense is that this offer is sincere, that Noriega does indeed
have the capabilities proffered and that the cost could be borne by Project
Democracy (the figure of $1M was mentioned) if other PD activities do indeed
proceed as planned. If, as in the past, Noriega refuses to deal w/ the CIA, we
might have available a very effective, very secure means of doing some of the
things which must be done if the Nicaragua project is going to succeed. The
way it is being approached now, these kind of internal actions will not
materialize until late next year - far too late to be effective when they are
eeded now. The proposal seems sound to me and I believe we could make the
ppropriate arrangements w/ reasonable OPSEC and deniability. Beg advise.
```

Poindexter facing Reagan in the Situation Room, NSC meeting 4-16-86
(Shultz, Meese, Casey on left, Weinberger, Crowe and Bush's hands on right)

Here are translations of some of the terms in the message: EPS (Ejercito Popular Sandinista) is the Sandinista Army; PDF is Panamanian Defense Force; CG is commanding general; Project Democracy (PD) is North's name for his off-the-books covert enterprise in partnership with retired general Richard Secord; and OPSEC refers to operational security, that is, both keeping Noriega from taping the meeting and keeping Congress and the American public from knowing about the meeting or the quid pro quo.

Poindexter responds less than two hours later (17:45 on August 23). He likes the idea of working a deal with Noriega: On "helping him to clean up his act," Poindexter says, "we should be willing to do that for nearly nothing." Poindexter demurs (as North did) on encouraging

Noriega to assassinate the Sandinista leadership, but "[m]ore sabotage would be another story." He endorses North's plan to meet with Noriega, saying, "I have nothing against him other than his illegal activities."!

Date: 11/22/86   User: NSJMP
NSJMP   --CPUA   NSOLN
Iran

FROM: NSJMP   --CPUA
To: NSOLN   --CPUA   TO: NSOLN   --CPUA   08/23/86 17:45:02

*** Reply to note of 08/23/86 15:52   UNCLASSIFIED
                                         -- SECRET --
NOTE FROM: JOHN POINDEXTER

On Noreiga -- I wonder what he means about helping him to clean up his act? If he is really serious about that, we should be willing to do that for nearly nothing. If on the other hand, he just wants to get us indebted to him, so that he can blackmail us to lay off, then I am not interested. If he really has assets inside, it could be very helpful, but we can not (repeat not) be involved in any conspiracy on assination. More sabotage would be another story. I have nothing against him other than his illegal activities. It would be useful for you to talk to him directly to find out exactly what he has in mind with regards to cleaning up his act.

WHITE HOUSE E-MAIL

North proceeds to set up the meeting with Noriega, in London, on September 22, 1986. In this September 20 e-mail, North says he has checked off the overture with Elliott Abrams, who in turn has cleared it with Secretary of State George Shultz, "who thinks we ought to proceed." Then, early on September 22, Poindexter greenlights North's trip to London—three months after the *New York Times* story exposing Noriega's criminality. While the e-mail trail apparently ends here, we know the details of the London meeting from North's notebooks (pried out of the government by a National Security Archive and Public Citizen Freedom of Information lawsuit). In fact, Noriega and North worked out arrangements for training and logistics support for the contras, as well as targeting Nicaraguan ports, an oil refinery, and other installations for sabotage. The North-Noriega plan came to naught, however, when three weeks later a Nicaraguan soldier shot down Eugene Hasenfus's plane, exposing North's contra-support network ("Project Democracy") and precipitating the Iran-contra scandal.

```
FROM: NSOLN    --CPUA     TO: NSJMP   --CPUA              09/20/86 12:04:15
To: NSJMP    --CPUA

*** Reply to note of 09/17/86 14:35
NOTE FROM: OLIVER NORTH

                                                              Noriega wants to
meet me in London on Tues. morning. Elliott and I have talked it over and he
has talked to Shultz who thinks we ought to proceed. UNODIR, will depart for
London on the 1845 flight Monday, Arrive London 0630 Tues. Dep London at 1345
Tues and be back here 1730 Tues. This shd serve to minimize time
lost/visibility and preserve OPSEC. V/R, North
```

```
MSG FROM: NSJMP    --CPUA     TO: NSOLN    --CPUA              09/22/86 08:37:02
To: NSOLN    --CPUA

*** Reply to note of 09/20/86 12:04    --UNCLASSIFIED
NOTE FROM: JOHN POINDEXTER

Ok on trip to London.
```

In the e-mail concerning Noriega, Oliver North mentions Panama's willingness earlier in 1986 to provide refuge for Filipino dictator Ferdinand Marcos, who fled Manila on February 25 after his military commanders defected to the People Power movement, led by opposition leader Corazon Aquino. The NSC staff, including North and Raymond Burghardt, worked hard to find Marcos a home, while providing running commentary on the melodrama. In this March 15, 1986, e-mail note, NSC Asia staffer Richard Childress nicknames Marcos "the Flying Dutchman" and notes Noriega's offer of assistance. To get to Poindexter, the note from Childress goes through the National Security Council Secretariat, headed by Rod McDaniel (RBM) and managed by Bob Pearson (WRP).

```
Date: 11/22/86 User: NSJMP      NoteLog: MAR186    Sequence: 185    Page 1 of 1
NSWRP    --CPUA      NSJMP    --CPUA                           03/15/86 15:05
Flying Dutchman and Panama   --  CONFIDENTIAL

FROM: NSWRP    --CPUA      TO: NSJMP    --CPUA              03/15/86 15:05:43
To: NSJMP    --CPUA      JOHN M. POINDEXTER

NOTE FROM: BOB PEARSON                        UNCLASSIFIED
Subject: Flying Dutchman and Panama  -- CONFIDENTIAL
From Childress.
```

```
                                            03/15/86 13:30 ***
To: NSRBM    --CPUA      JOHN M. POINDEXTER NSWRP    --CPUA      JOHN M. POINDEXTER
NOTE FROM: M. KAY LAPLANTE
SUBJECT: Flying Dutchman and Panama  -- CONFIDENTIAL    UNCLASSIFIED
NOTE FROM DICK CHILDRESS:

Although Ray and Ollie clearly do not want the flying Dutchman
in Panama, they do not believe it will cause the instability
predicted.  Noriega, in their view, will control the demonstrations
as he wishes.

Told State to prepare appropriate messages to Tokyo and Taiwan
even though it looks bleak.  Also told them if travel documents
are a problem on Monday, they should get the Secretary to press
Meese.

We will get the Spanish reaction this weekend, then focus on Panama
option and possible travel.
```

John Monjo called from Customs to report the 5:00 p.m. deadline was not met as they are still going through the documents. They had not been numbered and each had to be looked at to be sure no personal documents are turned over. He has indicated most do not appear sensitive. There is one listing political campaign contribution in the US, but it is also bipartisan.

They hope to finish the task overnight.

Childress 11-1-85

Two days later, Childress tells his colleagues about the U.S. Customs search of Marcos's luggage after his arrival in Honolulu, including mention of Marcos's political contributions in the United States. NSC Executive Secretary Rod McDaniel tags on the details of the Marcos contributions: "Reagan, Carter, [California Democratic Sen. Alan] Cranston, [San Francisco mayor and gubernatorial candidate Diane] Feinstein—could make a splash, but seems to balance out."

03/17/86 19:21:23
To: NSJMP   --CPUA   JOHN M. POINDEXTER NSDRF   --CPUA   DONALD FORTIER
NOTE FROM: ROD B. MCDANIEL
Subject: Marcos Documents (SECRET)
Childress sez the campaign contributions include: Reagan, Carter, Cranston,Fein
stein--could make a splash, but seems to balance out.
*** Forwarding note from NSRTC   --CPUA   03/17/86 19:09 ***
To: NSRBM   --CPUA   JOHN M. POINDEXTER NSWRP   --CPUA   JOHN M. POINDEXTER
NOTE FROM: RICHARD T. CHILDRESS
SUBJECT: Marcos Documents (SECRET)

To: NSJMP   --CPUA   03/18/86 09:32:07

*** Reply to note of 08/31/85 13:26

NOTE FROM: OLIVER NORTH   UNCLASSIFIED
Subject: PRIVATE BLANK CHECK
I just received a call from Panamanian President De Valle's chef de Cabinet
(an old acquaintance) who said that the Pres. had asked him to relay the
following: "We do not trustBurghardt, he is just a State Dept. flunkie in a
new suit of
  clothes. Please tell me if this is something that President Reagan wants or
is this something concocted at the State Dept. If it is what President Reagan
wants, we will do it though it will complicate things for us in the days
ahead."

I replied that Ray was in Panama at the specific direction of the President
and that the President had complete trust in him. We recognize that this is a
difficult matter for the Panamanian government and that RR wd be very grateful
ifthey could accept the visitor with the gracious hospitality for which Panama
is so well known. I urged that they listen carefully to Ray's message and to
be assured that this was indeed coming from the President himself and that RR
was personally grateful.

He replied that if this was the case further meetings would be unnecessary --
more unkind comments about Ray's parent company and assured that it would be
done and asked that this news be relayed to RR.

Despite the assurances, I wd urge that we wait to hear fm Ray, since the
Panamanian political is, if nothing else, dynamic. Warm Regards, North

North & McFarlane 12-16-85

But the Noriega offer to help
Marcos was not all smooth sailing,
according to Oliver North's e-mail
of March 18. Interesting is the
Panamanian slam of NSC staffer
Raymond Burghardt, a former
State Department official.

WHITE HOUSE E-MAIL

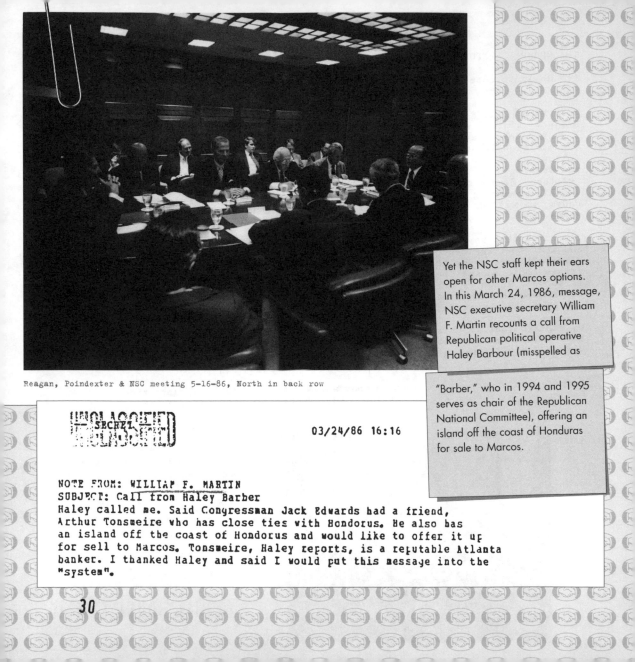

Reagan, Poindexter & NSC meeting 5-16-86, North in back row

Yet the NSC staff kept their ears open for other Marcos options. In this March 24, 1986, message, NSC executive secretary William F. Martin recounts a call from Republican political operative Haley Barbour (misspelled as "Barber," who in 1994 and 1995 serves as chair of the Republican National Committee), offering an island off the coast of Honduras for sale to Marcos.

03/24/86 16:16

NOTE FROM: WILLIAM F. MARTIN
SUBJECT: Call from Haley Barber
Haley called me. Said Congressman Jack Edwards had a friend,
Arthur Tonsmeire who has close ties with Hondorus. He also has
an island off the coast of Hondorus and would like to offer it up
for sell to Marcos. Tonsmeire, Haley reports, is a reputable Atlanta
banker. I thanked Haley and said I would put this message into the
"system".

Richard Childress weighed in on Marcos again in September 1986, with the good news that Marcos would "reimburse" the United States for his moving expenses. However, he "asked us to wait awhile in apparent reference to his non-liquid position."

09/05/86 15:10 ***
JOHN M. POINDEXTER NSWRP   --CPUA   JOHN M. POINDEXTER

NOTE FROM: RICHARD T. CHILDRESS
SUBJECT: Marcos Expenses (SECRET UNCLASSIFIED

President Marcos has agreed to reimburse the USG for the extraordinary expenses we computed were over and above the norm. He seemed relieved that the amount was reasonable. He asked us to wait awhile in apparent reference to his non-liquid position.

Meanwhile, State has received another letter from Congress asking what has been done to recover the expenses incurred. I told State to wait until after the Aquino visit to reply.

cc: NSJAK   --CPUA

One of the most revealing NSC e-mail messages on U.S. dealings with dictators went from National Security Adviser Poindexter to his top deputy, Don Fortier, in the midst of Marco's travels, on March 13, 1986. Poindexter wants Fortier to caution the State Department's Elliott Abrams against getting "carried away on Chile"—that is, fostering against the right-wing Chilean dictator Gen. Augusto Pinochet the kind of pressure that, for example, allowed People Power to triumph in the Philippines. Poindexter cites Henry Kissinger (HAK) as his authority and expresses confidence that NSC East Asian staffer Gaston Sigur will keep South Korea from getting "out of our control."

To: NSDRF   --CPUA   DON FORTIER   03/13/86 10:57:16

NOTE FROM: JOHN POINDEXTER   UNCLASS
SUBJECT: CHILE
IN ONE OF YOUR DISCUSSIONS WITH ELLIOT CAUTION HIM ON MAKING SURE HIS PEOPLE
DO NOT GET CARRIED AWAY ON CHILE AFTER WATCHING HOW WE HANDLED THE
PHILIPPINES. WE NEED TO HEED HAK'S CAUTION THAT STATE DEPT BUREAUCRATS DON'T
PLUNGE US INTO SITUATIONS THAT GET OUT OF OUR CONTROL. SAME HOLD TRUE FOR
SOUTH KOREA, BUT I THINK GASTON WILL WATCH THAT VERY CAREFULLY.

WHITE HOUSE E-MAIL

A similar "Flying Dutchman" extravaganza revolved around Haitian dictator Jean Claude "Baby Doc" Duvalier, who, like Marcos, flew the friendly skies of the U.S. Air Force on his way to exile in France on February 7,

1986. This March 11, 1986, e-mail note from Don Fortier to Poindexter says the Seychelles (an island republic in the Indian Ocean) is willing to take Duvalier for $2 million. Undersecretary of State Michael

Armacost and U.S. ambassador to France Joseph Rodgers are also on the case. Poindexter vetoes having the CIA pay the $2 million and suggests hitting up the French.

NOTE FROM: DONALD R. FORTIER  03/11/86 11:25 ***
SUBJECT: DUVALIER

ARMACOST CALLED. SAID SEYCHELLES WAS PREPARED TO TAKE DUVALIER. THE PRICE THOUGH IS TWO MILLION DOLLARS. FRENCH WANT TO GET HIM OUT AND SHARE THE BILL WITH US. THEY HAVE AGREED TO ATTACH HIS ASSETS IN FRANCE (E.G. PRESUMABLY A SEVEN MILLION DOLLAR CHATEAU) TO BE ABLE TO ENSURE THAT BOTH WE AND THEY ARE REIMBURSED. ROGERS URGES THAT WE GO ALONG WITH THIS. APPARENTLY, HE FEELS SO STRONGLY ABOUT IT THAT HE WAS PREPARED TO WRITE A PERSONAL CHECK TO SEAL THE DEAL. MIKE IS ANXIOUS TO HAVE GUIDANCE. THE EARLIER PROPOSAL HE PUT TO ME WAS THAT WE SIMPLY TAKE IT OUT OF CONTINGENCY RESERVE. I SAID I FELT WE OUGHT TO PRESS THE FRENCH ON GETTING REIMBURSED. THIS THEY HAVE NOW DOWN. I DIDN'T COMMIT YOU TO A POSITION, THOUGH. I WILL BE OUT OF THE BUILDING FOR AN HOUR. SUGGEST YOU HAVE TY PASS GUIDANCE BACK TO STATE IF YOU GET TO THIS BEFORE I GET BACK. THANKS.

DUVALIER

FROM: NSJMP   --CPUA   TO: NSPBT   --CPUA   03/11/86 11:34:46
To: NSTC   --CPUA   TY COBB

NOTE FROM: JOHN POINDEXTER
Subject: DUVALIER
THIS SOUNDS FINE TO ME, BUT I DON'T WANT TO TAKE THE MONEY OUT OF CIA. STATE SHOULD FIGURE OUT A WAY TO FUND AND GET REIMBURSED FROM THE FRENCH.

To: NSJMP   --CPUA

*** Reply to note of 03/11/86 11:34
NOTE FROM: Tyrus Cobb
Subject: DUVALIER

03/11/86 11:52 ***

Agree. Joe Rodgers just called. He had been trying to reach you. I passed your
guidance to him. I believe he still leans to securing the funds from CIA, but
I told him you explicitly ruled that out. Joe does indicate that the French
will work firmly with us to get reimbursement--they have their eye, for
example, on a lucrative chateau just outside of Paris that Duvalier owns. I
recommend that we have Armacost tell the French we agree to split the $2
million and get the funding from State. If it leaks we should describe the
funding as a necessary expenditure to ensure Duvalier's security, and that we
are seeking reimbursement. Then, we immediately move with the French to "bill"
Duvalier directly, or with the GOF to seize property.

Joe is right, however, that we must move immediately to take advantage of the
Seychelles option. If you agree with the above, I will contact Armacost's office
and Joe Rogers.

Later that day, NSC staffer Tyrus Cobb relates Ambassador Rodgers's news that the French "have their eye...on a lucrative chateau just outside of Paris that Duvalier owns."

Poindexter tells the NSC secretariat a few hours later that he has talked to George Shultz and says that "I don't understand why they can't attact [sic, attach] the chateau, keep 2 [$2 million] and give D [Duvalier] 5."

To: NSWRP   --CPUA

03/11/86 19:45:39

*** Reply to note of 03/11/86 14:13

NOTE FROM: JOHN POINDEXTER
Subject: DUVALIER
I TALKED TO GEORGE TODAY. I THINK WE HAVE TO HAVE A FIRM COMMITTMENT FROM THE
FRENCH ON REIMBURSEMENT. I GUESS I DON'T UNDERSTAND WHY THEY CAN'T ATTACT THE
CHATEAU, KEEP 2 AND GIVE D 5.

WHITE HOUSE E-MAIL

To: NSJMP   --CPUA

03/12/86 11:51:21

*** Reply to note of 03/11/86 19:45
NOTE FROM: Tyrus Cobb
Subject: DUVALIER

I just spoke with Armacost's office. Shultz talked with Dumas last night, as
you know, and categorically told him that we would not agree to put money up
front on this (He thereby agreed with you the we should not seek it from the
CIA, but also felt that the AID budget would not permit this
expenditure--hence, no available funding). As you know George pressed Dumas to
simply attach Duvalier's property. Dumas said the GCF could not do that;
however, the Quai told Rodgers that this was incorrect. ••••••••••••••••••
•• Shultz is a bit
miffed with the Ambassador--feels that he has gotten too far out front on this
(and other issues).

Strategy now is for State to work this with French, holding tough for the most
part and getting them to simply put the money up front and attach assets.
Duvalier may resist going to the Seychelles, but I would say that his
bargaining position is not the strongest at present.

Shultz, Keel, Reagan 11-19-86

The next day, Tyrus Cobb reports that
Secretary of State Shultz had spoken
with French foreign minister Roland
Dumas about Duvalier's chateau and the
reimbursement problem, and that Dumas
said the GOF [Government of France]
could not attach the chateau while the
Quai [d'Orsay] (the location of the
French Foreign Ministry) told the U.S.
ambassador otherwise.

To: NSTC   --CPUA

*** Reply to note of 03/12/86 11:51   UNCLASSIFIED

NOTE FROM: JOHN POINDEXTER
Subject: DUVALIER
DUMAS TOLD SHULTZ THAT THEY COULD NOT ATTACH DUVALIER'S ASSETS IN FRANCE. I
THINK A TOUGH LINE WITH THE FRENCH IS APPROPRIATE. SHULTZ ALSO TOLD RODGERS TO
CALM DOWN.

Five hours later, on March 12,
Poindexter's response is to
recommend "a tough line with
the French."

The finale of the Duvalier e-mail series
explains some of the tensions around the
role of the U.S. ambassador to France,
Joseph Rodgers. NSC staffer Tyrus Cobb
sings Rodgers's praises to Cobb's new
post-Iran-contra boss, Frank C. Carlucci,
the national security adviser. According
to Cobb, Rodgers is "[a] born-again
Christian, long-time Republican fund-
raiser and self-made millionaire, [and]
is in many respects the embodiment of the
President's personal philosophy."

02/10/87 13:22:08

[Doc 6]   SECRET   1-14-94

NOTE FROM: Tyrus Cobb
SUBJECT: Carlucci Memo

MEMORANDUM FOR: FCC

FROM: TWC

SUBJECT: Your lunch with Joe Rodgers

Partially Declassified/[...]
under [...]
by N. Menan, [...]

You hve invited Ambassador Joe Rodgers to have lunch with you Thursday,
February 12, to review issues in the Franco-American relationship and to
discuss his thoughts on the direction this Presidency should go in the next
two years. I don't know if you have met Joe--he is basically one of the finest
human beings on earth and an excellent representative of this Administration.
A born-again Christian, long-time Republican fund-raiser and self-made
millionaire, Joe is in many respects the embodiment of the President's
personal philosophy. Although he is not an experienced diplomat or linguist,
Joe has developed excellent ties with the French political establishment.

WHITE HOUSE E-MAIL

Tucked away between the lines in this heavily censored e-mail are some of the deep roots of the Persian Gulf War. Even though Iraq had been the aggressor and invaded Iran in September 1980, the United States began tilting in favor of Saddam Hussein against Iran during the 1980s. The American calculation was that revolutionary Iranian fundamentalism was a greater danger to American interests than was the bloody and repressive dictatorship of Saddam. The Reagan administration restored diplomatic recognition to Iraq (suspended in the 1970s because of Iraq's support for terrorists), and began encouraging allies to supply Saddam, and even secretly started sharing U.S. intelligence with the Iraqis. That's the subject of this February 24, 1986, e-mail message. NSC intelligence staffer Ken DeGraffenreid describes a still-classified item in that morning's Situation Room summary of U.S. intelligence that was shared with Iraq, but goes on to speculate that "the Iraqis either did not believe it or were unable or unwilling to act." The information may have been on Iranian military positions or an advance warning of a particular Iranian move in the war.

Later in 1986, on September 30, NSC Middle East staffer Howard Teicher asks for a copy of a State Department paper on U.S. intelligence sharing, mentioning battle management as one of the goals. At this point, the United States is actually helping Saddam Hussein run his battles with Iran, which involves giving him, for example, tactical intelligence, information on how the Iranian troops are lining up or preparing to advance, and the locations of Iranian supply lines.

Teicher & Poindexter 12-4-86

Given this kind of U.S. complicity in the war with Iran, one begins to see how Saddam might have thought in 1990 that he could get away with an invasion of Kuwait.
("Jim" probably refers to James Stark.)

To: NSWAC   --CPUA   09/30/86 08:41 ***

NOTE FROM: Howard Teicher
SUBJECT: gulf war
jim advises me that he gave a copy of a state paper on possible
u.s. assistance to the iraqis in the intelligence/battle management
area. i would appreciate getting a copy of this and discussing it
before you send anything forward to jmp. for what it's worth, i
have been working on this lousy war since the day iraq invaded
iran and would like to stay in the loop.

To: NSHRT   --CPUA
                                             09/30/86 20:59:55

NOTE FROM: Alton G. Keel
Subject: gulf war
What I want to know is whywe don't have a peace accord yet!
Howard, you're losing your influence!

WHITE HOUSE E-MAIL

Probably in reference to the same State Department paper, National Security Adviser Poindexter writes Oliver North that he needs "a thoughtful piece that lays out a rational scheme fro [sic] providing intel to both sides"—that is, both the Iranians with whom North was engaged in trading arms for hostages, and the Iraqis with whom the United States was engaged in battle management.

To: NSOLN   --CPUA

*** Reply to note of 10/02/86 17:04

-USECRET JON ILI   10/02/86 20:44:42

NOTE FROM: JOHN POINDEXTER
Subject: Iran
I talked to Casey tonight. This may be a problem. I need a thoughtful piece
that lays out a rational scheme fro providing intel to both sides. The Iraquis
are asking for the same sort of thing -- location of economic targets behind
the lines. I wonder if the Iranians are thinking of targetting with Scuds?

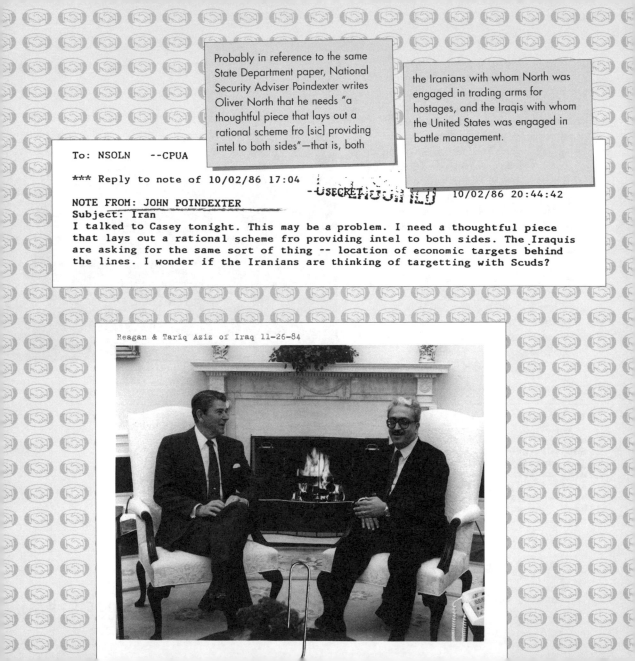

Reagan & Tariq Aziz of Iraq 11-26-84

On October 3, NSC Middle East staffer Dennis Ross writes Poindexter asking for a review of the consequences of the United States providing intelligence to the Iraqis on Iranian infrastructure targets. Presumably, the Iraqis would then go after these targets with bombs or missiles, which would be a dramatic escalation even from the battle management role already assumed by the United States. Ross says then-CIA director William Casey "clearly views this as non-controversial," while the White House staff is worried about possible Iranian or terrorist retaliation against American targets. This e-mail shows exactly how biased U.S. policy was in favor of Saddam and helps explain why high officials like Casey could rationalize the arms-for-hostages deals with Iran as sort of a balancing of the scales.

```
                                      10/03/86 10:44 ***
To: NSRBM   --CPUA    JOHN M. POINDEXTER NSWRP   --CPUA    JOHN M. POINDEXTER
FROM: Dennis Ross
SUBJECT: Expanding Intelligence Provided to Iraq
     Ken tells me that he feels that Casey may not have left your meeting
last night with a clear understanding of your position on providing Iraq
intelligence on strategic economic infrastructure targets in Iran--
specifically, on electrical power plants and kerosenemanufacturing
plants.  Casey clearly views this as non-controversial and in another
category from the other proposals ••••••••••••••••••••••••••••••••
     While it may not represent as much of a tilt toward the Iraqis,
it does need to be thought through as Iraqi attacks on these targets could
trigger Iranian retaliation--and not only against Iraq.  The recommendation
made in the memo to you on this subject is that we have some high-level
review of the consequences of taking the step Casey is proposing and
we not simply go ahead and adopt it.  You might want to be sure that you
and Casey are on the same wavelength.
```

WHITE HOUSE E-MAIL

On November 21, 1986, NSC staffer William Cockell warns Alton G. Keel, Poindexter's deputy, that a draft set of talking points (TPs) might "reveal some of the more sensitive aspects of our assistance to Iraq." For example, Cockell mentions that

U.S. intelligence helped the Iraqis set targets in Iran, and that "it is difficult to characterize this as defensive assistance." Keel responds the same evening: "Totally agree!! Who put this in? It's sensitive info and shd [sic] not be handled carelessly."

```
                                        11/21/86 13:39 ***

To: NSAGK    --CPUA      ALTON G. KEEL

NOTE FROM: William A  Cockell
SUBJECT: Iran Game Plan
Al, I have one comment on the package that was sent to you last
night.  The talking points, on page 9, address the fact that we have
provided Iraq with intelligence ••••••••••••••••••••••••••••••••••••••
•••••••••••••••••••••••••••••••••••••••••••••••••••••••••••••••••••••••
•••••••••• We have kept quiet about this up to now and, as you know, our
actions have gone even farther than the words in the TPs suggest.  While there
is some utility in pointing out that we have been even-handed, i.e.,
helped both sides, I question whether we want to inject what we have
been doing to aid the Iraqis into the discussion at this point.  The
intention is that the TPs be broadly used.  They would receive wide
circulation.  One would have to assume that they  would rapidly migrate
into the public domain, under these circumstances.  Additionally, while
we have cast our help to Iran in defensive terms, when we say we
helped the Iraqis target ••••••••••••••••••••••••••••••••••••••••
positions, it is difficult to characterize this as defensive assistance.
It also raises a new issue which the press could use to keep the story
alive for several more days and could lead to press probing which would
reveal some of the more sensitive aspects of our assistance to Iraq.
I would vote to leave it out of the paper.
```

```
To: NSWAC    --CPUA                    11/21/86 17:16 ***

NOTE FROM  Alton G. Keel
Subject: Iran Game Plan
Totally agree!! Who put this in? It's sensitive info and
shd not be handled carelessly.
```

On January 20, 1987, Frank C. Carlucci, the new national security adviser, tells the NSC secretariat that he has asked Secretary of State George Shultz to convene a Senior Interagency Group (SIG) meeting on the Iran-Iraq war, in light of the possibility that a key Iraqi city, Basra, might fall to the Iranians. As if intelligence sharing were not enough, Carlucci mentions that "CWW [Caspar Weinberger] would favor some overt tilt toward Iraq. GS [George Shultz] is more cautious."

Carlucci, Reagan, Weinberger 1-21-87

```
FROM: NSFCC    --CPUA      TO: NSWRP    --CPUA            01/20/87 13:21:31
To: NSWRP    --CPUA

*** Reply to note of 01/20/87 12:25
NOTE FROM: Frank C. Carlucci
Subject: Response on Waite and Status of Iran-Iraq War
I ASKED GEORGE S. TO CONVENE A MEETING OF THE SIG TO DISCUSS THE MESSAGE FROM
***** AND TO DO SOME CONTINGENCY PLANNING SHOULD BASRA FALL. HE AGREED. CWW WOU
LD FAVOR SOME OVERT TILT TOWARD IRAQ. GS IS MORE CAUTIOUS.
```

The Reagan administration's most celebrated war of the 1980s was the War on Drugs. But in the shady world of covert operations, according to the White House e-mail, sometimes the White House just said "yes," even to convicted drug traffickers. While the Noriega case has received the most media coverage, the largely unknown prosecution of an obscure Honduran general probably illustrates White House manipulation of the justice system in a far more pernicious manner.

From 1981 to 1984, Honduran general José Bueso Rosa served as a key asset in CIA activities in Honduras supporting the contra rebels against Nicaragua. Then, Bueso Rosa went over the edge, joining a 1984 coup conspiracy to assassinate the newly elected president of Honduras, Roberto Suazo Córdova. The conspiracy itself was to be financed by smuggling 760 pounds of cocaine, valued at $10 million, into the United States. After Bueso is caught and pleads guilty in mid-1986, on the assumption that his friends in high places will spring him, the just-retired general formerly in charge of the U.S. Southern Command, Paul Gorman, calls National Security Adviser John Poindexter to clear the way for a very important phone call, according to this Poindexter e-mail from September 17, 1986. The new Honduran president, Jose Azcona, is going to contact President Reagan directly about clemency for Bueso, and Poindexter orders one of his staff, Raymond Burghardt, to "work the issue" of getting Bueso off before he is sentenced.

Reagan & Azcona of Honduras 10-21-87

09/17/86 08:15:44

To: NSRFB   --CPUA   RAY BURGHARDT

UNCLASSIFIED
SECRET

NOTE FROM: JOHN POINDEXTER
SUBJECT: President Azcona
Paul Gorman called this morning and said that Azcona would be calling the President to ask for clemency in the case of the ex-chief of staff that we are trying here in the US. Please prepare a telephone memo for the President in case the call comes through. Paul recommends that the President grant clemency. Paul also says there is a 7 April letter from Azcona to the President on this subject. In the call I expect the President should just say that he will look into it and try to be helpful. Then we need to work the issue.

Oliver North supplants Ray Burghardt and takes charge of gathering representatives of the Pentagon, CIA, State and Justice departments to "cabal quietly" on how "to keep Bueso Rosa from feeling like he was lied to in legal process and start spilling the beans" [these last five words were censored from previous versions of this e-mail message released to the Congress] on his involvement in the CIA covert operations in Honduras on behalf of the Nicaraguan contras. To convey a sense of the importance

To: NSJMP   --CPUA

*** Reply to note of 09/17/86 08:15
NOTE FROM: OLIVER NORTH   **UNCLASSIFIED**
Subject: President Azcona
A Presidential call memo has been prepared, and after much wrangling w/ Ray, I
have concurred. The problem w/ the Bueso case is that Bueso was the man with
whom Negroponte, Gorman, Clarridge and I worked out arrangements ▓▓▓▓▓▓   1.3 (a)(4)

▓▓▓   5 A

▓▓▓▓▓▓▓▓▓▓▓▓▓▓▓▓▓▓▓▓▓ Only Gorman, Clarridge and I
were fully aware of all that Bueso was doing on our behalf. Subsequent to the
Alvarez ouster, Bueso was assigned as MilAttache in Chile and at one point
last year was invited to meet w/ a group of disgruntled Hondurans who it turns
out were plotting the assasination of Pres. Suazo. When the FBI broke the case
Bueso was indicted for conspiracy. His legal advice was apparently to keep his
mouth shut and everything wd be worked out. Although subpeonas were prepared
for Gorman, Clarridge, Negroponte and North, they were never issued because
Bueso pleaded guilty (on advice of counsel). Several months ago Azcona wrote
to the President, and was never answered. He now is going to call the
President to ask if Bueso can be pardoned. Bueso is due to report to Tallahase
Fla to start serving sentence on Sep 25. He apparently still believed up until
yesterday that he wd be going to the minimum security facility at Eglin for a
short period (days or weeks) and then walk free. Bueso's wife has implored
Azcona to do something and he now wants an answer to his letter. I do not know
who has action on the letter, but we (USG) should have answered same some time
ago. Our major concern - Gorman, North, Clarridge - is that when Bueso finds
out what is really happening to him, he will break his longstanding silence
about the Nic Resistance and other sensitive operations. Gorman, Clarridge,
Revell, Trott and Abrams will cabal quietly in the morning to look at options:
pardon, clemency, deportation, reduced sentence. Objective is to keep Bueso
from feeling like he was lied to in legal process and start spilling the
beans. Will advise.

attached to the case, North tells
Poindexter in this September 17, 1986,
e-mail that Bueso's trial would have
subpoenaed Gen. Paul Gorman,
Dewey Clarridge (former head of the
CIA's anti-Nicaragua covert operations
in Central America), U.S. ambassador
to Honduras John Negroponte, as well
as North himself. The "cabal"—
including the FBI's Oliver Revell and
Associate Attorney General Steven
Trott, in addition to the usual suspects,
Dewey Clarridge and Elliott Abrams—
weighs the options of a presidential
pardon, clemency, deportation, and
a reduced sentence.

WHITE HOUSE E-MAIL

```
To: NSOLN    --CPUA                              09/18/86  17:02:32

*** Reply to note of 09/17/86 19:28    UNCLASS~~SECRET~~

NOTE FROM: JOHN POINDEXTER
Subject: President Azcona
You may advise all concerned that the President will want to be as helpful as
possible to settle this matter.
```

In this September 18 e-mail, Poindexter alerts North and the others in the "cabal" that President Reagan wants to be "helpful" in settling the Bueso Rosa case. The implication is that the call from Azcona went through, and that Reagan was sympathetic.

An hour later, according to this September 18 e-mail, North alerts Ray Burghardt that most options on leniency for Bueso Rosa carry too much "political risk," but that "at the right time the right people" will quietly approach the judge and ask for a reduced sentence and deportation to Honduras. North notes that the leader of the conspiracy, American citizen and arms dealer Gerald Latchinian, received a thirty-year prison sentence. North casually notes that the Justice Department "will see to it" that

Shultz, Reagan, Weinberger, Elliott Abrams behind Shultz 5-13-87

To: NSRFB   --CPUA

NOTE FROM: OLIVER NORTH
SUBJECT: Bueso Rosa

According to what I have been able to put together, our best option appears to be to have Justice go back in to the U.S. Attorney and the Judge after the other defendants have been tried, convicted and sentenced and quietly discuss a petitiion from the Defense attorney that the sentence be further reduced and that he be remanded to custodial probation for the remainder of his sentence to a responsible authority in Honduras. He wd then be deported back to Honduras. None of this can take place until after the remaining trial has been held (the other four have been tried, convicted and sentenced w/ the American, Lechinian, receiving 30yrs). In the interim, Justice/FBI will see to it that Norm Carlson changes the venue of sentence from Tallahassee to Eglin (as the judge had originally recommended) and delay his surrender date for serving sentence until after the 25th of September. While there are other options (parole, pardon, clemency) they all have varying degrees of political risk attached in that the first wd require briefing the entire parole comission and the latter two wd involve the President in the matter. Justice has said that they will be back to us by the end of next week with definitive recommendations based on the remaining trial and discussions with the U.S. Attorney. This shd also be useful as input to the Azcona letter - though it might be best to have JMP, Meese, or even Elliott answer the April letter, rather than the President. Bottom line, the talking points appear to be about right. We just need to make sure that at the right time the right people go to talk to the Judge and U.S. Attorney. Gorman has volunteered to fill this role - and that may be just about right since he's no longer in the government.

Norm Carlson, the federal judge in the case, moves Bueso to the minimum security facility at Eglin Air Force Base, known in the federal prison system as "Club Fed." In other versions of this e-mail, declassified during the National Security Archive's lawsuit, this entire sentence about changing the venue is censored, presumably to disguise the manipulation of the criminal justice system.

Regan, Reagan, Poindexter 3-27-86

WHITE HOUSE E-MAIL

An hour later, North reports to Poindexter a summary of the deal put together by the White House to prevent Bueso from "singing songs nobody wants to hear." Again, in other versions of this e-mail, the sentence referring to the Justice Department is blacked out.

09/18/86 19:40:49

To: NSJMF /--CPUL

*** Reply to note of 09/18/86 17:02
NOTE FROM: OLIVER NORTH
Subject: President Azcona
Done. Good mtg this morning w/ all concerned, including Gorman who flew up
from Charlottesville. Bottom line: Justice will immediately change the venue
of confinement from Tallahassee to Eglin and delay Bueso's surrender date
until after the 25th of September. Four of the others involved in the
conspiracy have already been convicted and as soon as the last is tried,
convicted and sentenced, Justice, FBI and others as necessary will have the
defense atty. request that the judge review the sentence, and in camera have
Gorman, et al explain to the judge our equities in this matter. Revell/Trott
both believe that this will result in approval of the petition for
probationary release and deportation to Honduras. Discretely briefing Bueso
and his attorney on this whole process shd ameliorate concerns (both with us
and Azcona) that Bueso will start singing songs nobody wants to hear. Justice
is justifiably upset that none of this info was made available to them prior
to indictment or before/during the trial, but there is much blame to go around
on that score. Clarridge was totally unaware that CIA had responded to a
Justice query on the case with the terse comment that they "had no interest in
the case." Elliott was also somewhat chagrined to learn that some at State had
been urging rigorous prosecution and sentencing.Bottom line: all now seems
headed in the right direction.

Reagan & Poindexter in the Situation Room 11-12-86

In the end, as this September 20, 1986, e-mail describes, the White House efforts pay off: A drug smuggling conspirator in a plot to assassinate a foreign head of state receives a sentence of five years (with time off for good behavior) in a country club prison facility used for white-collar criminals. At no time in his short incarceration does Bueso Rosa "spill" the secrets of state that so concerned the Reagan White House. Bueso Rosa is now retired and living in the United States.

09/20/86 12:10:55

To: NSWRP   --CPUA

*** Reply to note of 09/20/86 11:43
NOTE FROM: OLIVER NORTH
Subject: Bueso Rosa
Bueso Rosa was convicted of conspiracy under RICO - which wd normally have gotten him 25-30 years. He was also convicted of conspiracy to do harm/assault a friendly head of State under the new C/T law - with a sentence up to life. He was "awarded" two concurrent 5 yr terms. The judge is on our side. I don't think we need to do anything right now, will keep you posted.

CHAPTER 2

WHITE HOUSE MESS

The conversational quality of the White House e-mail comes through in hundreds of items that have the candor of personal phone calls. Some people gossiped; others exchanged ethnic slurs. Practical and impractical jokes abound, often with imperfectly shared ideas of humor. The White House staff used e-mail to arrange office parties, to assign wine-buying tasks or tennis partners, and to threaten softball vengeance, among other social events. Via e-mail, they checked in with their colleagues on weddings, births, hospital stays, and funerals; they chatted with their support staff; they ordered flowers to be sent and documents to be read; they communicated electronically in what are recognizably distinct individual voices.

E-mail also provided an internal management tool, where those who hired and fired could query their staffs about personnel and performance. New job candidates, office assignments, support staff assignments, courier routes, and missing packages (especially when classified) all generated e-mail messages. Included in this chapter are some classics of the self-promotion genre, as well as more modest lobbying, if not for aggrandizement, then at least a clearer signal of future plans. Sometimes the pressure came from outside, and the e-mail often reflects highly mixed views of distinguished National Security Council alumni like Henry Kissinger and Zbigniew Brzezinski.

With most of the items in this chapter, at least one or two associated e-mail notes have come out or the context is clear from contemporaneous documents. But other messages remain a mystery. Bits and pieces more of the White House e-mail record will come out over the next few years, but it will be decades before the whole is publicly available.

This December 12, 1985, e-mail from NSC Latin America staffer Jackie Tillman shows that NSC counsel had to make fine judgments in areas other than international law and oversight of covert operations.

```
FROM: NSJT    --CPUA    TO: NSPBT   --CPUA              12/11/85 16:51:37
To: NSPBT    --CPUA

NOTE FROM: Jackie Tillman
SUBJECT: BOOZEY LEGAL ADVICE
A strange thing just happened to me.  I got a call from
Rm. 45 that I had a present to pick up.  So natch I ran
right down and it was a nicely wrapped bottle of booze.
An envelope with my name on it, when opened, revealed a
blank cark--not very revealing.  Don't know who it is
from.  I seem to recall that there are rules governing
this sort of thing; but I don't recall the specifics.
Question:  Can I e booze (it turns out to be
Bacardi Rum--Gold Reserve, yummy!)?  Can I keep it
anyway since I don't know who it is from and can therefore
made unimparied decisions about policy without the rum
unduly coloring my judgement?  I'll give you a drink if
you say yes......
```

U.S. Navy captain James R. Stark ordinarily tended the NSC's business related to subjects like terrorism and Libya (which involved freedom of navigation, or FON, challenges). In this December 5, 1985, e-mail to Oliver North (NSOLN), however, "Remember Pearl Harbor" seems to be Stark's motto, in his racially derogatory reference to a Japanese embassy staffer. "Ray" is Raymond Burghardt, a former State Department officer.

```
TO: NSOLN    --CPUA                                    12/05/85 11:39 ***

NOTE FROM: JAMES B. STARK
SUBJECT: Nip in the air
One of my Japanese visitors asked who on the NSC staff
worked on Central America.  I mentioned Ray's name, and
then yours when he asked who handled the military side.
Since he does Centam issues for the embassy, he asked if
he could see you sometime.  He asked if
though I suspect he will--they are very persistent.
    1  Nip in the air
```

North indulged in the same slur against Japan at a time when the Japanese were doing him and the Reagan administration a very large favor. On November 20, 1986, as the Iran-contra scandal was breaking, the Japanese foreign minister was visiting Tehran and at the behest of the U.S. government passed on reassurances to the Iranians in an attempt to keep open the lines of communication. In this e-mail message, North tells his aide, Coast Guard commander Craig P. Coy (NSCPC), that he's grateful to the "nippers."

```
*** reply to note of 11/19/86 15:57
NOTE FROM: OLIVER NORTH                              11/20/86 13:03:
Subject: Japan/Iran
We ought to tell the nippers that we really are grateful, that if it wd help
them, we are prepared to say so publicly, and how wd they like it?
       Japan/Iran
```

Then there were the practical jokes; in this case, one joke led by Paul B. Thompson, Poindexter's in-house lawyer. Thompson had started as a military assistant for the National Security Council staff (he held the rank of Navy commander) and worked his way up to the job of in-house legal counsel. This series of e-mail messages apparently began with a phony "eyes only" (meaning only the recipient is to see it) letter from National Security Adviser John Poindexter to Steven Steiner, a State Department foreign service officer detailed to the NSC. The letter announced that Steiner was under investigation for some alleged misdeed, which was not detailed in the flurry of e-mail that followed. We don't have the first e-mail in this sequence—on February 3, 1986 (at 17:25), from Steiner to Paul Thompson—but we do have Thompson's response (at 20:24) questioning whether Steiner would even be at the NSC in the morning. Thompson then cc.'s his note to Steiner with another note (at 20:27) to his co-conspirators, whose initials reveal them to be Mary Dix (NSMAD), William H. Wright (NSWHW), and Robert E. Linhard (NSREL). Steiner is meant to see this note as well.

```
*** Forwarding note from NSPBT    --CPUA     02/03/86 20:24 ***
To: NSSES    --CPUA

*** Reply to note of 02/03/86 17:25

NOTE FROM: PAUL THOMPSON
Subject: Investigation
Will you be here in the morning?  I assumed you would be in an
admin leave status til this thing gets cleared up
```

```
FROM: NSPBT    --CPUA     TO: NSMAD    --CPUA          02/03/86 20:2
To: NSMAD    --CPUA               NSREL    --CPUA
    NSWHW    --CPUA

NOTE FROM: PAUL THOMPSON                        WHITE HOUSE E-MAIL
Subject: Investigation
Is there some reason why we have foreign service officers on this staff?
```

Meanwhile, Steiner is appealing to his erstwhile friends and coworkers, including Linhard and Wright, who are in on the joke. First, at 17:47 Linhard rejects Steiner's overture of 17:35, saying, "What have you done for me lately?" Then at 17:52, Steiner posts his response "with friends like [these] . . . "

The next day, February 4, one of the friends, William Wright, forwards on the call-and-response to Mary Dix, who in turn sends the batch to Paul Thompson. The topmost e-mail message forwarded, from Thompson to Poindexter, reveals that the national security adviser himself is also in on the joke.

```
FROM: NSPBT    --CPUA     TO: NSJMP    --CPUA           02/04/86 11:12:47
To: NSJMP   --CPUA     JOHN M. POINDEXTER

*** Reply to note of 02/03/86 17:35
NOTE FROM: ROBERT E. LINHARD
Subject: Investigation
YOU GOT YOURSELF INTO THIS ONE.  GET YOURSELF OUT!  DO YOU THINK THAT I CARE
ABOUT YOU AS A PERSON?  WHAT HAVE YOU DONE FOR ME LATELY?
```

```
   NOTE FROM: Steven Steiner
   Subject: Investigation
   with friends like this, . . . . . .
                           Classification:   UNCLASSIFIED
   *** Forwarding note from NSREL   --CPUA     02/03/86 17:47 ***
   To: NSSES   --CPUA
```

```
NOTE FROM: WILLIAM H. WRIGHT
Subject: Investigation
*** Forwarding note from NSSES   --CPUA     02/03/86 17:52 ***
To: NSJEM   --CPUA                      NSHGS   --CPUA
                     Classification:   UNCLASSIFIED
```

```
   NOTE FROM: Mary Dix
   Subject: Investigation
   *** Forwarding note from NSWHW   --CPUA     02/04/86 08:15 ***
   To: NSMAD   --CPUA
```

```
NOTE FROM: PAUL THOMPSON
Subject: Investigation
glad we have time for humor around here.
*** Forwarding note from NSMAD   --CPUA     02/04/86 10:12 ***
To: NSPBT   --CPUA
```

- Later on February 4, one of the conspirators, Mary Dix, threatens to blow the whistle by sending Thompson, Linhard, and Wright a copy of a note she "could" send to Steiner. "[S]uch childish antics on the part of our professional staff...," she writes. Thompson replies to Dix within two hours and they both get a chuckle out of the references to the staff shrink.

Reagan & Thompson on Air Force One 5-3-87

```
FROM: NSMAD    --CPUA      TO: N
To: NSPBT    --CPUA
     NSREL    --CPUA
                                    NSPBT    --CPUA           02/04/86 18:17:04
                                    NSWHW    --CPUA
NOTE FROM: Mary Dix
SUBJECT: Your Invesitgation
Dear Steve, the large individual who plotted the entire plan and who is
leaving town tonight wanted me to inform you that he instigated and devised
the entire plan to wreck havoc in your well-ordered life. Yes, it is true; the
letter was in fact, signed by John M. Poindexter....and the signing of that
letter implicates Paul Thompson. It grieves me deeply to see such childish
antics on the part of our professional staff....to include Bill Wright
misusing poor Art Pridemore to hand delivèr the letter. I am shocked by
it all.

    How do you guys like this one?    I could send it????????????
```

```
FROM: NSPBT    --CPUA      TO: NSMAD    --CPUA          02/04/86 20:38:53
To: NSMAD    --CPUA

*** Reply to note of 02/04/86 18:17

NOTE FROM: PAUL THOMPSON
Subject: Your Invesitgation
i think we probably we should have gone with hiring that staff shrink
i wanted to get last year.
```

But the next day, February 5, the truth comes out. Thompson gets an e-mail note from Brenda Reger, manager of the NSC's Freedom of Information Act requests and other records, who reveals that legislative affairs director Ronald Sable had secretly let Steiner in on the joke. To save face, Steiner claims to have figured it out all along. No one else would have known about an "eyes only" message from Poindexter (JP) to Steiner, so having anyone ask about its delivery signals that maybe the message is a phony.

```
FROM: NSBSR    --CPUA    TO: NSPBT    --CPUA              02/05/86 10:26:10
To: NSPBT    --CPUA                        NSMAD    --CPUA
```

NOTE FROM: BRENDA REGER
SUBJECT: investigation

I am a covert source on this but didn't want you to get broadsided-- Sable
called Steiner this morning saying he had "overheard" a joke was been played
on him and wanted to be sure Steiner wasn't taking it seriously. Note he made
no mention of HIS involvement!!! Anyway Steiner told him when Art delivered
the letter he said he had eyes only from JP but then added that Wright had
wanted to be sure it was delivered ASAP so Steiner says he knew it was joke
all the time! Moral of this lesson---when involved in covert activities, the
choice of messenger is as important as the message!I recommend Sable be target
ted for your next effort in this area!

Oliver North was one of the most distinctive voices on the White House e-mail during the 1980s. This energetic Marine officer on detail to the NSC took on assignments to manage the contra war in Central America, deceive Congress, coordinate the government's responses to terrorist incidents, and trade arms for hostages with Iran; but he still found time for fun. In this December 5, 1985, message, Naval Academy graduate North grandiloquently informs fellow NSC staffer and West Point graduate Tyrus Cobb that the tables have been turned in a rather fishy practical joke coinciding with the Army-Navy football game.

Oliver North 12-16-85

MSG FROM: NSOLN   --CPUA   TO: NSTC   --CPUA   12/05/85 23:13:46
To: NSTC   --CPUA

*** Reply to note of 12/05/85 15:35

--UNCLASSIFIED

NOTE FROM: OLIVER NORTH
Subject: Beat Army present
Dear Col Cobb and Lance Corporal Ringdahl,

It has come to the attention of the management that certain aquatic items
were recently misplaced by you or others currently or formerly affiliated with
an institution of ill repute located on the banks of the Hudson River, downwind
of Bayonne, NJ. Our shipping office has had these misplaced aquatic items
returned to sender(s). Unfortunately, in that it is difficult to get good help
these days, the shipping agent now reports that it too has misplaced the
packages. We are certain, however, that your olefactory sensor systems,
primitive though they may be, will be able to locate the subject items in the
relatively near future. We are advised by knowledgeable consultants that when
exposed to normal atmospheric conditions these items will be readily detectable
by the normal primate. We would advise that under these circumstances, you
may wish to vacate the immediate premises and summon a fumigator who,
for a nominal fee, will provide a strong deodorant. We are further apprised
by our experts, that in a matter of twenty to thirty days the "odour" will
have passed and your spaces will again be fit for habitation. In lieu of
completelyvacating the area, you may choose to purchase one of our M-5A2
Chemical/biological warfare masks. These can be obtained by writing:
Commandant, U.S. Naval Academy
Annapolis, MD

                                    Regards,

                                    Oliver North
                                    USMC, USNA 68   WHITE HOUSE E-MAIL

Then there are the mystery notes. We don't have the preceding e-mail notes from February 5, 1987, on the subjects of "two people" or "READ MY LIPS," so why did a (male) senior NSC staffer write these two responses to a junior (female) NSC administrator? Or, for that matter, what kind of answer did he receive? Given the subject matter, we've left out the indentities of both pen pals to protect their privacy.

```
*** Reply to note of 02/05/87 17:07
NOTE FROM:                              02/05/87 17:46:20
Subject: two people
you slut!
```

```
*** Reply to note of 02/12/87 12:54                02/12/87 14:06:26
NOTE FROM
Subject: READ MY LIPS
which lips are these?
```

Another mystery note went from Oliver North to Jackie Tillman on November 14, 1986. He "lost the slip"? "Will return the wig on Monday"? We may never know.

But North's note a few minutes earlier to David G. Major is no longer a mystery. In fact, we now have Major's note to North describing an on-going prosecution of alleged arms dealers in a New York case involving Israelis and Iran. Major was the NSC's staffer for counterintelligence matters. North's response is characteristic bravado, but the New York dealers were claiming White House clearance, and after the Iran-contra scandal broke, prosecutors had to drop the case.

MSG FROM: NSOLN ---CPUA   TC: NSJT   --CPUA   11/14/86 18:34:34
To: NSJT   --CPUA

*** Reply to note of 11/06/86 09:18
NOTE FROM: OLIVER NORTH
Subject: YOUR PAL THE AYATOLLA
Oh Lord. I lost the slip and broke one of the high heels. Forgive please. Will
return the wig on Monday.
     YOUR PAL THE AYATOLLA
                                                                        B

To: NSDGM   --CPUA

*** Reply to note of 11/10/86 12:34
NOTE FROM: OLIVER NORTH
Subject: ARMS SALES TO IRAN
Hang the guilty bastards. They weren't working for me.
     ARMS SALES TO IRAN
                                                                        R

Another mystery note at least provides some of the context. On October 2, 1986, North writes to Ronald Sable, the NSC's legislative affairs director, about a phone call from Congressman Dick Cheney (future secretary of defense in the Bush administration) related to contra aid. Even with this context, that doesn't mean we can understand it.

                                                            10/02/86 15:14:10
To: NSRKS   --CPUA

*** Reply to note of 10/02/86 14:50
NOTE FROM: OLIVER NORTH
FILE: NOTE   OFSLCGE1 DO   WHITE HOUSE COMMUNICATIONS AGENCY

Subject: CONTRA AID/CHENEY CALL
He did. That doesn't mean I understood it. But then there is more and more
each day that I don't understand. I think I have Alzheimer's disease. Or do I?
 I don't know -- I forget. What did you say?

WHITE HOUSE E-MAIL

This June 1986 exchange between administrative officer Mary Dix and counsel Paul Thompson provides a sampling of the flavor of NSC management. "Some of the children," as Dix calls the NSC staff, have overspent on travel and the budget ceilings are looming closer.

To: NSPBT   --CPUA

*** Reply to note of 06/09/86 14:38   06/09/86 16:51:44
NOTE FROM: Mary Dix
Subject: FY86 TravelBudget Restrictions
Some of the children have been pulling some cute tricks to get
1st class travel...the travel ceiling is just too close to let
anyone else try it again....sometime, I'd like to share with
you some of the totals of what our people claimed while on the
Tokyo trip.

To: NSMAD   --CPUA

                                                    06/09/86 14:38:13
*** Reply to note of 06/09/86 13:00

NOTE FROM: PAUL THOMPSON
Subject: FY86 TravelBudget Restrictions
never mind the ceiling. will we have a roof over our heads?

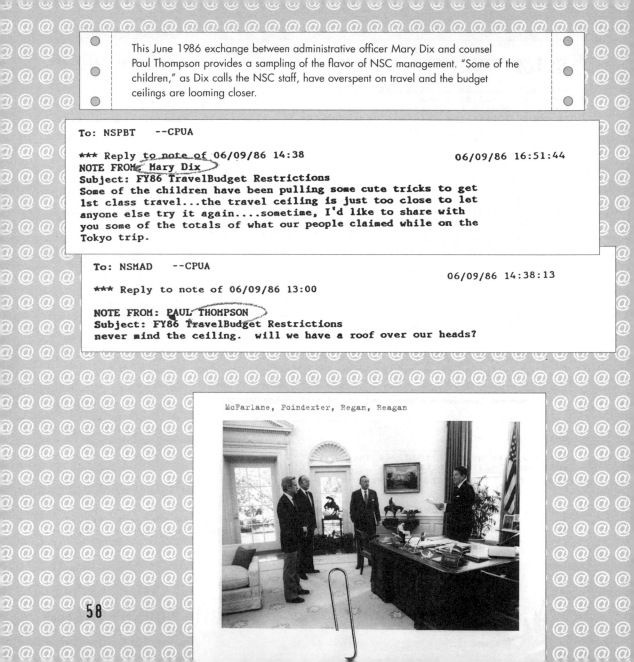

McFarlane, Poindexter, Regan, Reagan

The NSC staff also had their peeves. This exchange between Brenda Reger and Paul Thompson concerns what Reger calls a "Know Your Enemy" exercise, a trip to a luncheon to hear guest speaker Scott Armstrong. Reger's job at the NSC required that she search and process piles of documents for possible release in response to Freedom of Information Act requests and other declassification review queries. Donna Sirko and Nancy Menan were also part of that staff, which may explain their feelings toward Armstrong, who filed hundreds of requests at the NSC during his time as a *Washington Post* reporter, and from July 1985 through December 1989 as founder and first director of the National Security Archive. Armstrong has earned more NSC ire as the lead plaintiff in the Archive's suit to save these e-mail messages and get them released—*Armstrong et al. v. Executive Office of the President et al.*

```
To: NSPBT    --CPUA                              02/26/86 12:02:20

                        UNCLASSIFIED

NOTE FROM: BRENDA REGER
SUBJECT: S. Armstrong
The Def. Investigative Service is sponsoring a DOD Security luncheon on March
13 , 11:15-13:30 at Ft. Myer Officer's Club. The guest speaker will be Scott
Armstrong. Donna and Nancy want to go and I am going to insure they don't
trip him as he walks down the stairs or something! Are you interested in
joining us? (This is a "Know your Enemy" exercise!) The cost is $11.00 non-
refundable even if you don't like the speaker and the lunch! We need to do the
reservations today-- yes or no????
```

```
To: NSBSR    --CPUA                              02/26/86 12:04:40

*** Reply to note of 02/26/86 12:02

NOTE FROM: PAUL THOMPSON
Subject: S. Armstrong
yes
```

Day-to-day life at the NSC could be hazardous, particularly if you were a driver or courier. This May 7, 1986, request for a new government car recounts a series of major defects in the previous car assigned to the NSC, citing, among others, that "the accelerator pedal has a tendency to fall off." The memo originated with Robert Fishbourne, who worked out of Room 381 of the Old Executive Office Building, but apparently had a hard time spelling his boss's name correctly (George Van Eron).

```
.SE   AUTHOR      'fishbourne, robert'
.SE   TITLE       'fish'
.SE   INITS       'RTF'
.SE   COMP        'nsc'
.SE   DEPT        'secretariat'
.SE   ZIP         'room 381'
.SE   CITY        'wash dc'
```

SUBJECT   Incident Report on NSC leased Car

On April 23rd we observed the following. someone damaged the government car which the National Security Council Secretariat uses for Official Government Business.The car's lower left front quarter panel, just in front of drivers door has been dented in. This dent prevents the drivers door from opening. This is the second time the car has been damaged attached is the report of the first incident.

We need to return this car to GSA for repair of this damage

Other defects noted when car was received:

A. Horn button was missing.
B. The accelerator pedal has a tendency to fall off.
C. Dome light keeps falling out of the roof.
D. The passenger door does not open or close easily it has to be slammed to close it

We did not receive a proper replacement for the car we turn in.

We request that NSC be issued a newer vehicle without government markings on the doors. The only government reference should be the tags.
Since this vehicle is used by the White House to carry Professional Staff members and also to make courier runs throughout the Washington DC area.

                        George Van Iron
                        Director
                        NSC Secretariat
```
```

This exchange of e-mail notes involves the three top administrators in making sure that Fawn Hall does not get a job at the NSC, not since she admitted absconding with documents from Oliver North's office as the Iran-contra scandal was breaking. First, NSC general counsel Paul Schott Stevens relates a rumor that Fawn has been spotted in the White House complex. Deputy Executive Secretary Robert Pearson responds that it's not a matter for the NSC, although others in the Old Executive Office Building might be interested (Fawn's mother, Wilma Hall, still worked there). Finally, administrative officer Mary Dix weighs in with the assurance that NSC is not involved.

```
                                       02/17/87 13:39 ***

To: NSGSG    --CPUA

NOTE FROM: Paul S. Stevens
SUBJECT: Fawn Hall
  To your knowledge, is Fawn Hall (Ollie North's former secretary)
interviewing for a new position with anyone on the NSC staff?
My information is that she has been in WH complex on job interviews.
Please advise.
```

```
                                       02/17/87 14:20 ***

To: NSPSS    --CPUA

NOTE FROM: BOB PEARSON
Subject: Fawn Hall
She would not be interviewing for any NSC position - would not doubt that
otheres in OEOB might be interested.
```

```
                                            02/17/87 14:26:43

To: NSWRP    --CPUA

NOTE FROM: Paul S. Stevens
Subject: Fawn Hall
Bob, I share your conclusion that she shd not be. But is she? We need to
confirm she is not, at least at NSC. Rest of EOP is WH Counsel's concern.
```

```
To: NSPSS    --CPUA

*** Reply to note of 02/17/87 13:39          02/17/87 14:45 ***
NOTE FROM: Mary Dix
Subject: Fawn Hall
No. Fawn Hall is not interviewing with the NSC staff;  however,
I heard that she was trying for a WH support position...
```

```
                                            02/17/87 15:42:13

To: NSMAD    --CPUA

NOTE FROM: Paul S. Stevens
Subject: Fawn Hall
Thanks, Mary. Pls. advise if you hear anything to contrary viv-a-vis NSC
position.
```

WHITE HOUSE E-MAIL

It was only a few days before Christmas, after all, so why not get a jug of wine "to entertain the troops after what we hope will be a short meeting." This e-mail message from December 22, 1986, outlines the agenda for a meeting of the self-styled Star Wars mafia on the NSC staff, including Steven Steiner, Robert Linhard, and Will Tobey. Several points remain classified, but the key line is "WINE (AND CHEESE???) ACTION OFFICER IS TOBEY!!!!!!"

```
To: NSEEL    --CPUA                           NSGT    --CEUA 12/22/86 12:47:35
    NSFBP    --CPUA

                    Classification:      UNCLASSIFIED
NOTE FROM: Steven Steiner
SUBJECT: mafia agenda

Here is proposed agenda.

Flora, please print and give copies to Linhard, Tobey and me. Thanks.

Will: Bob mentioned possibility of our buying a jug of wine to entertain
troops after what we hope will be a short meeting, back in his office. Bob and
I will do the paying if you are willing to get a big bottle. Thanks. Advise.
```

```
INE (AND CHEESE???). ACTION OFFICER IS TOBEY!!!!!!

:: NSLSS    --CPUA

                    Classification:      UNCLASSIFIED
    mafia agenda
```

This October 3, 1986, message from former national security adviser Robert ("Bud") McFarlane (who kept his e-mail terminal at home even after leaving the NSC) reassures his successor, Admiral Poindexter, about the criticism he's facing from two predecessors, Henry Kissinger (HAK) and Zbigniew Brzezinski. The United States had just worked out something of a swap, sending home a Soviet spy arrested in New York on August 23, in exchange for the Soviets' release of *U.S. News* reporter Nicholas Daniloff, who was arrested in Moscow on August 30. The U.S. position was that Daniloff was set up and arrested precisely for such an exchange, thus the criticism. Needless to say, Poindexter is grateful for Bud's support.

To: NSJMP   --CPUA

*** Reply to note of 10/01/86 16:56   UNCLASSIFIED
                                       -- SECRET

NOTE FROM: ROBERT MCFARLANE
Subject: HAK & ZBIG
Their motives are entirely self-serving on this issue. Specifically, they are
both basically motivated by what they think it takes to please as much of the
press/congressional/public constituency as they can as often as they can. On
this issue the press was bound to be rushing to be very tough; thus it was an
easy way for Henry to ingratiate himself with them to be just as tough as they
are. If you were to ask him he would say, "I was just trying to help the
President as he goes to Iceland by showing some pressure from the right (for
Russian consumption)." There is also a touch of envy involved for both Henry
and Zbig. They like to posture about how they would have done it had they been
in your shoes but in fact, you clearly did better than the '78 outcome so
Zbig's comment is particularly egregious. Don't worry about it.

Separately you have seen another curious phenomena in the form of all this
tough rhetoric from Hil liberals. The reason for that is that they have all
just finished voting for a $30billion defense cut and now that they are going
home, they need to be able to point to something where they have been tough
and the Daniloff affair presents a convenient target. They hope people will
remember the last thig they did which now will be their tough rhetoric on
Daniloff. Pure sophistry. Don't let it get you down.

I am a little annoyed. I did a 40 minute telephone interview with Maureen
Santini (US News & World Report) laying out the President's strategy from 81
to date making the point (rather well I thought) that he hasn't flip-flopped
at all and why it was first necessary to restore ou7r economic and military
strength and now that it has succeeded in getting the Russians' attention, he
is ready to negotiate--as he always plannned to do. Today I got word that they
intend to use one sentence (from a three page, single spaced interview). I
intend to tell DAve GErgen what I think about it.

Hang in there.

To: NSRCM   --CPUA

*** Reply to note of 10/03/86 18:55   UNCLASSIFIED
                                       -- SECRET

NOTE FROM: JOHN POINDEXTER
Subject: HAK & ZBIG
Bud, thanks for the analysis. I really appreciate it. Tell Gergen that he owes
you one for the work we did for him on Daniloff.

WHITE HOUSE E-MAIL

Ironically, only a month and a half earlier, Brzezinski had won a major favor from the NSC staff, which hired his son Ian after a Zbig phone call. Guess what? "Ian turned out to be a fine, intelligent, young man with a superb attitude," says Mary Dix in this August 15, 1986, e-mail.

NOTE FROM: Mary Dix   08/15/86 13:06:05
SUBJECT: Brzezinski Action Status

I just wanted everyone who was in on Brzezinski's call to
Brenda requesting temporary employment for his son, Ian,
to be briefed on the results.

Rod said to proceed with a positive response if we had a
suitable vacancy. Paul Schulte was leaving and so George
Van Eron interviewed Ian Brzezinski for Paul's replacement.
Ian turned out to be a fine, intelligent, young man with
a superb attitude. George requested that Ian be selected
for Paul's replacement, with my strong recommendation, and
as of now, all paperwork has been completed and Ian will
begin to work in the Secretariat on September 2nd.

This e-mail note is a classic of employment negotiation, self-promotion, and personnel gossip. Poindexter had called Ronald F. Lehman, the deputy assistant national security adviser, on March 10, 1986, to let Lehman know of his impending appointment to replace former Senator John Tower (R-Texas) as the U.S. chief arms control negotiator in Geneva. In this e-mail, Lehman rolls out his concerns about senior arms negotiator Max Kampelman, about Secretary of State George Shultz, about getting the same pay grade and presidential access that Tower had, and about the competitors for the job. This kind of candid bargaining for job conditions is rarely found even in personnel files, demonstrating yet again how the White House e-mail system replaced oral communications. And Lehman certainly never intended for anyone but Poindexter to be privy to his thoughts.

*** Reply to note of 03/10/86 09:20
NOTE FROM: RONALD F. LEHMAN
Subject: TOWER SITUATION
I would be pleased and honored to relieve John Tower and have no problem
going whereever you think I can help the Administration most. But I have
mixed feelings. My wife Susan would prefer that I go to Geneva but she had
reconciled herself to my return to the NSC. Frankly, we've built a good team
and I'm enthusiastic about my new job here as well. At the same time, I understand the importance of continuity, of keeping a working team going, and of
demonstrating the interest of the President himself. I am identified with
the President, would be the only Republican, and am already John Tower's
understudy. All of that argues that I should go.

     If I do go to Geneva, I'd like your help on a number of items. First, I'd
like to go with the full support of the President. I have not really spent muc
h time with the President in the last two years and I would hope he would know
that it really his guy that we are sending. I know that you have been
frustrated by all of the negotiators, but I would really like to have the
same mandate and position that John Tower had (report to the President,
full Senate Confirmation, same pay grade, select my own deputy, accompanied
by my wife, etc.). Secondly, I would like to go with the support of the
Secretary of State. Paul indicated to me that Shultz and he would support
me if I wanted the job, but that if I did not want to go then Paul needed
to provide Shultz with alternative candidates. His list now includes
David Acheson (conservative democrat hawk), Walt Slocombe(bright Harold Brown
protege and critic of SDI, democrat), Gen John Voigt (friend of Bud's, not
bad and supports SDI --good candidate for this or some other job), and Jim
Woolsey. He also mentioned that some people had recommended Dick Kennedy,
the NP Ambassador at Large. Max gave me a somewhat different story this
afternoon. He says that Shultz thinks that the issue of Tower's replacement
is very much open and that Dick Kennedy is being pushed for the job. Max
didn't say that Shultz was negative on me but made it quite clear that he (max)
would prefer me to some senior and perhaps more difficult candidates.
The implication of course was that he might prefer a junior and more
submissive candidate. I think I can do a better job of working with Max
than either Tower or Glitman, but I hope you would agree with me that I
am not going there as Max's deputy and that I will have your supportjust
as you gave it to John Tower. I don't ask you or anyone simply to agree
with my views, only to make certain that I am not cut out of essential
START deliberations.

○ The next day, Poindexter responds to Lehman with maximum reassurance: "The President and I would like for you to relieve John Tower." He goes on to give Lehman the scuttlebutt on Shultz's seeming hesitation and says, "In fact if we could be sure they [the State Department] are not working a separate effort over there we would be a lot more comfortable."

Shultz & Poindexter 4-15-86

To: NSRFL   --CPUA

03/11/86 18:38:30

*** Reply to note of 03/10/86 20:19 UNCLASSIFIED

NOTE FROM: JOHN POINDEXTER
Subject: TOWER SITUATION
AS I TOLD YOU ON THE PHONE, THE PRESIDENT AND I WOULD LIKE FOR YOU TO RELIEVE
JOHN TOWER. CAP IS FULLY ON BOARD AND SO IT GEORGE. I THINK GEORGE'S CONCERN
IS HIS LACK OF CONTROL AND HIS FEAR THAT YOU WILL BE AN INDEPENDENT OPERATOR.
TODAY HE SAID THAT WHEN HE TALKED TO YOU HE WANTED TO DISCUSS MAX'S ROLE AS
CHAIRMAN OF THE DELEGATION AND HOW IMPORTANT IT IS THAT ALL OF THE DELEGATIONS
WORK TOGETHER. I AGREED, BUT WENT ON TO REMIND GEORGE THAT AS FAS AS THE
SOVIETS ARE CONCERNED WE HAD THREE SEPARATE GROUPS. GEORGE AGREED. YOU SHOULD
CALL HIS OFFICE TONIGHT OR TOMORROW FOR AN APPOINTMENT TO SEE HIM. WHEN YOU
SEE HIM DO NOT REVEAL THAT YOU KNOW THAT YOU ARE THE PRESIDENT'S CHOICE. LET
GEORGE TELL YOU THAT. YOU WOULD LOGICALLY KNOW THAT YOU WERE JOHN TOWER'S
RECOMMENDATION. GEORGE WILL WANT YOU TO KNOW THAT HE IS LOOKING FOR A TEAM
EFFORT. I THINK WE ALL ARE. IN FACT IF WE COULD BE SURE THEY ARE NOT WORKING A
SEPARATE EFFORT OVER THERE WE WOULD BE A LOT MORE COMFORTABLE. YOU WILL
CONTINUE TO HAVE THE FULL SUPPORT OF THE WHITE HOUSE AND THE NSC. YOU SHOULD
GET THE SAME TREATMENT AS JOHN TOWER IN TERMS OF CONFIRMATION ETC. AFTER YOU
HAVE TALKED TO GEORGE AND PRESUMABLY ACCEPTED, WE NEED TO TALK ABOUT THE
TACTICS OF THE ANNOUNCEMENT. OBVIOUSLY THE SOONER THE BETTER. I TALKED TO WILL
BALL LAST NIGHT. HE THINKS IT WILL BE HELPFUL ON THE HILL TO HAVE JOHN TOWER
CALL A FEW OF HIS KEY FRIENDS ON THE HILL AND TELL THEM IF HE HASN'T ALREADY
THAT YOU WERE HIS CHOICE AS REPLACEMENT. I AGREE ON ED ROWNY. WE NEED TO COME
UP WITH A GOOD NAME FOR THAT. ALSO I NEED YOUR VIEWS ON YOUR REPLACEMENT HERE.

Alton G. Keel, the new deputy national security adviser under Poindexter, must have gotten curious about Oliver North's middle initial, having seen NSOLN on dozens of e-mail messages in September 1986 about the imminent (but very secret) visit to the White House by the nephew of Iranian prime minister Hashemi Rafsanjani, as part of the arms-for-hostages deals.

```
09/18/86 20:27:02

FROM: NSAGK    --CPUA    TO: NSOLN    --CPUA
To: NSOLN    --CPUA

NOTE FROM: Alton G. Keel
SUBJECT: HUMINT
So, what the heck does the "L" stand for?
```

North responds to Keel early the next day (7:17 A.M.) with an ironic story about a maternal terrorist, as well as some details of the planned photo and tape recordings of the nephew's visit. North, a shrewd user of the e-mail system, saved Keel's note in his own user area, so that any time North wanted to write Keel directly, without going through the NSC Secretariat, all he had to do was title his note "HUMINT" (a CIA term for human, as opposed to electronic, intelligence).

```
To: NSAGK    --CPUA                              09/19/86 07:17:47

*** Reply to note of 09/18/86 20:27
NOTE FROM: OLIVER NORTH
Subject: HUMINT
The L. is for Laurence - name derived from maternal grandfather, an IRA
terrorist run out of Ireland by the "black and tans" in 1921. Thanks for the
note. Will save it for future returns. JMP said he did not want to have the
nephew meet w/ him/you on this visit. Will give you a picture for future use.
Will be taking several for I.D. purposes, in addition to recording today's
conversations.
```

Arms deals, spies, and terrorists had no monopoly on the NSC staff's attention. Occasionally, staffers even got into the import and export of exotica, as in this August 1985 e-mail exchange on the subject of nutmeg from Grenada. Walter Raymond, a career CIA psychological operations specialist, came to the NSC to run its so-called public diplomacy efforts (read propaganda and psyops). Helping the Grenadian economy was good PR after the October 1983 U.S. invasion of Grenada; and all he needed was approval by NSC lawyer Paul Thompson for a letter clearing the nutmeg deal. Raymond seems not yet comfortable with the e-mail keyboard, since this note has many mispellings and runover lines; the last word is "background."

To: NSPBT   --CPUA   08/07/85 16:42:30

NOTE FROM: Walter Raymond
SUBJECT: grenada nutmeg
It is time for a little exotica. I have been trying to help get Grenada nutmeg
 marketed in the US. One simple reason: it is critrical to the Grenadan econom
y, they have a lot harvested and they need to move it. I would hope that6 you
would be able to concur in the proposed letter as it is done in the bvest inter
ests of the US and Grenada. Fiurther, Vernazza is the only one trying to move t
he stuff. I have sent the draft over to ylou by tulbe, but theis is the back-go
d.

                                                               08/08/85 05:07:45
To: NSWR   --CPUA

*** Reply to note of 08/07/85 16:42

NOTE FROM: PAUL THOMPSON
Subject: grenada nutmeg
will act on it on friday morning.

The departure of an NSC staffer often meant long hours for the administrative staff, particularly for people like Brenda Reger, who were responsible for safeguarding classified information (and also for giving it out, under the Freedom of Information Act, which of course she did as rarely as possible). This June 10 and 11, 1986, e-mail exchange concerns NSC Latin America staffer Constantine Menges, who had transferred from the CIA to serve as something of an ideological commissar at the NSC, upholding the hardcore right-wing vision of the Reagan revolution until he departed in July 1986. Mary Dix and Bill Van Horn discuss the disposition of some mystery boxes, and Reger chimes in as the taskmaster, holding Menges to a tight schedule for reviewing all of his papers, so he has no "excuse for another week" hanging around the NSC.

To: NSWVH   --CPUA   06/10/86 17:25 ***

NOTE FROM: Mary Dix
SUBJECT: Constantine's Boxes

Constantine says he is not sure of what is in the boxes upstairs.
Let's discuss

To: NSMAD   --CPUA   06/11/86 06:51 ***

NOTE FROM: Bill Van Horn
Subject: Constantine's Boxes
It is all unclassified material from his time in Latin American
Affairs. He can have all of it to take with him.

To: NSBSR   --CPUA   06/11/86 08:13:01

NOTE FROM: Mary Dix
Subject: Constantine's Boxes
Is this true?
If so, let's simply have them taken with the others to Constantine's house.....

To: NSMAD   --CPUA
*** Reply to note of 06/11/86

UNCLASSIFIED

NOTE FROM: BRENDA REGER
Subject: Constantine's Boxes
It probably is but given his habits of mixing his files, I don't want to be
the one to send this out without his assurance that there is no classified in
it. I told him late yesterday that we would postpone those til later and bring
them down only after he completed the things in his office now--if he gets
those done, we can bring down the others--if not, I told him I would work out
an arrangement for him to come later to my office to go thru them!! Lets stick
to that-- otherwise he will try to use these as an excuse for another week!

WHITE HOUSE E-MAIL

Joan Yonaitis was secretary to Admiral John Poindexter, and the subtext of this e-mail exchange hinges on its date: November 26, 1986. The previous morning, November 25, President Reagan called an extraordinary press conference to announce the reassignment of Oliver North and the resignation of Poindexter, due to the revelations of the Iran arms-for-hostages deals and the diversion of funds to the Nicaraguan contras. Yonaitis's correspondent here is NSC counterintelligence staffer David Major.

```
                                              11/26/86 10:29 ***
To: NSJJY    --CPUA

*** Reply to note of 11/26/86 09:54
NOTE FROM: David Major
Subject: Last Evening
IF ONLY YOU HAD CALLED, I WOULD HAVE BEEN THERE. MOST ARE LEAVING
EARLY TONIGHT. I AM NOT.
```

```
                                            11/26/86 10:42:27
To: NSDGM    --CPUA

NOTE FROM: Joan Yonaitis
Subject: Last Evening
You silly goose.  You saw me last night as you were approaching
the elevator.  You even waved.
Anyway, I'll be leaving just after the boys tonight.  I plan to
drive up to Pennsylvania tomorrow morning, and will stay on
through Saturday (not that you asked).
```

Powell & Reagan 4-18-88

UNCLASSIFIED

MEMORANDUM FOR:

Paul S. Stevens   6-Jan-1989 09:33 EDT

FROM: Nicholas Rostow
                 (ROSTOW)

SUBJECT: Money

We're looking good for the Powell gift. I gather we can go
with the plaque or, if it cannot be attached, a brass engraved
paperweight to go with the desk. George Robinson supplied a
catalogue of things that might do for JDN. He also said he
might have money left over from the dinner, which he would be
happy to let us use to cover any additional gift costs! I'm
not too comfortable with that deal.

    FROM: NSPSS --CPUA   TO: ROSTOW --VAXC   01/06/89 10:33:01
    To: ROSTOW --VAXC   -UNCLASSIFIED-

    NOTE FROM: Paul S. Stevens
    Subject: Money   UNCLASSIFIED
    Yes, we do have to do something for John. Perhaps something from the
    Steuben catalog? Let's discuss before COB today.

WHITE HOUSE E-MAIL

The departure of a subsequent national security adviser, Colin L. Powell, at the end of the Reagan administration, was somewhat more orderly. In this exchange of e-mail between Nicholas Rostow, the NSC's lawyer, and Paul S. Stevens, the NSC executive secretary, they discuss the farewell gifts for Powell and his deputy, John D. Negroponte.

CHAPTER 3

PRESIDENTIAL SCHEDULES

The White House Daily Diary

The president's daily schedule for the most part is a public document, tacked up on bulletin boards in the White House press room and beamed around the world by the wire services. But the schedules the public never sees are those of the president's top staff, the people who write the agendas and briefing memos, who put together the arrangements for the meetings, and who make the decisions on how the president spends his day.

Thanks to the White House e-mail system, we now have a virtual daily diary of White House operations in the 1980s. E-mail solved a long-standing problem of setting up meetings, in that clearing the competing schedules of the VIPs on the White House staff could take days by phone or fax or paper memo, while the simultaneous communication made possible by e-mail found the open slots and instantly connected all the invited participants. Several daily calendars—shared through e-mail with other White House staff —for different national security advisers to the president are included here, the first time the public has ever seen this level of detail on the daily activities of the people at the top of the national security apparatus.

In addition to the calendar function, over time, White House staff wrote thousands of to-and-from e-mail messages arguing about whether to have the various meetings in the first place, and if so, why and how. One particularly revealing sequence of transmissions included in this chapter concerns the very sensitive issue of having President Reagan meet the families of Americans being held hostage in Lebanon. Beginning with the March

1985 abduction of Terry Anderson, the Associated Press's chief Middle East correspondent, the hostages became a major focus of the Reagan administration, at times verging on obsession, which ultimately produced the scandal of the arms-for-hostages deals with Iran. Reagan's top aides were well aware of how the protracted Tehran hostage crisis had weakened the Carter presidency and helped their electoral victory in 1980.

So when the hostage families asked for a meeting with the president in October 1985, the computer terminals at the NSC started humming. The resulting sequence of e-mail represents a classic example of the hashing-out of policy, of White House staff navigating the shoals of intensive media attention, emotional appeals from outsiders, the president's personal inclinations, pressure from the State Department, and their own temper tantrums. Through the magic of computers, this single e-mail sequence includes six senders on the NSC staff and fourteen recipients, including secretaries and other NSC staff designated for certain tasks, along with three looming offstage players: the president, Chief of Staff Donald T. Regan, and the White House scheduler, Frederick J. Ryan.

This chapter also includes a series of e-mail messages around a meeting that never took place, despite the best efforts of the president's staff. A delegation of Afghan freedom fighters, the *mujahideen*, were visiting the United Nations in New York City at the end of October 1985. The first extant e-mail note we have in this sequence bears the exuberant title "Pres Meets the Muj." Things quickly turn more serious, however, with vicious intramural battles within the Afghan delegation, as well as with their Pakistani sponsors.

The chapter concludes with an extraordinarily detailed e-mail note describing all the hoops the president's staff jumped through to organize and staff his "face time" with foreign leaders, in this case, King Hussein of Jordan.

The pecking order at the White House comes through clearly in this remarkable series of e-mail about setting up a meeting with the families of the hostages.
The gatekeeper of the paper flow from the National Security Council, William F. Martin (WFM), also winds up in the middle of much of the e-mail flow, especially when it concerns scheduling the president. This story begins on

Thursday, October 24, 1985. At 1:45 P.M., Martin receives Oliver North's recommendation, agreeing with the State Department, that President Reagan should not meet with the families of the American hostages (AMCITS, or American citizens) held in Lebanon. North gives three reasons: first, it is purely a matter of public relations; the second reason involves bureau-

cratic buck-passing; and only the third substantively concerns the hostages. The first reason refers to the terrorist hijacking of the cruise ship *Achille Lauro* (*see* "The Real War Room" below). U.S. Navy jets had forced down, in Italy, the getaway plane carrying the "ACHIrorists" [sic]. "Oakley's office" refers to Ambassador Robert Oakley, the State Department's lead staffer on the hostage issue.

10/24/85 13:45 ***

To: NSWFM   --CPUA

-- SECRET --

NOTE FROM: OLIVER NORTH
SUBJECT: Presidential meeting w/ Families of AMCIT Hostages held in
      Lebanon.
State has advised that hostage families will be here in Wash D.C. on
28 October and that they wd like to meet w/ the Pres. State is NOT rpt
NOT recommending a meeting w/ the President. NSC concurs in this recommendation for the following reasons:
-- The President is currently seen in a positive light as having
   acted against the ACHIrorists. Attention focused on
   a meeting w/ the hostage families will again emphasize the frustration
   and inaction criticism we have set aside for the time being.

-- Sec Shultz met w/ some of the hostage families in May and since then
   all meetings have been here at the White House (McFarlane, VP or
   President. It is time for State to again act on this issue. They
   (Oakley's office) agree.

-- Finally, it must be noted that a Presidential meeting would be
   well publicized, as was the meeting with the VP, encouraging the
   captors to hold out hope that they may finally be getting through
   and that their demands might finally be met. Thus such a meeting
   at this point could well result in further prolonging the captivity
   of our citizens.

Bill, would you please pass this to JMP and RCM. If, in spite of
recommendations above, it is decided to have a meeting w/ the Pres,
we will need some time to do a meeting memo, etc.

WHITE HOUSE E-MAIL

At 1:55 P.M., Martin forwards North's note to their boss, Deputy National Security Adviser John Poindexter (JMP), who seems to have been in a meeting at the time. By 4:45 P.M., however, Poindexter has sorted through his e-mailbox

and sends the whole package on to his boss, National Security Adviser Robert C. ("Bud") McFarlane (RCM), with a cover note: "I agree with State and Ollie."

```
                                              10/24/85 16:45 ***
To: NSRCM    --CPUA    BUD MCFARLANE

                        -- SECRET --
NOTE FROM: JOHN POINDEXTER
Subject: Presidential meeting w/ Families of AMCIT Hostages held in
I AGREE WITH STATE AND OLLIE.
*** Forwarding note from NSWFM   --CPUA    10/24/85 13:55 ***
To: NSJMP   --CPUA    JOHN M. POINDEXTER


                        -- SECRET --
NOTE FROM: WILLIAM F. MARTIN
Subject: Presidential meeting w/ Families of AMCIT Hostages held in
John, I've only forwarded this to you. You may wish to pass to Bud with
your views.
*** Forwarding note from NSOLN   --CPUA    10/24/85 13:45 ***
```

Martin & McFarlane 6-18-85

At 5:20 P.M., the fireworks start. One of the cc. recipients of North's original e-mail note intervenes with a note to Martin. Johnathan Miller serves at the time as manager of the president's foreign travel and handler of

visits by foreign leaders to the United States. (Miller had been "Tour Director" for Reagan's presidential campaign in 1980.) So the implication of Miller's message is that a meeting might already be in the works.

```
                                                              10/25/85 09:32:59
TO: NSFM    --CPUA

*** Resending note of 10/24/85 17:20          UNCLASSIFIED
To: NSWFM   --CPUA

NOTE FROM: Johnathan Miller
Subject: Presidential meeting w/ Families of AMCIT Hostages held in

Bill, as much as I usual agree and support Ollie, I think RCM favors this
based on the President's own feelings.
Thanks
```

At 7:52 P.M., North fires an e-mail cannon across Miller's bow, among other choice phrases calling him "untrainable" and the meeting "a disaster for RR" (Ronald Reagan). In current Internet parlance, one might say that Miller is being "flamed."

```
To: NSJSM   --CPUA                                      10/24/85 19:52:51

NOTE FROM: OLIVER NORTH                  -- SECRET --
SUBJECT: Mtg w/ hostage families
As usual Miller, you are incredibly screwed up. I believe you may fall into
the category we Marines refer to as "untrainable." Instead of trying to make
work for me (and what I perceive to be a disaster for RR and the possibility
of an early release of the hostages) wd you please answer the following
questions to save me from having to leap through my bung hole:

-- Did you read the prots notent you on this matter earlier today? -- Did
you see Adm Poindexter's concurrence that no mtg take place? -- If so, why the
hell didn't you answer? -- Is such a meeting now being planned? -- If so, when,
where, why? -- If not who, what?

Regards, North p.s. Please call, soonest.
     Mtg w/ hostage families
```

McFarlane, Reagan & Regan 10-10-85

North's flamethrower is soon extinguished, however, because at 11:18 P.M., Bud McFarlane gets around to his e-mailbox (perhaps from the computer terminal the NSC had installed in his home, to maintain continuous communication capability) and replies to Poindexter's package.

Interestingly, McFarlane cites both public relations and the president's own feelings in favor of a meeting and tells Poindexter to check with Fred Ryan, the president's scheduler. Ollie North is on the cc. list. So presumably he saluted and went to stand on his head in the corner.

```
*** Resending note of 10/24/85 23:18
To: NSJMP    --CPUA

*** Reply to note of 10/24/85 16:45

-- SECRET --
NOTE FROM: ROBERT MCFARLANE
Subject: Presidential meeting w/ Families of AMCIT Hostages held in
Still, at the end of the day, if they come, and ask for the meeting (publicly)
and we refuse it will be a big story. And in fact, I kind of think the Pres
would like to meet with them. So please ask Fred Ryan to raise it. Many thanks.
```

UNCLASSIFIED

The next day, Friday the 25th, they get their marching orders. At 1:53 P.M., Poindexter relays McFarlane's wishes to Ollie and the NSC staff. Bud is calling from "AF1" (Air Force One); the White House chief of staff, Don Regan, has decreed a meeting; Ollie is to write up the meeting memo for a "drop by format"; and State's Oakley is included.

```
TO:  NSOLN   --CPU1    OLLIE NORTH

NOTE FROM: JOHN POINDEXTER
SUBJECT: HOSTAGE FAMILIES                    -- SECRET --

BUD CALLED FROM AF1. DON REGAN HAS AGREED ON A MONDAY MEETING FOR THE
PRESIDENT WITH THE HOSTAGE FAMILIES. BILL, PLEASE GET A TIME FROM FRED RYAN.
OLLIE, BUD WANTS A PRESIDENTIAL DROP BY FORMAT. HAVE BOB OAKLEY, YOU OR BUD
TALKING TO THE FAMILIES IN THE ROOSEVELT ROOM AND PRESIDENT COMES IN, MAKES
SHORT REMARKS, GREETS EACH ONE AND HAS PHOTO OP.
```

At 3:38 P.M., the NSC's staff gets more details through an e-mail note addressed to the key secretaries such as Wilma Hall (McFarlane's aide and Fawn's mother) and cc.'d to North and Fawn, among others. The meeting with the hostage families is to begin at 4:45 P.M.

on Monday, October 28, and even after the president leaves the drop-by, McFarlane will stay until six. One of the family members attending the meeting, Terry Anderson's sister Peggy Say, later writes: "I didn't know it at the time, but I was told later that this

unusual largesse was a deliberate attempt by the people who were running the show to miss the evening news. The whole White House press corps was waiting outside for us, but by the time we could speak to them their deadlines had passed."

```
TO:  NSWGH   --CPU1    WILMA         NSKVZ  --CPU1   KAY
     NSJJY   --CPU1    JOANIE        NSKMH  --CPU1   KATHY
                         -- SECRET --
NOTE FROM: DON PICCTCE
SUBJECT: President's Meeting with Families of Hostages Abducted
  in Lebanon, Monday, 10/28 at 4:45 PM
Fawn has already advised you of this meeting.  This is additional info:
At 4:30 there will be a briefing for the meeting in Oval Ofc.  Fred
Ryan asks that when the President leaves mtg at 5PM RCM remain with
hostages until 6 PM. This should appear in Ollie's memo/sp for this dropby.
```

WHITE HOUSE E-MAIL

Reagan & hostages' families 10-28-85

At 6:35 P.M., North has finished his meeting preparation and lets Poindexter know. But the tinniest note is sounded by the "plaudits" to Jon Miller.

To: NSJMP   ---CPUL   UNCLASSIFIED   10/25/85 18:35:49
                                       --(SECRET)
NOTE FROM: OLIVER NORTH
Subject: HOSTAGE FAMILIES
Done. Meeting memo enroute to you as this is typed. Plaudits to Fawn and
Jon Miller for the prep. Wd like ten min. w/ you before you leave on Mugniyah
and the Nic Resistance legislation if at all possible.
        HOSTAGE FAMILIES

Meetings and more meetings make up the daily grind of White House life, so much so that the national security adviser's daily calendar in the 1980s often listed only a single hour each day, outside of meetings, labeled "work time." And these were not short days, often beginning at 7 or 7:30 A.M. and going well into the evening, with events from 8 P.M. even to midnight all too common. This January 9, 1987, e-mail calendar outlines one of Colin Powell's early days (beginning at 6:55 A.M.) as deputy national security adviser to President Reagan (under Frank C. Carlucci, who is listed as FCC on the calendar). While Carlucci has breakfast with Don Regan, the White House chief of staff (an item in parentheses generally means that Powell does not attend but needs to know about it), Powell chairs a meeting (ODSM) of the senior staff (Office Directors) of the National Security Council. Grant Green (GSG) appears repeatedly on the calendar in his role as chief aide and administrator for Carlucci and Powell.

Many of the other names are familiar White House e-mail users. Among the most interesting items are the National Security Briefing (NSB—a daily event) for the president at 10:30 A.M. in the White House Residence; a 10:05 A.M.

"prebrief" on an upcoming Crisis Pre-Planning Group (CPPG) meeting; the CPPG itself at 1 P.M. on Chad; an 11:05 A.M. briefing on covert action (CA) procedures and a 5 P.M. briefing on "black programs" (secret programs not even acknowledged

in the U.S. government's budget); and a 2 P.M. briefing on the Single Integrated Operational Plan (SIOP), the TOP SECRET targetting plan for nuclear war.

The day ends with an 8 P.M. cocktails event, the description of which is censored on personal privacy grounds—(b)(6) refers to the sixth, or privacy, exemption from the Freedom of Information Act.

```
01/07/89: CP      -- NSPWR, NSPBT, NSCLP, NSFCC

01/09/87
  6:55AM                  Arrived in Office
  7:30AM                  (FCC/Bkfst with Don Regan)
  7:30AM    8:00AM        ODSM (Powell to chair)
  8:05AM    8:15AM        Grant Green
  8:15AM    8:30AM        Col Sam Watson, VP's National Security Office (x6013)
  8:30AM    8:35AM        FCC
  8:35AM    8:45AM        Michael H. Mobbs/Marybel Batjer/GSG
  8:45AM    9:20AM        Joined FCC/Bob Linhard/Fritz Ermarth
  9:20AM    9:32AM        Bob Linhard
  9:34AM    9:50AM        Bob Pearson
 10:05AM                  Ron St. Martin/GSG/Cobb/CPPG's in general and CPPG Prebrief
 10:28AM   10:35AM        Bob Linhard and Fritz Ermarth
 10:30AM                  (P/FCC - NSB - Residence)
 10:45AM                  (FCC/Sensitive Brfg by Col Hallager & Lt Loeber)
 10:50AM                  (P/Personal Time - Photo working on SOU-Res)
 11:00AM   11:02AM        FCC (debrief on mtg w/President)
 11:00AM   11:30AM        (FCC/Bob Hormats)
 11:02AM   11:05AM        Barry Kelly
 11:05AM   11:30AM        Brfng on CA Procedures by Cannistraro/B. Kelly  SEE PG 2
 NOON                     (FCC/Lunch w/Ed Feulner, Paul Weyrich at Heritage Foundat'n)
 NOON       1:00PM        Planning Group Lunch - Roosevelt Room (STAY FOR 1 HR)
  1:00PM    2:00PM        CPPG on Chad - Room 208
  1:55PM                  (FCC/Marvin Fitzwater (VP's Press Secretary)
  2:00PM    3:00PM        FCC/GSG/SIOP Brfg-PEOC, East Wing Basement(Col Brown escort)
  3:15PM                  (FCC/Dep for mtg w/Cong Bob Michel - Capitol)
  4:00PM                  LTG(Ret) Julius W. Becton, William Tidball & Heidi Mayer
  4:35PM    4:46PM        FCC
  5:00PM    5:20PM        (FCC/Backgrounder w/Magazines w/press & Dan Howard)
  5:00PM    5:49PM        Brfg w/Ron St. Martin (CMC) re Black Programs w/GSG-Sit Rm
  5:30PM                  (FCC/Judge William P. Clark)
  5:50PM    6:00PM        John Douglass
  6:45PM                  Grant Green
  8:00PM                  LTG&Mrs Powell/Cocktails w/Jack & Patty Woodmansee,
                          Sport Coat & Tie                           (b)(6)
```

WHITE HOUSE E-MAIL

This October 21, 1987, e-mail calendar for Frank Carlucci shows how the national security adviser keeps up on White House happenings even while he's in a foreign country—in this case, Finland. While Carlucci has breakfast in Helsinki with Secretary of State George Shultz, Colin Powell (CLP) is standing-in back in Washington for the regular weekly breakfast with the secretaries of the State and Defense departments (S-W-C means Shultz, Weinberger, Carlucci). Powell also handles five other meetings in Carlucci's absence that same day, including the National Security Briefing of the President (P/NSB) in the Oval Office. Carlucci's calendar notes the prominent

```
10/21/87
    7:30AM              Bkfst w/Sec Shultz - His Suite/Guest House
    7:30AM    8:30AM    (S-W-C Breakfast - CLP)
    8:30AM              Motorcade from Guest House to Amb Residence at Embassy
                          Upon entering Emb Compound, your driver will leave
                          motorcade and you will be escorted to conference rm
                          to hold while Shultz addresses employees
    8:30AM    8:45AM    (HHB Meeting - CLP)
    9:00AM              (Sec Shultz addresses Embassy Helsinki employees)
    9:15AM   12:45PM    Mtgs in Embassy annex
    9:30AM    9:45AM    (P/NSB w/CLP - Oval - CLP)
    9:45AM   10:00AM    (P/Brf mtg w/King Moshoeshoe II of Lesotho - Oval - CLP)
   11:00AM   11:30AM    P/Mtg w/Pres Azcona of Honduras - Oval
   11:45AM    NOON      (P/Dropby Brfg on Foreign Affairs Funding - 450 EOB)
   12:55PM              Motorcade from Embassy to Palace
    1:00PM    2:30PM    Shultz/Carlucci Luncheon w/President Koivisto, inc Roz
                          Ridgway, Chuck Redman, Mike Durkee (notetaker) --
                          1:05 to 1:20 - Tete-a-tete/1:20 to 2:30 - Luncheon
    2:30PM    2:45PM    (Intelligence Directorate Briefing - CLP)
    3:00PM              (Shultz Press Conference at Kalastajatorppa Hotel Conf Rm)
    3:30PM    6:30PM    Private Time
    5:00PM    5:30PM    (NSC Staff Mtg - CH Conf Rm - CLP)
    6:30PM              Buffet at Guest House
    6:30PM    8:30PM    (P/Cabinet Dinner    Res - second of two)
NOTES:                  RON:  Kalastajatorppa (011-358-0-488011)
                        Time:  EDT +6
                        HOURS:   LOCATION, NOT EDT
```

visitors to the White House that day, including Lesotho's king and Honduras's president, as well as President Reagan's hosting of half the Cabinet at dinner in the White House Residence (meaning upstairs instead of in the state rooms) that evening. The notes remind Carlucci that Finland time is six hours in advance of Eastern Daylight Time (EDT) and give the phone number for the hotel where he's spending the night.

This sequence of e-mail about planning a presidential event begins with an exuberant title, "Pres Meets the Muj" (meaning the *mujahideen* rebels fighting Soviet troops in Afghanistan), in a message from senior NSC staffer Donald Fortier to Soviet specialist Steven Sestanovich on October 3, 1985. An Afghan delegation is coming to New York for the opening of the United Nations General Assembly.

The discussion, however, quickly turns serious, as in this e-mail from travel scheduler Johnathan Miller to Fortier later the same day, referring to William Martin ("Bill"), Robert McFarlane ("Bud"), and the upcoming Geneva summit meeting with Gorbachev. Fortier is appropriately

sobered, and he raises more problems, including information from CIA liaison Vince Cannistraro about Admad Shah Masoud ("Masood"), a key *mujahideen* leader noted for his independent base in northeast Afghanistan.

```
10/03/85 08:00:53

NOTE FROM: DONALD R. FORTIER
Subject: Pres Meets the Muj
```

```
To: NSDRF    --CPUA

NOTE FROM: Johnathan Miller                    10/03/85 12:33 ***
SUBJECT: Pres. Mtg. with Afghans

Bill and I like the idea and I would like to include it in the master
Presidential pre Geneva events calendar that I am crafting for Bud. There is,
however, a problem with the President's schedule in New York; i.e. there is no
open time.Is there anyway that we could move this event to the White House o/a
October 28?
```

```
                                               10/03/85 13:37:13

To: NSSRS    --CPUA


NOTE FROM: DONALD R. FORTIER              --UNCLASSIFIED
Subject: Pres. Mtg. with Afghans
Give me your thoughts on how we should proceed from here.  I expected that
this would be the problem.  Doing it at the reception gives them short shrift.
Vince thinks getting Masood here is going to be tough, for reasons that
appear to me to be legitimate.  I'll explain in person.
```

WHITE HOUSE E-MAIL

By the end of October, the White House staff are running into major political problems with the Afghan delegation, in spite of "a firm appointment on the President's schedule." This extraordinary October 28 e-mail from Walter Raymond to Fortier describes Gulbuddin Hekmatyar (the most radical Islamic fundamentalist of the group) as also the most favored by the Pakistani military and the least interested in the embrace by the United States. "Gen. Akhtar" refers to the head of the Pakistani Inter-Services Intelligence Directorate (ISI), which managed the Afghan war and distributed U.S. and other military aid. Vernon "Dick" Walters, U.S. ambassador to the United Nations, is the key player on the New York end. Raymond recommends a "back channel" cable to the Pakistanis for pressure on the Afghans.

10/28/85 16:47:49

To: NSDRF   --CPUA

NOTE FROM: Walter Raymond
SUBJECT: Afghan Delegation
    We have a problem getting the delegation to Washington. 5 of the 7 will come, but Gulbuddin--the delegation head--said that given current instructions he is not prepared to come to Washington. Zal has not explicitly told the group that they have an invitation to see the President because he is certain that they will feel compelled to turn it down without Pakistani endorsement. Zal adds that Gulbuddin is concerned about too close an identification with US policy; he does not want to bve seen as a too' of US policy. Gulbuddin told Zal today, in response to a trip to Washington, that General Akhtar had given him guidance and told him that he was only to go to NYC.
    I had intended to have Dick Walters formally invite the group when they visit him at USUN tomorrow at 2:30, but at this point Zal is afraid this may be a disaster--i.e. a turndown. (NB: As you know we have a firm appointment on the President's schedule for the group to see him 1130-1150 AM Wed 30 October.
    I think we need to send a cable to Islamabad back channel to tell Ahktar to instruct the delegation to do three things: (1) Go to Washington for meeting with President; (2) authorize that they stay in US until 10 Nov and (3) authorize their participation in Congressional meetings, including a reception. Could you send a cable to this effect--night action--to Islamabad crafting in whatever else is needed to tie this with what happened in NYC when you were present. Key is that we should get a greenlight so that Walters can formalize the process on Tuesday PM. (FPO please print)

Fortier responds to Raymond about a two-track approach—through "our intelligence channel" and through the Pakistani ambassador in Washington—to bring the Afghans around. The "Additional Secretary" is apparently the Pakistani official escorting the Afghans. Zia refers to the Pakistani dictator Gen. Mohammad Zia-ul-Haq, who apparently had spoken with President Reagan about the Afghan war. Shirin refers to National Security Council staffer Shirin Tahir-Kheli.

Fortier, Reagan & Bush 3-2-86

To: NSWR   --CPUA

10/28/85 17:25:54

NOTE FROM: DONALD R. FORTIER
SUBJECT: Afghan Meeting

I have asked our intelligence channel to get the word through to the Paks. Separately, at Shirin's suggestion, I called Amb. Azim, the Pakistani Ambassador here in Washington. He had already been advised of the problem and said he had just gotten off the phone with their Additional Secretary in New York. He said he had relayed the Zia-Reagan conversation to clear the air. He said he also told the Additional Secretary to "go and pump some bloody sense into their heads. They have been invited by the President of the US and for that they were damned lucky." Azim is a good man.

But by noon the next day, October 29, the deal still is not done, writes Raymond in this e-mail to Fortier.

To: NSDRF   --CPUA   10/29/85 12:19:33

NOTE FROM: Walter Raymond
SUBJECT: Afghans
    As of 10:00 AM the Additional Secretary had not bveen in touch with the Afghans and they (Gulbuddin and co) had not changed their positions re coming to Washington. The whole thing may change when Walters formally invites them at 2:30PM, but yoiu may want to call Azim and be sure everything is in place.

WHITE HOUSE E-MAIL

```
                                          10/29/85  18:56:07
To: NSDRF    --CPUA

NOTE FROM: Walter Raymond
SUBJECT: Afghan Update
     State (Peck) advises that the Paks have gotten the word that the Afghan
Council has voted in favor of the meeting. Shanawaz has been instructed to
advise Gulbuddin of this development.  On the surface this might suggest our
mini-crisis is over. On the other hand, many slips are possible: 1) Afghans
may reject instructions unless they come from Ahktar; 2) Gulbuddin may have a
"loss of face" problem to deal with; 3) Paks may have a secret agenda.  I am
advised that the Paks (presumably Shanawaz and possibly the Additional Secy are
to meet with Gulbuddin and his boys at 7PM. We should know the results relative
ly soon.
     Analytically, I have tried to reconstruct. I havce the following thesis:
The Paks and some Afghans (notably the fundamentalists) have never been very
enthusiastic about the trip: The Paks because they are concerned that we will
start playing a more active direct h the Afghan Resistanceand the
Fundamentalists because they are not "pro-American" and furthermore do not want
to be seen as on our string. At any rate, there was something to be gained from
the Pak/Afghan side in having Gulbuddinhead the delegation, as he was least
likely to work closely with us. I suspect it was more than accidental that
Gulbuddin headed this delegation. When the alliance was formed, the spokesman
was to rotate every two months, yet Younis Khalis remained in situ for 4 plus
months. Then when it was time to send a delegation to the U.S. they resumed
rotation and who pops up: Gulbuddin. At any rate, initially it probably worked
to the advantage of both the Paks and the Afghans to keep one's distance. When
it became clear that we were very serious about themeeting with the President
the Paks began tointo gear, although there may still be some spoilers in
the Pak system somewhere.  Now, however, they have some difficulties because
 having unleashed the "monster" they may not be able to control him, i.e.
Gulbuddin--particularly if he thinks that within the Pak structure there are
those who favor an arms length relationship with the U.S. Time will tell.
```

By 8 A.M. the next day, the meeting is scrapped, and Raymond is busily constructing high-level spin to cover up the fiasco. UNGA refers to United Nations General Assembly; Steve is Steven Sestanovich; Don is Don Fortier; JMP is Poindexter, and Ed Djerejian (Raymond spells it phonetically) is NSC spokesman.

To: NSEPD   --CPUA

NOTE FROM: Walter Raymond
SUBJECT: Scrub of Afghan Meeting
    If asked whether there will be a meeting with the Afghan Alliance Group: We are aware that an important group of Mujaheddin leaders are in New York. This group which represents all major elements of the Afdghan Resistance have been at the UN where they are making their brave fight for freedom known to many representatives at that international body. If there schedule had permitted a trip to Washington the President and key members of Congress would have been happy to have met with them. Unfortunately the timing was too short to lay on such a session. If at some time in the future such a meeting can be arranged we would be pleased. The President, as you know, strongly supports the brave fight for freedom being waged by the Afghan peoples against heavy odds. He also deeply believes, as expressed in his speech to the UNGA last week that the mujaheddin must be part of any process leading to peace in Afghanistan .This is contingency guidance. Do not use unless asked. If Steve, Don or JMP ha have any edits, pls pass directly to Ed Deregian. I have told Zal to use the same line in NYC and have advised State.

WHITE HOUSE E-MAIL

This e-mail gives an inside account of the actual logistical arrangements that the White House makes for presidential face-to-face meetings. In this case, White House staffer Mary Kay Stults is writing NSC staff counsel Paul Thompson in April 1987 about the impending visit of King Hussein of Jordan and about the importance of "toe markers" (indicating where VIPs are to stand during particular ceremonies, such as departures and arrivals and speeches). William Burns and Dennis Ross are NSC staffers on Middle East issues. WHCA refers to the White House Communications Agency, a Pentagon-sponsored outfit based at the White House, which arranges presidential phone lines, computers, e-mail, and the like. DAS, in this case, is deputy assistant secretary for Public Affairs at the State Department. Such is the detail work that creates good television footage.

04/11/87 21:09:11
Declassified/Released on AUG 27 199_
by NARA on the recommendation of the NSC.

To: NSPBT   --CPUA

NOTE FROM: MARY KAY STULTS
SUBJECT: Hussein

Bill Burns has agreed to do the participants memo, and I've also asked him to contact Kathy Fenton, First Lady's Social Office 7064, and notify her who is coming to lunch and who will be at the departure statements. They need this because they do toe markers for the departure statements and name tags/chairs for the lunch. When I first had this job I didn't realize they worried about lunch and toe markers and I failed to tell them that Secry Weinberger was coming to lunch. They scrambled & got him a chair, plate and lunch at the la st minute as well as a toe marker - and I've always kept them informed since. I've sent him a sample participants memo which is usually submitted the day before the meeting (sooner if participants are firm) and then ldx'd to the appropriate Exec Secs. I also put a copy of the memo in a folder on my desk for you and Jackie.

Bill/Dennis Ross will do the meeting memo, but may come to you for numbers. I also sent him, and have in the folder, the numbers that the rooms will hold. We traditionally hold the one-on-one to Pres/Hussein and two notetakers. You may have to bar the door, Paul. Sometimes people crash. Of course, if the entire party remains small the plenary can take place in the Oval as well - that's really up to you and Dennis/Bill - just depends on what flavor you want to give the meeting.

If interpretation is required WHCA wires the Oval office, they will need to be notified since there is no coordinating meeting. State wires the cabinet room and Jackie will need to clear in the technicians with TSD as well as with waves (but call 4311 rather than 6742 because they are considered workers). She needs to call Cathy Osborne and ask when it will be conven- ient for the technicians to come from State to wire the room - usually it's

after 4:00 the day before. She will have to meet them at the gate, call
TSD to tell them they are here, escort them to the Cabinet Room. Same
procedure applies for the day of the visit, except they will come back about
9:30 to check equipment. (TSD's # is 4044).
I've asked Jackie to reserve the Roosevelt Room (I don't remember if I've alrea
dy done it) so you have a place for strap hangers. She will also need to clear
in any State Protocol people who will be coming in Advance. I don't know who
has the Hussein assignment at State Protocol, but Julie Andrews 647-3064 or
Bunny Murdock 647-1676 will know as soon as Hussein decides to come.
We need to check with Dan Howard and DAS at State to see who will do the
Backgrounder and Press Readout in the Press Room. Also need to determine
what there will be in the Oval and at the Departure Statement. Lastly, need
to decide if there is going to be a backgrounder at the Foreign Press
Center. State DAS and Dan Howard really work these, the decisions just
need to be tied together. Again, WHCA may need to wire for the departure
Statements and it needs to be determined where the departure statements
will be done - Dip entrance or Rose Garden.

I call and notify or remind the appropriate offices (VP's Secry, Baker's,
Shultz, etc) of the prebrief and meeting. Their numbers are on my rolle-
dex. I also remind LT Sexton WHSS 4420 because he likes to be remembered
by us. He saves us lots of hassle - Protocol also touches base with him
so he knows the cars are coming in.

King Hussein of Jordan & President Reagan 9-30-85

WHITE HOUSE E-MAIL

CHAPTER 4

THE REAL WAR ROOM

The election of Bill Clinton as president has turned the phrase "war room" into slang for any boiler room quick-response operation, slinging crisis-management spin at the media and any political opponent. The White House e-mail from the 1980s shows that all of President Reagan's staff did more than their fair share of spin control (see chapter 6 on "Spin Doctors"). But the real nerve center of the presidency during a national security crisis is the Situation Room, a nondescript little conference room slightly below ground level in the west wing of the White House. It has none of the grandeur you might expect from the only remaining superpower; in fact, even the renowned "hot line" to Moscow is a basic consumer-model telephone set (a Merlin from AT&T when I saw it in 1993) inside a pull-out drawer at the head of the government-issue conference table in the center of the SitRoom.

Around that modest conference room is a warren of offices staffed twenty-four hours a day—all plugged into the government's electronic circuits of cable traffic and intelligence reports and newswires and, yes, CNN. From the SitRoom issues a constant flow of intimations, warnings, notices, and updates. At the beginning of every day, over the White House e-mail system comes the Situation Room Morning Summary of key cables and news; and the sun sets on the Situation Room Evening Summary of the same. Hundreds of e-mail messages testify that the readers of these summaries in the Reagan-Bush White House worked on a remarkable range of real wars, from Libya to Honduras, from Afghanistan to Costa Rica.

America's most popular war of the 1980s took place in Afghanistan, where tribally based *mujahideen* "freedom fighters" took on the Soviet Union's occupation forces, with the help of hundreds of millions of U.S. dollars, often appropriated by Congress in excess of the administration's requests. Inside the White House, the president's staff welcomed all the support, a relief from the incessant controversy over Central America. But sometimes the support verged on the farcical, as with the episode chronicled herein of the "Buffalo" gun.

The controversial war was against Nicaragua, resulting in censure from the International Court of Justice at The Hague, and causing a series of bitter and divisive Congressional debates over aid to the contra rebels. Included here are only a few of the newest items, detailing how the White House staff tried (and failed) to bully Costa Rican president (and later Nobel Peace Prize winner) Oscar Arias into covering up one of Oliver North's "Project Democracy" secret airstrips.

Another major war effort revolved around terrorist incidents, perhaps the most prominent of which was the hijacking of the Italian cruise ship *Achille Lauro* in the Mediterranean in October 1985. The terrorists killed a disabled American, Leon Klinghoffer, and wrangled an escape plane out of Egyptian president Hosni Mubarak, only to be forced down in Italy by U.S. jets. The can-do White House action officer for the operation was Oliver North, and the e-mail traffic around the event helps explain how its success provided North a launching pad for his subsequent covert dealings. Other e-mail detail a failed Israeli attempt to duplicate the *Achille Lauro* success, and provide highly interesting discussions of proposed U.S. actions against foreign governments, like Syria, seen as supporting terrorists. The chapter ends with a candid commentary on another agency's SitRoom, the Department of Justice's Operations Center.

This Situation Room Morning Summary from November 12, 1985, previously classified SECRET, wraps up the overnight international news in eleven short paragraphs, leading with a coup in Liberia. The source is censored from the Liberia item, but we can take an educated guess at the information under the black blotch. The designation (b)(3) means that the authority for the censorship is the third exemption to the Freedom of Information Act (FOIA), which allows withholding of information required to be kept secret by a specific statute, and the (C) means it's only classified at the confidential level, the least sensitive secret. In this case, given that the CIA is quoted in the text of the item and that the CIA is required by law to keep secret its sources and methods, the deletion probably just gives the cable number or other qualifier of the CIA's report to Washington. The citations for other entries reveal a primary source for the SitRoom—cables from U.S. embassies abroad—ranging from Beirut 6402 (the cable number) to Tegucigalpa 5470. Reuter newswire is also represented. One of the paragraphs is completely censored on grounds of national security, the (b)(1) meaning the first exemption to the FOIA for records that are properly classified and would damage national security if released. Still, the level of secrecy is merely confidential, so it's hard to guess what's under this blotch, other than that it relates to the Near East or South Asia and was still seen as sensitive in 1994, when this e-mail was declassified.

SITUATION ROOM MORNING SUMMARY SECRET 12 November 1985

HIGHLIGHT

LIBERIA: Successful coup last night. General Quiwompka seized executive mansion and declared himself head of state, jubilant crowds and soldiers in streets, and Doe reportedly in hiding. Sporadic shooting continues in Monrovia but countryside quiet. All U.S. citizens safe. CIA describes Quiwompka as fervently pro-U.S. and he has considerable support in Liberia. ███████ (b)(3) (c)

USSR/EUROPE

GERMANY-US: Stern Magazine reports all 108 Pershing-2s are now in place in West Germany ahead of schedule...claims U.S. concerned Geneva summit could produce an immediate halt to deployment, therefore, the decision to accelerate. (U) Reuter 70

NEAR EAST/SOUTH ASIA

JORDAN-PLO: King Hussein's statements (to NYT, Le Monde, et al.) on Arafat's Cairo Declaration given widespread coverage in Jordanian multi-media...with emphasis on Hussein's comment that while Arafat's move is welcome, it's not enough...Arafat must renounce all acts of violence inside and outside Israel, as well as accept 242/338 (U) Amman 0751

WHITE HOUSE E-MAIL

LEBANON: Carbomb exploded in East Beirut this morning (0315 EST) outside a monastery, where weekly meetings of Christian Lebanese Front are held...roughly a quarter mile from U.S. embassy annex. According to preliminary report, President Chamoun, his son Dany, and Phalange Party Chairman Elie Karamah were slightly injured. Additionally, two of our foreign service nationals and a U.S. foreign service officer were slightly injured...required no hospitalization. The Front was left out of last month's peace talks between Moslem and Christian militias in Damascus and its members have criticized a peace accord militias were to have signed (u)(c) Beirut 6402; State NOIWON; Reuter 193

LEBANON-SYRIA-US: In series of increasingly explicit statements, Syria blames U.S. for delays in concluding Syrian-sponsored accord among Lebanon's three militias....accusations now heralded in front-page, headline articles. Embassy Beirut notes this is typical for Syria.(u)(c) Beirut 6400

EGYPT-ISRAEL: Mubarak has suggested to Peres that trilateral talks on Taba be resumed early next month (u)(s) Cairo 8563

EGYPT-US: Mubarak letter to President focuses on moving forward on peace process and healing U.S.-Egyptian relations...closes out Achille Lauro affair by repeating Egypt's justification for its actions. Mubarak will reveal letter during speech Wednesday. Full text available (u)(s) Cairo 8565

(b)(1)

(c)

LATIN AMERICA

HONDURAS: Embassy reports media campaign is intensifying against alleged government support for Contras. Government has yet to be provoked into public reaction; however, Embassy attempting to determine if tolerance level has now reached the point whereby government will feel compelled to respond. Embassy believes connection exists between Honduran media criticism of government support for Contras and Nicaraguan media campaign linking CIA, FDN, and Honduran armed forces in a military alliance (u)(c) Tegucigalpa 5470

AFRICA

SUDAN: Moratorium on refugee departures to all nations of resettlement has been imposed for an indefinite period...may be
lifted at end of former VP Tayyeb's trial. Move reflects unease within government over refugee resettlement outside of Sudan (u)(c) Khartoum 5887

SOUTH AFRICA: Pretoria said consideration given to contingency plan to expel some 1.5 million foreign black workers
because of international economic sanctions....said there is no immediate desire or need to instigate plan. (U) Reuter 64

This Morning Summary from November 18, 1985, features two very interesting deletions, as well as a buried commentary on the Liberian coup mentioned above. First, we see a variety of information sources in addition to cables from U.S. embassies abroad. Here, we have reports from the Foreign Broadcast Information Service (FBIS), a CIA-run media monitoring effort that listens in on radio and TV broadcasts outside the United States from regionally based listening posts (which also collect print sources), translates the most newsworthy items from a U.S. perspective, and cables the English-language versions back to Washington for policymakers (outsiders can subscribe through the National Technical Information Service, but there are major copyright problems standing in the way of broad dissemination). The two censored paragraphs, one on the U.S.S.R. and the other on "Libya-U.S.," both signal a different source (some form of U.S. intelligence surveillance in those countries): either overhead photography or electronic or voice intercepts. The give-away is the level of classification—Top Secret/Codeword (TS/CW), which in the context of an information source almost certainly means the most sensitive methods of stealing information. Finally, the last item in the summary reveals that the "successful coup" announced in the November 12 Morning Summary wound up failing. By November 18, Gen. Samuel Doe was back in power, blaming neighboring Sierra Leone for helping the coup attempt. So much for the CIA's assessment that coup leader Quiwonpka had "considerable support in Liberia."

SITUATION ROOM MORNING SUMMARY   November 18, 1985
SOVIET UNION/EUROPE

USSR-US: Press sources report Soviets have accepted principle of
new summit next year if current talks prove inconclusive...State
has no further information on these reports. (U) FBIS 88, 90,
State Telecon

USSR-US: Moscow television said U.S. delegation in Geneva gave
unintelligible answers at first news conference...U.S. proposals
would lead to buildup of strategic arms and evade key space
militarization issue. Also, USA Institute's Arbatov cited Weinberger letter as proof conservatives want to destroy all arms
limitation agreements. (U) FBIS 100, 102

USSR: ██   (b)(1)
                                                         (b)(3)

FRG-NATO: West Germany's "Der Spiegel" magazine reports
documents on the NATO Wintex-85 maneuvers have been missing since
August from the Kiel civil defense office. (U) FBIS 35

USSR: Georgian dissident arrested Friday...family had appealed to
President to intervene with Gorbachev in Geneva on their behalf.
(U) FBIS 067

WHITE HOUSE E-MAIL

NEAR EAST/SOUTH ASIA

SAUDI ARABIA: Saudis voiced to Charge opposition to press
accounts of a summit agreement on emigration of Jews from the
USSR directly to Israel...urged U.S. not pursue such an agreement
since it would be prejudicial to the peace process. (C) Riyadh
0424

LIBYA-U.S.: ██ (b)(1)
██ (b)(3) (TS/CW)
██

LEBANON: Shi'ite group "The Victimized" announced in Beirut it
holds four Lebanese Jews kidnapped seven months ago. Proposing
their release in exchange for 300 Lebanese detainees in southern
Lebanon. (U) FBIS 81

EGYPT: Briefed ambassadors from UK, FRG, France, Greece, Italy,
Austria, and Nigeria concerning Libya's terrorist plans in

Europe and Africa revealed by recently arrested Libyan
terrorists. (U) FBIS 38
LATIN AMERICA

COLOMBIA: Government has ended emergency operations in wake of
volcanic eruption...no one believed left to rescue. (U) AP N027

ASIA

PHILIPPINES: Cory Aquino told Ambassador she is seeking to be
opposition standard bearer in presidential election and will not
support Doy Laurel for that office or vice president. Sees U.S.
support as crucial for her. Laurel reaffirmed to Ambassador
intent to run for president with or without Aquino. Ambassador
comments Aquino/Laurel friction could lead to easy Marcos
victory. Suggests if U.S. wants more active role in urging
opposition unity, the time is now. (U)(C) Manila 5735,5736

AFRICA

LIBERIA: Charge made human rights demarche to Doe. Doe gave
assurances intends no military retaliation against Sierra
Leone, which he accuses of complicity in aborted coup, but
requested map of Sierra Leone and information on its troop
deployments. Embassy to provide map but to obfuscate on
deployments. Press reports Liberian ambassador to Sierra Leone
recalled, border closed. (C) Monrovia 3325, FBIS 101
                         (U)

On June 10, 1986, former CIA officer and intelligence specialist Vincent Cannistraro sent this e-mail to his bosses at the National Security Council about Rep. Charles Wilson (D-Texas), the leading Congressional backer of the *mujahideen* fighting the Soviets in Afghanistan. This note not only gives away a fascinating Congressional tactic—members have a quota system of securing protection for one selected area of federal funding by giving up the fight in advance on any other item—but also starts a sequence of e-mail about an intriguing episode in the annals of superweapons, on the so-called Buffalo gun.

```
                                           06/11/86 08:41:13

To: NSKED    --CPUA

NOTE FROM: Vincent Cannistraro                    UNCLASSIFIED
Subject: Charley Wilson
*** Forwarding note from NSVMC    --CPUA    06/10/86 17:18 ***
To: NSRBM   --CPUA    JOHN M. POINDEXTER NSWRP    --CPUA    JOHN M. POINDEXTER
NOTE FROM: Vincent Cannistraro
SUBJECT: Charley Wilson
I went to see Congressman Charley Wilson (Texas) at his request.  He
wanted to discuss his efforts to insert money into the defense budget
for weapons development, specifically for use of freedom fighters such
as the Mujahedin.  Wilson had just been briefed by CIA which ••••••••••
•••••••••••••••••••••••••••••••••••••••••••••••••••••••••••••••••••••••
•••••••••••••••••••••••••••••••••••••••••••••••••••••••••••••••••••••••
•••••••••••••••••••••••••••••••••••••••••••••••••••••••••••••••••••••••
•••••••••••••••••••••••••••••••••••••••••••••••• Interesting that
CIA informed Wilson before telling us- assume they will brief me on Friday
when I go out for program update on Friday, in anticipation of the PCG
on Afghanistan scheduled June 20. Wilson asked me to tell you that the
program would need $300 million again in September as a DoD reprogramming.
He said he had already cut his deal with Congressman David Obey to "fence off"
the Afghan money from any DoD budget cuts.  He noted that this meant he
personally was not available to carry water to protect other Defense areas,
but that he had made the deal because of the importance he attaches to the
Afghan program.  I told him I understood.  Inter alia, Wilson said he wanted
to cooperate closely with the White House on Afghanistan and said he would
be calling on us frequently. He invited me out to see a test firing of
the "Buffalo" gun, a pet project which is designed to create a man portable
field anti-tank weapon which can penetrate armor at ••••••••••••• and fires
a •••••••••••••••••••••••••••••••••••••• I accepted.
```

The "Buffalo" gun not only made the White House e-mail, it also made the local news, as attested by this September 3, 1986, e-mail from Peter Rodman to Cannistraro. (USG means U.S. government.)

```
To: NSVMC   --CPUA                                  09/03/86 14:22:51

NOTE FROM: Peter Rodman
SUBJECT: Hand-Held Rocket for Afghans
  I meant to ask you: When I was on leave I read newspaper reports of the guy
whose home-made bazooka went off by accident at a Virginia gas station. The
inventor was said to be a consultant to the USG. Is that the same weapon you
once showed me a picture of?Have we bought any??  Looks like a good buy --
no danger of jamming or other excessive difficulties in firing....
```

Cannistraro replied the same day, admitting that there was this little problem with the trigger mechanism, for example.

```
To: NSPWR   --CPUA                                  09/04/86 08:50:08

*** Reply to note of 09/03/86 14:22
NOTE FROM: Vincent Cannistraro
Subject: Hand-Held Rocket for Afghans
Yes, Dilger's weapon is the same one of which you saw a picture. ••••••••
•••••••••••••••••••• The committee turned it down on the basis that the
weapon had technical problems.  DoD was not entirely happy with the
decision, maintaining that the weapon could be perfected with some
development money (it needed a new trigger mechanism, for example).  In
any event, although there is ten million in the new DoD appropriations
bill for development of unconventional weapons, courtesy of Congressmen
Bill McCollum and Charley Wilson, none of this is likely to be spent on
Dilger's "Buffalo Gun" because of the Arlington incident and the
resulting publicity.  Dilger is a good guy but is surprisingly
unsophisticated- carrying around a loaded 30 mm cannon in downtown
Arlington is not very smart.
```

UNCLASSIFIED
CONFIDENTIAL

The "Buffalo gun" dialogue continued for days in the White House e-mail, no doubt occasioning many chuckles, including this Cannistraro repartee to yet another Rodman note.

```
To: NSPWR   --CPUA                                  09/18/86 09:52:46
*** Reply to note of 09/10/86 10:45
NOTE FROM: Vincent Cannistraro
Subject: Stinger
Actually, they do have a countermeasure to Dilger's missile system- its
called the Arlington Police Department.
```

UNCLASSIFIED

This September 25, 1986, e-mail marks one of the major turning points leading to the public revelation of the Iran-contra affair. Oliver North is alerting John Poindexter about the blown cover of their contra resupply operation. Dick refers to Richard Secord, the NSC's contractor for the operation; Olmstead's real name is William Haskell, a military buddy of North's; Fiers is Alan Fiers, head of the CIA task force on Central America, who ran the contra war along with North and Elliott Abrams, assistant secretary of state for Inter-American Affairs. Other versions of this e-mail have been declassified for various legal investigations of the Iran-contra affair, but all previous ones completely censored the discussion of Costa Rican president Oscar Arias in the second paragraph. In fact, the Arias visit with Reagan was canceled, and Arias went on to win the Nobel Peace Prize for his role in mediating a settlement to the Nicaraguan war.

09/25/86 11:23:45

To: NSJMP   --CPUA

*** Reply to note of 09/13/86 12:01
NOTE FROM: OLIVER NORTH
Subject: Public Affairs Campaign on Central America
Elliott Abrams has just called from New York, followed by an urgent call from Fiers. Last night Costa Rican Interior Minister Garion held a press conference in San Jose and announced that Costa Rican authorities had discovered a secret airstrip in Costa Rica that was over a mile long and which had been built and used by a Co. called Udall Services for supporting the Contras. In the press conference the minister named one of Dick's agents (Olmstead) as the man who set up the field as a "training base for U.S. military advisors." Damage assessment: Udall Resources, Inc., S.A. is a proprietary of Project Democracy. It will cease to exist by noon today. There are no USG fingerprints on any of the operation and Olmstead is not the name of the agent - Olmstead does not exist.
 We have moved all Udall resources ($48K) to another account in Panama, where Udall maintained an answering service and cover office. The office is now gone as are all files and paperwork. The bottomline is that Arias has now seriously violated the understanding we have had with his administration since shortly after his inaugeral. Elliott has said that he and the Secretary want to cancel the Arias visit with the President and replace him with Cerrezo. They are due to meet with Arias at 1145. I strongly urge that you concur with the Secretary's recommendation. Arias has screwed us badly - and we should not gove him what he so obviously wants.

WHITE HOUSE E-MAIL

Poindexter's response to North refers to Lewis Tambs, the U.S. ambassador to Costa Rica, along with a question about Interior Minister Hernon Garrion, which was censored from all previous versions of this e-mail.

To: NSOLN   --CPUA

09/25/86 16:06:46

*** Reply to note of 09/25/86 11:23   --SECRET-- UNCLASSIFIED

NOTE FROM: JOHN POINDEXTER
Subject: Public Affairs Campaign on Central America
I agree. Why didn't Lew Tambs know that this was coming? Is Interior Minister a leftist?

North's answer to the question was only released in April 1995. Here, he gives Lew Tambs's excuse, thumps the table a bit on Arias, and says that he and Elliott Abrams and the CIA chief of station in Costa Rica are on top of the situation, and they are prepared to cover it up. The CIA official (known under the pseudonym Tomas Castillo during the Congressional Iran-contra hearings) is Joseph Fernandez, now in business with Oliver North making bulletproof vests for sale to police departments around the United States. (On privacy grounds we have deleted one libelous North phrase about Arias.)

MSG FROM: NSOLN   --CPUA
To: NSJMF   --CPUA

*** Reply to note of 09/25/86 16:06
NOTE FROM: OLIVER NORTH
Subject: Public Affairs Campaign on Central America
The Interior Minister, like most of Arias' cabinet, is a commie symp socialist who used to be the head of public sanitation in San Jose. Lew has been on annual leave for two weeks. He put this thing back in its box two weeks ago when I called you in the middle of the night to threaten that Arias would not get in the door of the oval office if this case came out. Arias is just a kid who believes so much in cabinet government that he doesn't even pay attention to what is going on in his own government. ~~for his involvement w/~~   On top of that, he apparently gave instructions to the minister to make this announcement after he left for the U.N. in hopes that he would not get blamed. He's not quite as smart as he thinks he is. Believe we have taken all appropriate damage control measures to keep any USG fingerprints off this and with Elliott and the COS, have worked up appropriate "if asked" press guidance. V/R North
    Public Affairs Campaign on Central America

Two weeks later, the Sandinistas shot down the plane carrying Eugene Hasenfus, and the U.S. government went into major denial. This October 8, 1986, e-mail gives the core anatomy of the cover-up. Written by Cannistraro, it lists the lies decided on by the Restricted Interagency Group (RIG) managing the contra war. Note especially that first the U.S. government decided that El Salvador should deny everything, and then the president of El Salvador, Jose Napoleon Duarte, agreed! The RIG also decided that UNO (United Nicaraguan Opposition), the front group for the contras, should take credit for the flight, to deflect attention from the actual sponsors in North's operation. ARA refers to the Inter-American bureau at State. HPSCI and SSCI are the House and Senate committees purportedly overseeing intelligence.

```
                                          10/08/86 16:08 ***
To: NSRBM    --CPUA    JOHN M. POINDEXTER NSWRP    --CPUA    JOHN M. POINDEXTER
NOTE FROM: Vincent Cannistraro
SUBJECT: Downed Plane
At RIG meeting with Elliott Abrams today the question of the captured American
held by the Nicaraguans was discussed. Following decisions were made:
     --Demands for consular access would continue. Elliott thought Nics would
accede to our request today. (He later called me to say the Nics had still not
responded and we should be prepared to escalate tomorrow if there is no
movement. Believes we may have to make this a "hostage crisis" to exert
leverage on Sandinistas.
     --El Salvador will deny any facilitative support to contra flights. By
secure phone to Embassy, we received notice Duarte agreed that GOES would deny
everything. Salvador asked that USG not refer newsmen to El Salvador for
followup.
     --Press Guidance was prepared which states no U.S.G. involvement or
connection, but that we are generally aware of such support contracted by the
Contras.
     --UNO to be asked to assume responsibility for flight and to assist
families of Americans involved. Elliott will follow up with Ollie to
facilitate this.
     --ARA will attempt to identify appropriate legal counsel and ask UNO to
engage him. Lawyer will be asked to donate services pro bono. Alternatively,
private money can be found, according to Elliott.
     --HPSCI and SSCI have been briefed and there were no problems.
     --Elliott said he would continue to tell the press these were brave men
and brave deeds. We recommended he not do this because it contributes to
perception U.S.G. inspired and encouraged private lethal aid effort.
```

This e-mail sequence details the *Achille Lauro* terrorist incident story from the inside for the first time. Several journalists have written news accounts based on leaked information (*Newsweek* revealed during North's denunciation of Congressional leaks during the Iran-contra hearings that its prime source for *Achille Lauro* stories had been North himself, Mr. Anonymous Source). But never before have the internal dynamics within the White House been revealed as they are in the e-mail. Early during the hijacking episode, NSC staffer James Stark complains in this October 8, 1985, note that the Joint Chiefs of Staff at the Pentagon are not proceeding at "best speed" even to locate the *Achille Lauro*. (Sara refers to the *Saratoga* aircraft carrier and its associated battle group.)

```
To: NSWFM    --CPUA    JOHN M. POINDEXTER NSWRP    --CPUA    10/08/85 18:44
NOTE FROM: JAMES R. STARK                                    JOHN M. POINDEXTER
SUBJECT: Location of Achille Lauro
I understand our reluctance to tell the JCS how to run their
show, and am not suggesting that we do so.  But I am concerned
that 24 hours after the start of the hijacking, we still do not
have a good fix on the ship, and the two naval surface units in
the area do not appear to be attempting to close it, •••••••••
••••••••••••••••••••••••  While we may not want to make any
suggestions, would it be in order for you to call JCS and simply
discuss the locating problem and how they intend to solve it?
My understanding is that Sara has not been ordered to proceed
at best speed to the Eastern Med.
```

Within twenty-four hours, practically the whole U.S. government had swung into action, according to this October 9, 1985, e-mail from Jock Covey to the NSC higher-ups. Covey's e-mail gives an extraordinary shorthand review of the pressure cooker of policy during a major crisis. DCM is the deputy chief of mission, the number-two embassy staffer in Egypt, slated to see Egyptian president Hosni Mubarak, who was contemplating allowing a quiet getaway for the hijackers, for his own reasons of state (for example, relations with the Palestinians, the rest of the Arab world, his own Islamic militants in Egypt). Klinghoffer is the wheelchair-bound American tourist killed by the hijackers; Shultz is secretary of state; Essepsi is the Tunisian ambassador; Hussein is the king of Jordan; Veliotes is the U.S. ambassador to Egypt; Port Said is the location of the *Achille Lauro* after the hijacking; Moreau refers to Admiral Arthur Moreau at the Joint Chiefs of Staff; and *Scott* is one of the American ships in the vicinity.

Reagan & Mubarak of Egypt 10-5-81

Reagan & Covey 4-10-86

10/09/85 15:44:21

To: NSWFM --CPUA   JOHN M. POINDEXTER NSWRP   --CPUA   JOHN M. POINDEXTER
NOTE FROM: Jock Covey
SUBJECT: Achille Lauro: update as of 1530

DCM Clarke has been instructed to see Mubarak urgently, and say that given
reports about Klinghoffer it is imperative that the pirates not be permitted
to leave Egypt. ●●
●●●●●●

Shultz sees Essepsi this afternoon. Tunis has already volunteered to help
however it can. Shultz will tell Essepsi they can help by making sure the
pirates stay in Egypt.

Similar message will be sent to Hussein asap.   UNCLASSIFIED

Veliotes still enroute Port Said. Situation there very confused. Not yet clear
when to expect he will be able to eyeball situation (and pax) and report
back.

Moreau still trying to get more direct contact via the SCOTT and its
bridge-to-bridge commo. Embassy Rome trying to get to ship's agent in Genoa,
who may be in direct commo via its own radio.

STATE sending over draft guidance asap on two contingencies: either there is a
victim of violence or everyone is safe. Guidance will address the two key
questions: (1) How are the hostages (2) What was the deal (did we play a role,
etc). Because of confused situation -- anarchy in Port Said plus conflicting
public statements by Egyptians and Italians, press is being reasonably patient
with our insistence on knowing the facts before we go out for another
briefing.

WHITE HOUSE E-MAIL

By noon the next day, Jock Covey's e-mail update has reduced the crisis down to a core point: Will the Egyptians let the hijackers get away? The deleted portion, because of how highly it is classified (Top Secret/Codeword), almost certainly refers to information gained from intercepts, in this case, presumably electronic or voice intercepts picked up by U.S. intelligence revealing the hijackers making plans to abscond and the Egyptians making plans to let them. "Spector" [sic; actually Specter] refers to the Republican senator from Pennsylvania; Armacost is undersecretary of state; and the image of working over the Egyptian ambassador forcefully is definitely not one found in most diplomatic cables.

```
                                                    10/10/85 12:04:27
To: NSWFM   --CPUA     JOHN M. POINDEXTER NSWRP    --CPUA    JOHN M. POINDEXTER
NOTE FROM: Jock Covey
SUBJECT: Achille Lauro: Update as of 1200

STATE working on fast instruction to Veliotes follow-up letter from President
to make two main points:
                                                              (b)(i)
-- We have ...............................................................
........................................................................  (TS/CW)

-- Letting the pirates go will surely rock the US-Egyptian relationship. Just
today, Spector put up an amendment to the Debt Ceiling recinding a billion in
aid for Egypt. This is just the beginning. Etc.

Armacost has the Egyptian Ambassador in his office now, working him over
forcefully.

We should consider sending the same message down the intel pipeline, as well.
```

Later on October 10, U.S. Navy jets intercept the Egyptian passenger plane carrying the hijackers en route to Tunis and force it to land in Sicily. After somewhat of a standoff with Italian authorities, the United States allows Italy to arrest the men; four are held for trial, but the Italians release two against U.S. wishes, while Egyptian president Hosni Mubarak denounces the forcedown as an "act of piracy." At the White House, however, the mood was joyful—the NSC staff had proposed and honcho'd the forcedown, and kudos came from Executive Secretary William Martin, from White House Chief of Staff Donald Regan, from Robert McFarlane to his staff, and from McFarlane's deputy, John Poindexter, specifically for Oliver North. This kind of backing from above helps explain North's ability to run covert Iran-contra operations from his office just next to the White House.

```
FROM: NSWFM   --CPUA     TO: NSHRT   --CPUA        10/11/85 09:20:51
To: NSOLN   --CPUA                  NSJC    --CPUA
    NSJRS   --CPUA                  NSRCM   --CPUA     ROBERT C. MCFARLAN
    NSJMP   --CPUA     JOHN M. POINDEXTER
```

NOTE FROM: WILLIAM F. MARTIN   ~~SECRET~~ UNCLASSIFIED
SUBJECT: White House Staff meeting

It was NSC day today. Regan said that McFarlane, Poidexter and the NSC staff ware to be congratulated for keeping their cool and pulling off this gutsy action. Once again we have done in the tax reform message of the day.

Key follow up action today is telephone call to Klinghoffer family in New York. The wife is still in Cairo and will not return until tomorrow but it was felt that a call to the rest of the family was desirable today. Ollie is tubing telephone call memo and we have tentatively worked out 10:45 with the schedulers for the oval office call.

```
FROM: NSRCM   --CPUA     TO: NSHRT   --CPUA        10/11/85 10:15:06
To: NSWFM   --CPUA
```

*** Reply to note of 10/11/85 09:43

~~SECRET~~ UNCLAS

NOTE FROM: ROBERT MCFARLANE
Subject: White House Staff meeting
I couldn't agree more. This is unfortunately not the stuff of which Colonels and Generals are being made nowadays--and that is all the more testimony to Ollie's guts and determination. Separately, John Poindexter was a giant throughout. The pressures and cautious resistance were immense--although Bill Crowe and 6th Fleet deserve very high marks--and it was an example of courage and leadership of which the President--who, by the way, never wavered--can be deservedly proud. Bravo Zulu to all hands.

WHITE HOUSE E-MAIL

*** Reply to note of 10/11/85 10:15

NOTE FROM: JOHN POINDEXTER
Subject: White House Staff meeting
I AGREE WITH THE CRITICALITY OF OLLIE'S ROLE. HE PROVIDED THE SYNERGISIM THAT
MADE IT ALL WORK.

cc: NSHRT   --CPUA   HOWARD TEICHER   NSOLN   --CPUA   OLLIE NORTH

                                                    10/13/85 10:38:58
To: NSWFM   --CPUA   JOHN M. POINDEXTER NSWRP   --CPUA   JOHN M. POINDEXTER
NOTE FROM: Jock Covey
Subject: US ship visit to Kuwait

Agree we should quietly press on with business as usual in the Arab world. It
is right that counter terror prep should be meticulous and imaginative. At
same time, we should expect some weaseling and snubs from our 'friends', who
will not yet have figured out how to cope with complex pressures generated by
Mubarak's wacky behavior, the PLO's "big lie" approach to the Klinghoffer
murder, and our own resolute, mostly successful, pursuit. These terrorists
have slimed everything they have touched in the last few days, creating
enormous tensions between us and some good friends. It shouldn't be surprising
if they are able, for now, also to complicate some of our less intimate
relationships. The simple fact of the capture speaks volumes; the confused
reactions to it pass. It will just take a bit longer to get on to the next
chapter if these creeps succeed in getting between us and a lengthening list
of our partners.

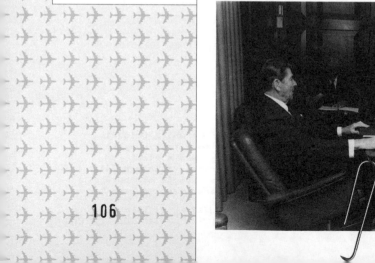

Reagan & Shultz 10-29-85

Bush, Reagan, Shultz, Weinberger et. al., Situation Room 10-23-83

This sequence of e-mail from February 4, 1986, shows the White House staff swinging into action after a Situation Room alert. Israeli jets had intercepted a Libyan civilian jet over the Mediterranean and forced it to land in Israel, apparently on the belief that the plane carried Abu Musa, a key Palestinian leader. National Security Council staffer Jock Covey's first e-mail, at 9:58 A.M., lets his boss, John Poindexter, know that it was the "wrong plane."

```
                                              02/04/86 09:58:21
To: NSRBM    --CPUA    JOHN M. POINDEXTER NSWRP    --CPUA    JOHN M. POINDEXTER
NOTE FROM:  Jock Covey
SUBJECT: Israeli Sky-capture

Possible that Israelis got wrong plane.  Abu Musa (Syrian-backed anti-Arafat
Palestinian) was supposed to be enroute Syria, but appears Israelis may have
pulled down a 15-seat exec jet carrying only Syrian Baath Party officials.
State on open line with Tel Aviv now trying to clarify.
```

WHITE HOUSE E-MAIL

By 2 P.M., members of the whole Middle East section of the National Security Council staff were relaying e-mail to each other, weighing in to shape the U.S. response to the Israeli action. Jock Covey continues at the center of the action, passing on notes from Howard Teicher (HRT) and James Stark (JRS) to others like Oliver North (OLN) and Elaine Morton (ELM), suggesting editorial changes in the official "guidance" in which the U.S. government would take its stance. Ultimately, the White House not only changed its language to "regret" the incident, but also ordered the U.S. delegation to the United Nations to veto on February 6 a Syrian-backed UN Security Council resolution condemning the Israeli action.

```
FROM: NSJC     --CPUA     TO: NSELM    --CPUA              02/04/86 14:25:08
To: NSOLN    --CPUA                    NSJRS     --CPUA
NOTE FROM:  Jock Covey
Subject: Israeli sky-capture


The problem the lawyers are wrestling with seems to go something like this:
We came out okay on Achille Lauro because we got the right plane -- where
would we have been if it had been the wrong plane?  Would the principle
of no-hiding-place-for-terrorists still apply?  Or does the more basic
rule of life apply: you're only right if it works?

There is no appetite for condemning the Israeli action.  Everyone understands
what motivated it.  Neither do we want to condone fishing in the air, however.
The proposed guidance may not be so far off if we drop the "irresponsible"
and emphasize the "regretable."
```

```
                                            02/04/86 14:18 ***
To: NSJC     --CPUA

*** Reply to note of 02/04/86 14:01
NOTE FROM: JAMES R. STARK
Subject: Israeli sky-capture
I think "deplorable" ought to be substituted for "irresponsible" to
soften it a bit.  The Israelis were not irresponsible in
their goal, and I don't think the fact that they screwed up the
operation shows irresponsibility either.
```

The White House was unable to enjoy many victories in counterterrorism other than the *Achille Lauro* operation. E-mail on other terrorist issues mostly reflects constant frustration —sometimes directed at allies, sometimes within the U.S. government, and almost always at the foreign governments who either did not share the U.S. government's antipathy or actively supported the black hats. In this sequence of e-mail, staffers Robert Earl, Craig Coy, Oliver North, and Howard Teicher weigh in on the subject of "Syria Bashing." A mad bomber named Hindawi (who had planted a bomb in his fiancée's suitcase before she boarded an El Al flight) was on trial in London, but the British were about to "wimp out on us," as Earl writes on October 20, 1986, by declining to name the Syrian ambassador as an accomplice. Also included in Earl's extraordinarily candid e-mail is a blast at the Treasury Department, the "poor dears."

```
                                                       10/20/86 15:01:23
To: NSOLN    --CPUA              NSCPC    --CPUA
NOTE FROM: Robert L. Earl
SUBJECT: SYRIA BASHING
Dave Long chaired a meeting at State today to try to get the bureaucracy
moving in developing a range of USG unilateral options for possible use at
the end of this week -- after the Hindawi trial reports out tomorrow and the
Brits wimp out on us.  One issue is whether we risk pissing off the Brits by
attacking their interpretation of the facts head on -- ie. if the Brits say
tomorrow (as one rumor has it) that there is no evidence of Syrian govt
involvement (ie the Syrian Ambassador to the UK acted as an "individual"),
do we say that our interpretation of the same set of facts is different from
the Brits (as in, we DO think there was Syrian govt involvement)?
    The political steps being considered by State are:
1. strong White House statement
2. additional high-level approach to the Syrians
3. a high-level approach to the Soviets on the activities of one of their
   "clients", and
4. a political campaign in Europe on Syrian support, similar to our Libyan
   campaign.
The economic steps are outlined in the draft State paper I've circulated, but
consist of some import sanctions (either just GSP or ALL imports, which
only total to $2m), and some export steps (ban Ex-Im Bank credits to Syria
and steps against Syrian Arab Airlines (affecting their purchase of parts
for their 3 727s and 2 747s...).
Treasury, in their inimitable fashion, didn't even want to touch the subject
until AFTER there had been a "high level" USG decision to impose some sort of
sanctions, because they were terribly overworked implementing Libyan, South
African, and Nicaraguan sanctions....  Poor dears.
```

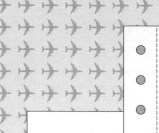

Craig Coy responds within the hour with more Syria bashing, but he mounts a defense of the British, especially since Syrian president Hafiz Assad seems to have helped with the release of Lawrence Jenco, an American hostage in Lebanon.

10/20/86 15:45:12

To: NSRLE   --CPUA

*** Reply to note of 10/20/86 15:01
NOTE FROM: Craig P. Coy
Subject: SYRIA BASHING
I agree that Syria is a bad actor and should be highlighted as a terrorist
state, but I'm confused by the debate.Why should we be bashing the Brits for
what
  happens in their court, for a attempted bombing of an Israeli airline from a
British airport? The Brits (Thatcher) has, albeit somewhat reluctantly, joined
with us every step of the way in our policy against terrorism. Before we go
off and impose sanctions and break diplomatic relations I think we better show
some nasty Syrian activity against U.S. interests. Talking tough and publicly
chiding them is good, but after our infamous disinformation campaign we should
not start down the bashing road before we have laid the groundwork for a case
against Syrian terrorist support. As it is now some at State are thanking
Assad for his latest help in gaining the release of Jenco, we do not need to
again send mixed signals from various places in the government on the pro or
cons of Syria. Am I missing something here?

To answer Coy's question—"Am I missing something here?"—Oliver North lobs in one e-mail to Coy and a rousing second-the-motion to Robert Earl.

*** Reply to note of 10/20/86 15:01   10/20/86 18:59:51
NOTE FROM: OLIVER NORTH
Subject: SYRIA BASHING
Bash the bastards!
     SYRIA BASHING

*** Reply to note of 10/20/86 15:45   10/20/86 19:04:22
NOTE FROM: OLIVER NORTH
Subject: SYRIA BASHING
Yes. There were 233 AmCit on the plane Hindawi tried to blow up.

```
To: NSRLE    --CPUA                          11/12/86 09:22:42

*** Reply to note of 11/12/86 07:38
NOTE FROM: Howard Teicher
Subject: syria
fuck the syrians! can we get together to coordinate our various affairs.
```

Weinberger, Bush, Reagan, Shultz, Casey, Regan, Situation Room 6-16-85

WHITE HOUSE E-MAIL

Sometimes the news from the Situation Room kicked off despair, as in this plaintive e-mail from Howard Teicher to Latin America specialist Jackie Tillman on October 29, 1986. At issue were British plans (announced by Foreign Secretary Sir Geoffrey Howe) to consolidate their control on the Falkland Islands—a slap in the face for Raul Alfonsin, the democratically elected president of Argentina, who came to power in large part because the military dictatorship there had lost so badly the 1982 Falklands war.

```
To: NSJT    --CPUA                              10/29/86 09:30:27

NOTE FROM: Howard Teicher
SUBJECT: argentina
i note that howe plans to announce an exclusionary zone around
the falklands this morning. did we have any warning of this?
i doubt it will encourage alfonsin to agree to talk about a
cessation of hostilities. anything we can do? do we plan to
say anything in public or private? maybe a silver lining. shit.
```

Reagan & National Security Council briefing 4-15-86

Then there was the phenomenon of SitRoom envy. In this September 29, 1986, e-mail, Craig Coy gives a trip report to his boss, Oliver North, about an excursion with the NSC's intelligence programs staff (Major, DeGraffenreid) over to see the Justice Department's SitRoom. St. Martin and McDaniel were top NSC Secretariat officials; the CMC is the Crisis Management Center at the Old Executive Office Building honcho'd by North and his gang; Larkin ran the White House SitRoom. When North replies on September 30, he gives Coy the appropriate spin to put in their counterterrorism (C/T) report to Alton Keel, that the Justice Department's success is a result of their good coordinating work at the Operations Sub-Group (OSG-207), but admits it really came from "just trying to find Meese in a hurry...."

```
                                                                   09/29/86  17:16:54
To: NSOLN    --CPUA                    NSRLE    --CPUA
NOTE FROM: Craig P. Coy
SUBJECT: Justice OP Center
Went over w/ Grimes, Major, deGraffenreid to see DOJ's new command center. It
is very impressive with a whole host of link ups to their agencies, Chosun,
Flashboard,secure phone, secure video to FBI, two secure conference rooms,
space s for translators, teletype, I mean everything!They did it for $500K:
furnitu re, equipment, construction, material, everything. It makes our
sitroom and the CMC led work look like child's play. St. Martin and McDaniel
should go over there. (problem is they would fire Larkin,, is that a problem?)
secure number is 633 5477 ID#03921 open line 633 5000.
```

```
                                                                   09/30/86  14:18:44

To: NSCPC    --CPUA

*** Reply to note of 09/29/86 17:16
NOTE FROM: OLIVER NORTH
Subject: Justice OP Center
Pls write this up in our next little C/T update for Keel. This is a direct
result of our efforts to get a real inter-agency process going on C/T - and
came out of the work of the OSG/207 coordination (actually it came out of just
trying to find Meese in a hurry, but we might as well make note of itin a
positive w ay.
```

CHAPTER 5

GUNS'T'BOMBS

During World War II, the United States earned the title of "arsenal of democracy" for our prodigious production and worldwide shipment of weapons. Over the past five decades, the distinction of being the world's biggest arms dealer (occasionally second to the Soviet Union) has also been a source of almost constant discomfort to top U.S. policymakers, not so much on moral grounds (one author memorably described this function as that of "merchants of death") as on political and alliance relations grounds. Supplying the world with arms meant constant pressure from domestic interest groups and especially weapons contractors, pressure from allies not to sell their neighbors particular weapons systems, and flare-ups of regional arms races that probably reached their duplicitous and deadly peak in the mid-1980s when the United States was helping both sides in the Iran-Iraq War.

The National Security Council serves as the umpire on U.S. arms deals. The staff's e-mail describes intricate balancing acts among the various competing interests, including hashing out compromises with the foreign countries as well as the domestic contractors. Some of the e-mail details juicy tidbits of impending scandals or legal investigations into arms deals, while others essentially assign the Good Housekeeping Seal of Approval to certain arrangements. A major theme throughout is the NSC role in quarterbacking the public relations and lobbying efforts necessary to get Congressional approval of major arms sales abroad, since all deals over $14 million have to be reported to Congress.

Included in this chapter are some vivid samples of the NSC's role in overseeing the world circulation of guns'n'bombs. Israeli spy operations to steal U.S. cluster-bomb technology quickly fade into Israeli offers to donate captured Soviet-bloc weapons to the contras. NSC staff scheme to arrange the sale of Israeli warplanes to Honduras and British-made antiaircraft missiles from Chile to El Salvador (fronting for the contras).

Of course, now we know that the NSC staff got into the arms dealing business themselves. For example, when President Reagan told his men to keep the Nicaraguan contras together "body and soul" after Congress cut off aid, the NSC staff hustled to set up a "private" support operation, run from the White House and the Old Executive Office Building. When Congress resumed aid, the same staff schemed to sell back the "private" assets to the CIA. The arrangements made by these staffers and detailed in the White House e-mail are about as close as most Americans will ever get to the shady lives led by "merchants of death."

Regan, Reagan, Bush, McFarlane (daily national security briefing) 6-20-85

This July 9, 1986, e-mail from NSC counterintelligence specialist David Major to his NSC superiors gives them a heads-up about an extraordinary arms deal allegedly put together by Israeli agents to obtain cluster bombs, so-called anti-personnel devices that explode and scatter a deadly cloud of shrapnel. The case is extra-sensitive because indictments are imminent for senior Israeli intelligence officials who had recruited American Navy analyst Jonathan Jay Pollard to spy for Israel (Pollard was arrested in November 1985).

```
FROM: NSDGM    --CPUA        TO: NSDGM    --CPUA              07/09/86 10:16:09
To: NSRBM     --CPUA    JOHN M. POINDEXTER NSWRP    --CPUA        JOHN M. POINDEXTER
NOTE FROM: David Major
SUBJECT: ISRAELI CLUSTER BOMB CASEAND POLLARD UPDATE
AS YOU KNOW YESTURDAY,CUSTOMS, AFTER CONSULTATION WITH DOJ AND STATE
EXECUTED SELLED SEARCH WARRANTS ON VECTOR CORPORATION AND BEXCO
INTERNATIONAL IN IOWA AND ASSEMBLY MACHINES, INC IN PENN AS WELL AS, 15 OTHER
COMPANIES WERE SERVED WITH SUBPOEANS FOR TESTIMONY AND THE PRODUCTION OF
DOCUMENTS BEFORE A GRAND JURY IN AUGUST.ALL RELATE TO AN INVESTIGATION
THAT OFFICIALS OF THE ISRAELI DEFENSE  PROCUREMENT MISSION AND ISRAELI
MILITARY INDUSTRY(IMI) HAVE BEENINVOLVED IN EFFORTS TO OBTAIN BLUEPRINTS
AND PLANS FOR CLUSTER BOMBS IN VIOLATION OF THE PRESIDENT'S 1982 POLICY
BARRING SUCH TRANSFERS.IT IS MY UNDERSTANDING THE CASE AGAINSTIMIIS
SUBSTANTIAL.I HAVE ADDITIONAL DETAILS RE THIS CASE IF YOU NEED IT.
```

Less than two weeks later, the Israeli cluster-bomb case turned "wierd" [sic] with an apology from the U.S. government, according to this e-mail from NSC press officer Karna Small to David Major. Major was apparently out of the office at the time, so Small repeated the gist of her e-mail on July 28, so Major wouldn't do "anything drastic."

```
To: NSDGM    --CPUA

NOTE FROM: KARNA SMALL
SUBJECT: Cluster bombs                                  07/23/86 15:34:20

I thought you might be interested in an item on the afternoon wires:

(AP) The Reagan Administration has apologized to Israel for publicity
surrounding allegations that Israeli agents smuggled cluster bomb
technology, US and Israeli officials said today. The US official, who
spoke on condition of anonymity, said "the State Dept. expressed regret for
apparently unauthorized disclosure of confidential information regarding
an ongoing investigation."

(Translation: State Dept. apologizes to people who steal technology --
or did I get that wrong?)
```

WHITE HOUSE E-MAIL

To: NSDGM   --CPUA   07/28/86 19:13 ***

NOTE FROM: JAMES R. STARK
SUBJECT: Apology to Israel
I checked with State, who said that Armacost called
in the Israeli ambassador last week to notify him that
the subpoenas and search warrants had been issued. Since
ASD Dick Murphy had earlier told the Israelis that the
subpoenas/search warrants were supposed to be secret,
and since they were issued under an order of confidentiality,
Armacost told Amb Rosenne that he regretted that the news
had been made public by Customs and DOJ spokesmen.
I don't know if anyone at NSC cleared on this; I doubt it.

To: NSDGM   --CPUA   07/29/86 09:11

NOTE FROM: Howard Teicher
Subject: Apology to Israel
nsc has zero involvement in this caper to the best of my knowledge.

At this point, the NSC staff were in a mild uproar—and NSC Middle East staffer James Stark was on the case. According to Stark's July 28 e-mail, the problem was the publicity around the case, which embarrassed the Israelis. Undersecretary of State

Michael Armacost apparently apologized for not keeping the cluster-bomb investigation confidential! NSC senior Middle East staffer Howard Teicher quickly e-mailed the file about "this caper."

Stark & Reagan 11-13-86

Regan, Reagan, Bush, McFarlane, Poindexter 6-20-85

Ironically, the NSC staff were busily plotting another Israel-related arms deal during the same period as the cluster-bomb scandal, this one to encourage the sale of Israeli Kfir jet fighter-bombers to Honduras, to counter the Soviet-supplied air force of Nicaragua. In this May 2, 1986, e-mail, NSC Middle East staffer Peter Rodman invokes the NSC's Don Fortier, Oliver North, Ray Burghardt, and Jim Stark, along with the State Department's Elliott Abrams and the CIA's Alan Fiers, in a bid to approach Israeli defense minister Yitzhak Rabin.

```
05/02/86 09:44:30
To: NSHRT    --CPUA

NOTE FROM: Peter Rodman
SUBJECT: Rabin Meeting
    At a meeting last week on Central America (with Don, Ollie, Elliot Abrams,
Fiers), Elliott suggested offering Kfirs to the Hondurans. The Hondurans are
apparently seeking US aircraft, and Elliott saw many advantages in getting the
Israelis engaged -- including Congressional advantages. (One problem was that
the Israelis had gouged the Hondurans on some earlier supply contracts and we
would have to ensure that the Israelis behaved themselves on this one.)
    Check with Ollie and perhaps Ray Burghardt to see where this stands and
whether it is ripe yet to discuss with Rabin.  I have mentioned this to
Jim Stark.
```

WHITE HOUSE E-MAIL

Reagan & Rabin 1-30-85

By August 1986, the Kfir dealing was in full swing, as Oliver North's two aides, Robert Earl and Craig Coy, exchange e-mail about possibly using Foreign Military Sales (FMS) subsidies for the transaction.

To: NSOLN   --CPUA   08/19/86 17:33 ***
NOTE FROM: Robert L. Earl
SUBJECT: KFIR SALES TO HONDURAS
Jim Stark called. He had a meeting w/ a representative of the Israeli
aircraft industry, who pumped him for info on whether the USG was favorable
toward Kfir sales to Honduras. Supposedly, Rabin had had a meeting w/
Shultz and/or Weinberger on the issue. Also, an unidentified NSC staffer
(Jim wonders if it was you) also met in late June w/ Israeli officials on
the subject. All this according to the unidentified Israeli, who apparently
thinks that the USG is not only favorably disposed toward the idea, but also
that FMS money can be used to finance the transactions.... Jim said he was
noncommittal in response, making the general observation that sometimes the
Israelis could provide things in areas where we could not, but also expressing
doubt about the FMS angle.

To: NSOLN   --CPUA
                                              08/19/86 19:24:22

NOTE FROM: Craig P. Coy
Subject: KFIR SALES TO HONDURAS
interesting, stark called me too. same conversation although i said that i tho
ught i'd heard something like that a while ago but couldn't be sure and pass it
on to oln.

To: NSJMP   --CPUA

*** Reply to note of 09/10/86 13:15   09/12/86 21:50:26
NOTE FROM: OLIVER NORTH
Subject: Iran
Have just returned from mtg w/ Rabin, who called at 1910 and asked me to come
by his hotel. Mtg lasted abt 1.5hrs. Summary: Vy complementary to you & noted
that the hostage operation had to be the longest running no-leak operation of
its kind in history. Said he was vy pleased w/ yr reaction & SecShultz re Kfir
to Honduras. He finally got to point of inviting me over. He noted press
stories and other intel on lack of supplies for Contras and wanted to know if
we had any need for SovBloc weaps and ammo he could make avail. I told him
that we wd vy much like to have whatever he cd spare and he asked "has your
shipload left the Med yet?" (This is the one I tried to get Casey's people to
pay for as a means of covering some of Dick's debts). At this point I cd see
no reason to dissemble, and told him it was in Lisbon. He then suggested that
if it is "your ship, not the CIA's," it shd come to Haifa and he wd have it
filled w/ whatever they cd have assembled in the next five days. He went on at
some length about his low opinion of our intel service - both in terms of
covert ops and intelligence collecting (I noted that maybe we were getting
better at counterintelligence than they thought - and he allowed that was
probably true and that there would "be no more Pollards). Bottom line: Don't
quite no what to do. Did not want to turn down offer - since it includes
recently seized PLO shipment captured at sea. We can go ahead and move the
whole shipment to Honduras or El Salvador - but still won't have any money to
pay off rapidly growing debts. Hate to turn away offers like this - it will
really help in long run. Any advice? V/R North P.S. pls look at today's NID re
Contra resupply effort. All flights being flown - including three msns last
night and three more tonight at last light have been vy successful. All being
done by Dick's pilots w/ borrowed $.

WHITE HOUSE E-MAIL

To: NSOLN   --CPUA   09/13/86 12:09:04

*** Reply to note of 09/12/86 21:50   -- UNCLASSIFIED

NOTE FROM: JOHN POINDEXTER
Subject: Iran
I think you should go ahead and make it happen. It can be a private deal
between Dick and Rabin that we bless. As I told you in the other note I talked
to Casey this morning about Secord. Keep the pressure on Bill to make things
right for Secord.

Poindexter and Reagan 4-15-86

North's boss, National Security Adviser
John Poindexter loved the idea of an
Israel-PLO donation and approved the
use as the middleman retired U.S.
general Richard Secord—the NSC's
(sole source and noncompetitive bid)
secret contractor on the arms deals
with Iran.

To: NSJMP   --CPUA   09/15/86 11:20:39

*** Reply to note of 09/13/86 12:09
NOTE FROM: OLIVER NORTH
Subject: Iran
Re the Israeli arms. Orders were passed to the ship this morning to proceed to
Haifa to pick up the arms. Loading will be accomplished during one night and
the ship will be back at sea before dawn. Loading will be accomplished by
Israeli military personnel.

To: NSDRP   --CPUA

*** Reply to note of 04/03/86 15:43

NOTE FROM: OLIVER NORTH   UNCLASSIFIED
                                           UNCLASSIFIED
Subject: Stingers

There are currently only two weapon systems which are effective against the
HIND -- the STINGER and the older version of the BLOWPIPE. The political and
training problems with our system are significant and do not obtain in the
case of the BP. We wd have considerable difficulty in passing ours to the
Resistance unless the Hondurans already had sufficient numbers to allay their
fears of attack. Last week's SWP breakfast decision NOT to send STINGERs to
Honduras is a serious set-back for this plan. The STINGERs for Honduras idea
was specifically intended to lay the groundwork for an eventual transfer to
the Resistance and now we have walked back from that promise. Unless we get
them to the HAF - and soon - we will never get them to the Resistance. The
DiConcini protocol is simply a tactic to get us beyond the vote and to
demonstrate a need later on. We can then go back to DiConcini and explain that
the situation has changed enough to warrant the provision of the weapons.
Meanwhile, the resistance is moving to acquire BPs and AA MGs in sufficient
quantities to defend themselves.

Sometimes the arms deals were not direct, but featured NSC staff as brokers among third parties, as in the case of Oliver North's attempt to move antiaircraft missiles to the contras. This April 7, 1986, e-mail from North to his supervisor, Don

Fortier, describes the demise of an elaborate pass-through mechanism in which U.S. Stingers would first go to the Honduran armed forces, and eventually to the contras.

McFarlane, Reagan & caddy 10-23-83

North was pushing this arrangement because his first choice, a deal for Blowpipe missiles, fell through. This March 26, 1986, e-mail to North's former boss, Bud McFarlane, tells the tale of a failed attempt to acquire Blowpipes from Chile through the manufacturer, the British firm Short Brothers. Unfortunately for North, the abysmal human rights record of the Chilean regime headed by General Augusto Pinochet came up in an international tribunal the same week the deal was to take place, and the U.S. government joined the condemnation, thus killing the Blowpipe deal. Note the covert help from the Salvadoran government, in the form of a fake end-user certificate (EUC).

*** Reply to note of 03/20/86 23:04

NOTE FROM: OLIVER NORTH
Subject: Anything New??

After the House vote on aid to the resistance, I plan to take a few days just to get re-acquainted w/ the family. Meanwhile, we are trying to find a way to get 10 BLOWPIPE launchers and 20 missiles from Chile thru the Short Bros. Rep. The V.P. from Short Bros. sought me out several mos. ago and I met w/ him again in London a few weeks ago when I was there ███████████ Short Bros., the mfgr. of the BLOWPIPE, is willing to arrange the deal, conduct the training and even send U.K. "tech reps" fwd if we can close the arrangement. Dick Secord has already paid 10% down on the delivery and we have a Salvadoran EUC which is acceptable to the Chileans. Unfortunately, the week all this was going to closure we decided to go fwd in Geneva w/ our human rights paper on Pinochet. The arrangement is now on ice and we are casting about for a way to tell the Chileans that we wd be pleased if this all went thru. Ur thoughts wd be appreciated.

(b)(1)(s)

UNCLASSIFIED

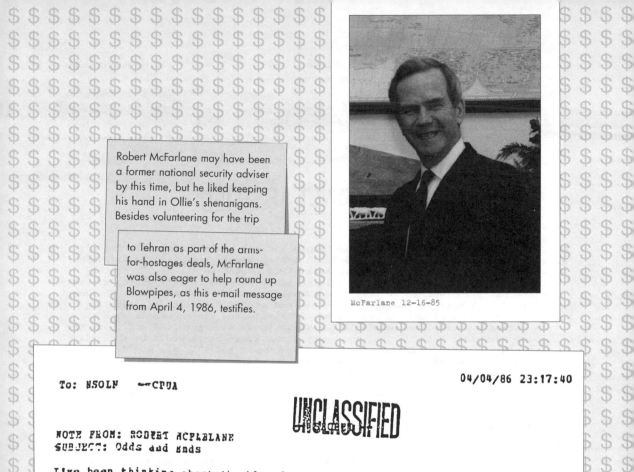

Robert McFarlane may have been a former national security adviser by this time, but he liked keeping his hand in Ollie's shenanigans. Besides volunteering for the trip to Tehran as part of the arms-for-hostages deals, McFarlane was also eager to help round up Blowpipes, as this e-mail message from April 4, 1986, testifies.

McFarlane 12-16-85

To: NSOLN   --CPUA

04/04/86 23:17:40

UNCLASSIFIED

NOTE FROM: ROBERT MCFARLANE
SUBJECT: Odds and ends

I've been thinking about the blowpipe problem and the Contras. Could you ask the CIA to identify which countries the Brits have sold them to. I ought to have a contact in at least one of them.

How are you coming on the loose ends for the material transfer? Anything I can do? If for any reason, you need some mortars or other artillery--which I doubt----please let me know.

WHITE HOUSE E-MAIL

Intimations of the ultimate Iran-contra blowup radiate from this May 3, 1986, e-mail from National Security Adviser John Poindexter to Oliver North. Aside from the U.S. ambassador to Great Britain, Charles Price, the note catalogs

a veritable rogue's gallery of shady characters, including Amiram Nir, North's partner from the Israeli prime minister's office in the arms-for-hostages deals; Adnan Khashoggi, a Saudi financier who served as

a middleman in the transactions; Manucher Ghorbanifar, the notorious Iranian expatriate who spark-plugged the deals and lied to both sides on a regular basis; and the dictator of Zaire, Gen. Sese Seko Mobutu.

05/03/86 06:59:51

To: NSOLN   --CPUA   OLLIE NORTH UNCLASSIFIED
-- SECRET --

NOTE FROM: JOHN POINDEXTER
SUBJECT: Iran
Charlie Price called me with a wild story tonight. A Bob Frasure on Price's staff met with Tiny Rowlands, a British entrepreneur. Tiny said he met this week with Nir, Khashoggi and Ghorbanifar. Nir wanted to use Tiny's company Lonhro to provide management for a large scale program to sell grain, military spare parts and weapons to Iran from countries as far away as China. Khashoggi claimed that very big money was involved and showed Tiny receipts for large scale transfers of cash to Swiss banks. Nir said the scheme was ok with the Americans and only four people in the White House were involved and I was the point man. Zaire was involved and weapons and spare parts would be channeled through Kinshasa and Mobutu was witting and would get 10%. Nir would cut Tiny in for 7%. Tiny checked this out with Mobutu and he confirmed it. Tiny also called Kimche who also confirmed it.

I told Charlie that there was only a shred of truth in this and the US connection was highly distorted. Tiny told Frasure that he didn't like the deal and did not want to get involved unless it was an American operation. I told Charlieto advise him not to get involved.

What in the hell is Nir doing? We really can't trust those sob's.

Ranking with the most unusual arms deals documented on the White House e-mail system is this July 1986 prospectus, written by North to Poindexter, advocating that a reluctant CIA be forced to purchase the contra-support assets run by his "overseas companies with no

U.S. connection." Note North's final argument for the sale—that the contras (North calls them the "DRF" or democratic resistance forces) were about to run out of food unless the sale happened.

At the time this e-mail was written, Swiss bank records show that the North-Secord-Hakim Enterprise (a.k.a. "Project Democracy" or "PRO-DEM") had assets of over $8 million in arms-sale profits. Perhaps North was just warming up for his ultimate career as a direct mail fund-raiser.

Date and time   07/24/86 13:55:53.

To: NSJMP   --CPUA

*** Reply to note of 07/15/86 14:07
NOTE FROM: OLIVER NORTH
Subject: PRIVATE BLANK CHECK

We are rapidly approaching the point where the PROJECT DEMOCRACY assets in CentAm need to be turned over to CIA for use in the new program. The total value of the assets (six aircraft, warehouses, supplies, maintenence facilities, ships, boats, leased houses, vehicles, ordnance, munitions, communications equipment, and a 6520' runway on property owned by a PRODEM proprietary) is over $4.5M.

  All of the assets - and the personnel - are owned/paid by overseas companies with no U.S. connection. All of the equipment is in first rate condition and is already in place. It wd be ludicrous for this to simply disappear just because CIA does not want to be "tainted" with picking up the assets and then have them spend $8-10M of the $100M to replace it - weeks or months later. Yet, that seems to be the direction they are heading, apparently based on NSC guidance.

  If you have already given Casey instructions to this effect, I wd vy much like to talk to you about it in hopes that we can reclama the issue. All seriously believe that immediately after the Senate vote the DRF will be subjected to a major Sandinista effort to break them before the U.S. aid can become effective. PRODEM currently has the only assets available to support the DRF and the CIA's most ambitious estimate is 30 days after a bill is signed before their own assets will be available. This will be a disaster for the DRF if they have to wait that long. Given our lack of movement on other funding options, and Elliot/Allen's plea for PRODEM to get food to the resistance ASAP, PRODEM will have to borrow at least $2M to pay for the food. That's O.K., and Dick is willing to do so tomorrow - but only if there is reasonable assurance that the lenders can be repaid. The only way that the $2M in food money can be repaid is if CIA purchases the $4.5M+ worth of PRODEM equipment for about $2.25M when the law passes. You should be aware that CIA has already approached PRODEM's chief pilot to ask him where they (CIA) can purchase more of the C-135K A/C. The chief pilot told them where they can get them commercially from the USAF as excess - the same way PRODEM bought them under proprietary arrangements. It is just unbelievable. If you wish I can send you a copy of the PROJECT DEMOCRACY status report which includes a breakdown of assets. It is useful, nonattributable reading. Warm Regards,
North

WHITE HOUSE E-MAIL

CHAPTER 6

SPIN DOCTORS

The White House press corps amounts to the largest group of reporters in Washington D.C., and probably the largest media group focused on a single institution anywhere in the world. Much of White House life revolves around "feeding the beast," as the White House public affairs staff calls the process of giving news to journalists, and for most of the 1980s, the White House succeeded in keeping the beast fed and purring. President Reagan won the nickname "The Great Communicator," partly for his script-reading abilities and partly for his staff's ability to script events that drove home the White House message and drowned out the critics.

The White House e-mail system records hundreds of these manipulations of the media into reporting the White House version of world events, including a classic succinct definition of the process: "[P]ut our own spin on the story—in other words, what points you would wish him to make, regardless of the question." These e-mail notes invite the reader to sit in on the electronic meetings in which White House staff debated and worked out their official public relations reactions to crises worldwide, including breaking scandals. Staff members answer interview requests, lobby for placement of op-ed articles, prepare for questions, wince from criticism, and argue with other agencies and their own press spokespeople about the ways and means of various announcements.

Perhaps most importantly, these e-mail messages profile a style of dealing with the press. Not only was the style routinely manipulative, but the White House staff of the mid-1980s went even further than spin, into what the military and intelligence community call "psychological operations," thus turning on the American people the personnel and techniques honed in three decades of Cold War propaganda overseas.

```
FROM: NSKS    --CPUA    TO: NSHRT   --CPUA        01/08/86 18:38:03
To: NSJRS    --CPUA                   NSHRT    --CPUA
    NSOLN    --CPUA

NOTE FROM: KARNA SMALL
SUBJECT: Fortier press session

Don Fortier is going to be meeting with the three news magazines Thurs.
afternoon for a little background session on the whole Libyan story.  He
has asked that I work with you to come up with some quick points that would
do two things: (1) answer (to the extent we want to) questions they are
likely to ask and (2)put our own spin on the story - in other words, what
points you would wish him to make, regardless of the question.
```

Karna Small served as a primary operator of the National Security Council's spin switchboard during the mid-1980s. As press liaison, she was the first point of contact for reporters and often the last. Some e-mail shows that she was kept out of the loop on much of the most covert operations, but this particular item demonstrates that she certainly understood the First Commandment of Spin—make your points no matter what the question is.

Reagan & Small 9-1-86

Sometimes effective spin meant making sure any blame attached elsewhere than the White House. In this e-mail, the NSC deputy executive secretary, Bob Pearson, enlists his boss, John Poindexter, to rein in the White House press secretary, Larry Speakes. Speakes was briefing the press corps sitting around in Santa Barbara (SB), California (where Reagan took frequent vacations on his ranch) about certain "Cuban initiatives" related to immigration levels of Cubans fleeing to the United States.

Since any limits on immigration were potentially controversial with President Reagan's hard-core backers in the Miami Cuban-American community, the NSC staff preferred that the State Department take the heat, not the White House, if any was forth-coming. PDT is Pacific Daylight Time.

Reagan & Small 5-6-82

08/22/86 11:08:13

To: NSJMP   --CPUA   JOHN M. POINDEXTER

NOTE FROM: BOB PEARSON
SUBJECT: Cuban Initiatives Announcement today

One issue remains in the announcement/notification plan. To keep the story at the right level, it needs to be kept as a State Department lead, not a WH lead. The execution of the legal steps requires a Presidential proclamation - up until last night, we had agreement from Speakes' office that the proclamation would be posted tomorrow at SB. Last night Speakes passed word he would post the proclamation and announce the 'nitiatives TODAY at 1030 PDT. That would make the story a WH lead, of course.

What we would like is that State retain the lead (announce at 0900 PDT of a backgrounder at 1100 PDT). If Larry wishes to say something at 1030 PDT concerning the State briefing and even have it carried to WH press corps in SB, still no problem. But to post the proclamation at 1030 PDT would focus the issue on t he President. Posting the proclamation after the State briefing today (anytime after 1200 PDT) would cover the bases and avoid hyping.

Have talked to Dan Howard, but anything which could be done to cover this directly with Larry would be very helpful. He may not agree otherwise.

WHITE HOUSE E-MAIL

Spin-doctoring begins with good intelligence: What is the reporter after? What questions will be asked? These three e-mail messages, sent by Karna Small to various White House staffers, focus on muckraker Jack Anderson's partner,

Dale Van Atta, and an upcoming interview with President Reagan. They're worried, they're scrambling, they're afraid Van Atta will focus on cost overruns and the rumored ineffectiveness in the "stealth" radar-evading airplane program.

Ultimately, we now know, Van Atta asked Reagan about information from disgruntled CIA sources that the United States was dealing with Iran over the hostages in Lebanon, and Reagan got Van Atta's pledge not to write further about the story.

                              --CPUA   02/18/86 10:32 ***

To: NSPBT   --CPUA

NOTE FROM: KARNA SMALL
SUBJECT: Van Atta update

More on our backing and forthing on Dale Van Atta and the question of
his columns on stealth. I am just now going through the new two-week
Presidential schedule and I note that Speakes has laid on an interview with
the President with Dale Van Atta at 2:30 PM next Monday, Feb. 24...I don't
know why -- but we've GOT to figure out what our position is on this
ASAP or he will surely hit RR with this subject fast and hard...what's
the latest? Please advise. (Separately, Van Atta is big on the terrorist
situation - our hostages in Lebanon etc. -- I will get together with
Jock et al on this and work up some talking points in advance of that
interview - but I would appreciate your discussing the stealth issue
with JMP. Many thanks.)

Reagan & Van Atta 2-24-86

To: NSRFL   --CPUA   NSJC   --CPUA
    NSGPH   --CPUA   NSOLN   - CPUA
NOTE FROM: KARNA SMALL
SUBJECT: President and Dale Van Atta

The President is scheduled to be interviewed by Dale Van Atta (Jack
Anderson's partner) on Monday. This was evidently a long-standing
request/promise which Speakes has just now put on the schedule. Since
he has a rather long lead-time (a week) he does not want to deal with
headline issues, but wants to talk to the President about "his feelings"
about a number of issues...e.g., how did he "feel" in Grenada, any
anecdotes, poignant moments, etc. How does he "feel about arms control?"
Not the numbers or specific responses but his general attitude toward
the possibilities of an agreement, working with Gorbachev, etc. He says he
doesn't really intend to ask about stealth, but I'm concerned about that one
since they've been writing some damaging columns on that issue and John
Douglas is doing a few talking points just for insurance. Also, he didn't
mention Mid-East, but as Jock knows, he has done damaging columns on
our hostage situation, saying Buckley and Kilborn are dead etc...and
emphasizing Iranian connections to terrorism, so could well ass how the
Pres. feels about terrorism and our inability to bring our hostages out.
Bottom line: could you all put together just a few very BRIEF talking
points on these issues by tomorrow afternoon - say 3:00 PM - so I can
get them retyped and up to Poindexter for his clearance as soon as he
returns from Grenada.(I realize Phil would be in Grenada, but perhaps
he could be thinking about it and jot down a few points on the return
flight so we could have them first thing Fri. - perhaps at ODSM -
I'll be glad to have them typed so a few notes would suffice).

To: NSPBT   --CPUA

NOTE FROM: KARNA SMALL
Subject: President and Dale Van Atta

I wanted you to be aware of what's going on with respect to Van Atta.
I talked to him about stealth, after talking to John Douglas -- Douglas
suggested that I suggest that Van Atta talk to Don Hicks at DOD - and
get him to hold off on writing on stealth -- I think I've done that,
at least for now. Then in the course of the conversation, Van Atta told
me roughly what he had in mind for his Mondayinterview - thus the
attached taskings.

WHITE HOUSE E-MAIL

03/20/86 14:15:36

To: NSJMP   --CPUA   JOHN M. POINDEXTER

NOTE FROM: KARNA SMALL
SUBJECT: Question from NY Times

Gerald Boyd of the NY Times called again today to "renew our request to
talk to Admiral Poindexter now that he has been out talking to a network."
Quite frankly, Gerald has called alot of late complaining about a lack of
access, saying that the NYT has good access to others in the White House and
yet is unable to talk to the NSC adviser or others on the staff...and he has
almost threatened to "write a story about how you people at the NSC handle
the press." Yesterday I pointed out to him that I had arranged for him and
his colleague (Bernie Weinraub - who is more reasonable) to see Ron Lehman,
Shirin, and Jack Matlock, that a request was in for Don Fortier, and that the
only one saying no recently was Dick Childress (who declined to talk to press
of late on Marcos). But Boyd is persisting - with today's call he says they
are going to write an item about how you were on the morning show and they
would like a quote from you on your attitude toward dealing with the press and
if today's appearance "marks a new attitude now." He says all he has on the
subject is what you have said on background at briefings. Is there a line you
wish me to use now about why you (1) appeared this morning and (2) do not
wish to accept other interviews?(Sorry to bother you, but he's been awfully
hostile and probably the toughest one for us to handle right now). I did tell
him that you felt strongly about the President's program on contra aid - but
he persisted in wanting a quote regarding your general attitude now. Please
advise - many thanks.

This exchange of e-mail between Karna Small and National Security Adviser John Poindexter illustrates some prime reportorial techniques, as well as unvarnished hostility toward the press. Gerald Boyd, a *New York Times* reporter, threatens to write a story about bad press management by the NSC if Poindexter doesn't give him an interview or at least a quote. Poindexter then blasts back saying he "won't speak to the press... on their agenda."

To: NSKS   --CPUA

*** Reply to note of 03/20/86 14:15

UNCLASSIFIED

03/21/86 09:22:24

NOTE FROM: JOHN POINDEXTER
Subject: Question from NY Times
WHAT I WOULD LIKE TO SAY IS THAT I CONTROL MY AGENDA AND NOT THE PRESS. WHEN I
THINK IT IS HELPFUL TO OUR OBJECTIVES, I WILL SPEAK OUT. I WON'T SPEAK TO THE
PRESS TO ANSWER QUESTIONS ON THEIR AGENDA. I STILL FEEL THAT IN THE WHITE
HOUSE THAT THE PRESIDENT IS HIS OWN BEST SPOKESMAN ON NATIONAL SECURITY. FOR
DAY TO DAY AFFAIRS, IT IS THE RESPONSIBILITY OF THE PRESS SECRETARY. MY
POSITION IS AS PERSONAL ADVISOR TO THE PRESIDENT. APPROPRIATELY THAT ADVICE IS
PRIVATE.
  THE ADMINISTRATION SPOKESMAN FOR FOREIGN POLICY IS SHULTZ AND FOR DEFENSE
POLICY IS WEINBERGER. TAKE ALL OF THIS INTO ACCOUNT AND PROPOSE TO ME WHAT YOU
SHOULD TELL HIM.

To: NSJMP   --CPUA   03/21/86 15:48:01

*** Reply to note of 03/21/86 09:22
NOTE FROM: KARNA SMALL
Subject: Question from NY Times
I think we are over this particular hump - as the NYT did run a short story
on you and your press activities on today's Washington Talk page (although
they got the details of your TV appearance wrong) - it's in your clips today.
But in general, when he and others press me again, I would suggest the
following general line - with your approval:
--The Admiral has an extremely full agenda. He feels that the President
  is the best spokesman on national security. He feels that Sec. Shultz
  is the appropriate spokesman on foreign policy issues and Sec. Weinberger
  on defense policy. As for day to day events, commenting on those is the
  responsibility of the Press Secretary. From time to time, probably on
  rather rare occasions, the Admiral may choose to speak out on an issue
  of particular national importance, but this would be the exception rather
  than the rule. However, when there are legitimate questions where
  reporters may need a bit more historical or extensive information for
  their background and analysis, we do try to make some members of the NSC
  staff available to handle those requests, commensurate with their busy
  schedules - although again, we feel that on a day-to-day basis, either
  the Press Office or the Departments of State and Defense are the appropriate spokesmen. The Admiral is a personal advisor to the President,
  and appropriately that advice is private.

Note: I did not want to emphasize that you won't answer questions "on their
agenda" as many in the press would take umbrage and argue that people in
government do have a responsibility to explain Admin. policy to the
American people - I think the above more or less handles that. Is this OK?
Thanks.

To: NSKS   --CPUA   03/22/86 11:26:41

*** Reply to note of 03/21/86 15:48

NOTE FROM: JOHN POINDEXTER
Subject: Question from NY Times   UNCLASSIFIED
YES, THAT IS FINE.

WHITE HOUSE E-MAIL

```
                                                      05/05/86 16:05:16

To: NSJMP   --CPUA    JOHN M. POINDEXTER

NOTE FROM: KARNA SMALL
SUBJECT: Op-ed on Saudi arms

I wanted you to know that we made all the changes and send the op-ed on
Saudi arms sales to Meg Greenfield at the Washington Post. I talked to her
about it this morning and she said she wouldconsider it immediately upon
receipt. Her office just called to say that she likes the piece very much and
it WILL RUN IN WEDNESDAY'S EDITION.   Since Ron Sable now advises that the
Senate vote may slip to Wed., and since the House vote is also scheduled for
Wed., we are very pleased that the Post is running it in such a timely fashion.
Many thanks for your edits and support at such a busy time.
```

Traditional spin doctors generally drew their satisfaction from anonymous roles—the rewritten leads or the questions unasked as the result of behind-the-scenes handling. But the rise of newspaper op-ed pages publishing syndicated columnists and other outsiders has provided a new arena for spin—the placed and often ghostwritten opinion article. These two e-mail messages from Karna Small, regarding a Poindexter op-ed promoting arms sales to the Saudis, provide some inside details as to how the *Washington Post* negotiates op-eds.

```
                                                      05/06/86 16:12:53

To: NSDRF   --CPUA    DONALD FORTIER

NOTE FROM: ROD B. MCDANIEL
Subject: Saudi arms op-ed
*** Forwarding note from NSKS    --CPUA    05/06/86 15:08 ***
To: NSJRS   --CPUA

NOTE FROM: KARNA SMALL
SUBJECT: Saudi arms op-ed

Just wanted you to know that the Wash. Post Editorial page people just
called to confirm that the Poindexter piece will run tomorrow and also
told me that his will be the ONLY piece on that issue tomorrow...which
is great as often times they run an opposing viewpoint -- but not this
time. (They also wanted to be sure I didn't give it to anyone else --
but I assured them that it was my policy to offer it to Meg first and
give her the option to run and they have an exclusive). So we're all
on track. Regards.
```

To: NSDRF   --CPUA

*** Reply to note of 05/07/86 12:37
NOTE FROM: ROD R. MCDANIEL
Subject: Casey & the Leaks article
Talked to Roche--he thinks the press performs an essential modulating function
that we tamper with at our peril. Thus his first instinct is don't do this.
When I pointed out that there were real sources and methods issues in these par
ticular cases, he agreed they are different. Problem is how to ensure that onl
y such cases become the subject of serious moves against the press--no ready an
swer (a non-partisan board, or something?).
He had a few other thoughts on leaks in general:
    -- We should forthrightly restrict some officials from talking to the press
    particularly those with extremely sensitive access.
    -- Don't just go after the junior people (pillsbury, et al)
    -- Need President/agency heads to frequently rearticulate to their people w
hy leaking is bad--in other words precept and example.

Every administration periodically erupts in an outcry over leaks of inside information, usually blaming Congress or the press for damaging national security. During the Reagan administration, CIA director William Casey was especially vigilant, proposing that they prosecute reporters who published leaks (at the same time as Casey himself gave secret access to *Washington Post* reporter Bob Woodward). This e-mail message from NSC executive secretary Rod McDaniel to Deputy National Security Adviser Donald Fortier shows a little more realism, citing John Roche, a member of the President's Foreign Intelligence Advisory Board, against Casey's proposal to prosecute reporters. The implication is clear—a certain lack of "precept and example" against leaking on the part of the highest officials. The reference to "pillsbury" is Michael Pillsbury, an assistant to the undersecretary of defense for policy from 1981–86, who was fired for supposedly leaking classified information about U.S. support for the *mujahideen* in Afghanistan. Congressional supporters of the *mujahideen* promptly hired Pillsbury and described the firing as a political retaliation by "go-slow" officials resisting Pillsbury's all-out advocacy of the *mujahideen*.

WHITE HOUSE E-MAIL

TO: NSSHS   --CPD'
    NCLFB   --CPUA
NOTE FROM: DONALD C. MAHLEY
SUBJECT: Q&A For INF Treaty Tabling "Leak" -- if one occurs

02/27/87 13:26 ***
NSSMI   --CPUA
NSSFK   --CPUA

Since, in the wake of the Tower Commission Report, I am certain that
PROFs notes have a life of their own, I will draft a couple Q&A's for a
possible "leak" of our efforts to table an INF treaty and submit them for
consideration.

Q: We hear reports the US is about to put a draft INF treaty on the table in
Geneva. Is this true?

A: During the current round in Geneva, there has been considerable work and
progress by both the US and Soviet INF delegations in discussing areas where
we agree and disagree on the principles of an INF treaty. Given the work that
has been done, we believe the next logical step in progress toward an INF
agreement would be a draft treaty, to allow the Soviet side to study in greater
detail the US-NATO positions on provisions of an agreement. The US is
therefore hard at work and consulting closely with NATO Allies to prepare and
present a draft treaty as soon as possible.

Q: Is it true that the US will try to table a treaty draft before the end
of the current round?

A: As you know, the current round is scheduled to conclude on March 4. Even
though that is only days away, if we can complete our work and consultation,
we would consider it useful to present a treaty to the Soviet side, so they
could study the proposal between rounds.

Q: Isn't the sudden rush to table a treaty in Geneva an attempt by the

Reagan administration to divert attention from the Tower Commission Report and
the Iran situation?

A: Absolutely not. The timing of a draft treaty is based on the progress made
during the current round of negotiations, based on the areas of agreement
reached at Reykjavik, where we believe the most logical way to maintain the
momentum of the negotiations toward achievement of an equitable and verifiable
INF treaty is to table a US draft text.

National Security Council arms control staffer Donald Mahley wrote this e-mail on the day after the Tower Commission report on Iran-contra came out, February 27, 1987. The Tower report reprinted several hundred key e-mail messages between Oliver North and John Poindexter and Robert McFarlane, pulled from the backup computer tapes, since the electronic originals had been blipped out. Mahley is making a preemptive spin strike, assuming that e-mail on the Intermediate-range Nuclear Forces (INF) negotiations in Geneva will also leak, making the Reagan administration look bad in its effort to put a draft treaty on the table. Mahley suggests some classic "diplo-speak" as a response, and his colleague Steve Steiner agrees, recommending only that they be "less defensive."

To: NSDAM   --CPUA   02/27/87 15:53:24
                    Classification: UNCLASSIFIED
NOTE FROM: Steven Steiner

Subject: Q&? For INF Treaty Tabling "Leak" -- if one occurs
I think your answers are excellent and very informative. I would only suggest
that in third answer you may want to refer as well to progress made at
Reykjavik and our follow up in R. VI. Also I would make that Q less defensive,
deleting ref. to "sudden rush." Just ask: Is timing related to . . . . . .

I make the latter point because these things end up in hands of alot of
people, and we will be seen by some as on the defensive if we pose Q that way.

Occasionally the spin doctors tripped over each other. After the hijacked Pan Am 72 airplane wound up in Pakistan, White House assistant press secretary J. Dan Howard relayed an allegation that the Pakistanis were not cooperating with the FBI investigation into the hijacking. In the first message, on September 11, Robert Earl tells Howard he's all wrong, the Pakistanis are cooperating, and that he should tell the press "to pound sand (nicely, of course)." In the second message, on September 12, Earl finds out it was his own boss, Poindexter, who started the allegation about the Pakistanis.

                                    09/11/86 17:35 ***

To: NSJDH   --CPUA

NOTE FROM: Robert L. Earl
SUBJECT: PAN AM PRESS GUIDANCE
I've checked with Ollie, State, CIA, and FBI -- your allegation from the
press that the Paks are not cooperating is completely wrong. (What
would the Dept of Justice know about this anyway? It's the FBI who is in
Karachi doing the investigating....) Regarding the substance of
"whodunnit" -- we simply still do not know. I know the press can't sit
still for two days in a row with the same answer (i.e. it's going to take
some time), but that happens to be the truth of the matter. Tell 'em to
pound sand (nicely, of course). I've passed your questions on to State
for them to develop formal coordinated guidance.

                                    09/12/86 15:14:21
To: NSOLN   --CPUA   NSCPC   --CPUA
NOTE FROM: Robert L. Earl
Subject: PAN AM PRESS GUIDANCE
When I picked up the Kauffmann videotape from Dan Howard this afternoon, he
mentioned that it was NOT the press that he had heard that the Paks weren't
cooperating, but from JMP on Monday at a meeting he had attended w/ Speakes.
What's the Admiral doing...?

WHITE HOUSE E-MAIL

The White House e-mail is perhaps most revealing when the spin doctors contrast their real motivations with their planned verbiage. In this case, Robert Earl recommends against confirming the death of William Buckley, the CIA officer held hostage in Lebanon, because press coverage of the CIA connection would scare off the Iranians with whom the White House was negotiating the infamous arms-for-hostages deals. Earl's recommended language sounds reasonable, except that the United States already knew from other released hostages that Buckley had taken sick and died in captivity. Roman refers to Roman Popaduik, one of the White House spokespeople.

```
                                                              11/20/86 10:12:23
     To: NSOLN    CPUA                        NSCPC    --CPUA
     NOTE FROM: Robert L. Earl
     SUBJECT: BUCKLEY DEATH
     Speakes got a question whether the President's statement that we expected
     two more back meant that the USG was now officially accepting that Buckley
     was dead.  Speakes apparently waffled that we didn't know, that we still
     had hope, but that the statement might have meant that -- he'd have to
     check....  Roman is seeking guidance.
     The only problem I can see w/ acknowledging that we think Buckley is
     dead (from lack of medical treatment, not execution) is that it will
     signal to the press who have to this point been unusually responsible in
     not printing his CIA connection, that "the gloves are off" and they can
     freely speculated all they want about his employment, the circumstances
     of his death, etc.  Lot's of press on the CIA bogeyman would not be helpful
     in retaining the channel....
     How about if we tell the press that our official position remains that since
     we haven't seen a body, we simply do not know.  On background, of course, we
     tend to believe that he is dead but that we simply cannot say that publicly
     because of risk to other hostages, possibility we might be wrong (ie.
     terrorists could interpret it as a signal that we have "written him off" and
     use it as an excuse to kill him now, if he is not already dead, etc.).
```

Then there were the press handling strategies. One can find in the e-mail all the different techniques of spinning, and this November 1986 message from Dennis Ross to the NSC higher-ups McDaniel and Keel notes the tried-and-true tactic of sending emissaries to editorial boards of major newspapers. Ross's first line hints at the dimension of the problem, though, as the Iran-contra scandal was breaking with the news of arms-for-hostages deals with Iran. The American public's opinion of the Ayatollah Khomeini was so low that during November 1986, President Reagan's own poll approval rating set an all-time record for a one-month decline.

To: NSRBM   --CPUA   ALTON G. KEEL   NSWRP   --CPUA   ALTON G. KEEL
FROM: Dennis Ross
SUBJECT: Public Affairs Strategy on Iran
       Obviously, it will take some time to turn things around on the
Iran connection. To this point we haven't had the time or the manpower
to do something that is very necessary; namely, send people to do backgrounders
for the editorial boards of key papers around the country. Getting together
with these boards will begin to effect not only the editorials in major state
and local papers but also the stories they choose to run. I think we ought
to pick 20 or 25 papers around the country and send people to talk to those
boards. That is, of course, why we need State D. involvement--for the money
to send people around and to provide some bodies. (I can tell you who would
do it well besides people like me.) At this point, I have been invited to
speak to a Jewish group in Los Angeles on January 5; I haven't said yes yet,
but I am thinking about it and if I did it, I would recommend that I meet
with the LA Times editorial board.

When spin turns to deliberate leaks that are lies, it often bites the spinners in the rear. On August 25, 1986, the front page of the *Wall Street Journal* featured a lead story, based on high administration sources, declaring that the United States and Libya appeared to be "on a collision course." Not only was Libyan dictator Col. Muammar el-Qaddafi back in the terror business, the story said, after a hiatus due to the U.S. bombing of Tripoli in April, but the United States was gearing up for more action against Libya.

This September 3, 1986, e-mail from National Security Adviser John Poindexter to NSC Middle East specialist Dennis Ross indicates that the story was a leak with a purpose—presumably to threaten Qaddafi and keep him on the defensive—but may have backfired.

To: NSDBR   --CPUA   Dennis Ross

NOTE FROM: JOHN POINDEXTER
SUBJECT: QADHAFI
I would like an analysis done of the relationship between the WSJ article and
Qadhafi's return to an agressive public stance including his decision to go to
Harare. In other words did the leak and subsequent discussion about it have
the reverse impact from what the leaker intended? Tough question, but see what
you can make of it. It could be an interesting object lesson. Do it in house.

WHITE HOUSE E-MAIL

A month later it really backfired. On October 2, *Washington Post* reporter Bob Woodward exposed what he called a disinformation campaign, in which the *Wall Street Journal* article was the opening shot. Using his own leaked documents and anonymous administration sources, Woodward wrote that the White House was putting out the "collision course" story specifically to convince Libyan dictator Muammar el-Qaddafi that the United States was coming after him, even though no action was really planned. The White House staff (not to mention the *Wall Street Journal*) went ballistic and counterattacked, accusing Woodward of damaging the national security and providing aid and comfort to Qaddafi. This e-mail message from Robert Earl to David Major lists several alleged examples of "damage" from the Woodward article, ranging from the French and Libyan role in the border struggle in Chad to the compromising of CIA sources and methods.

10/02/86 10:09:47

To: NSDGM   --CPUA

NOTE FROM: Robert L. Earl   UNCLASSIFIED
SUBJECT: DAMAGE
To answer you question about what damage to our national security interests
from the Woodward article might be "documentable":
-- Damage to our relations with our allies, particularly the French regarding
   Chad policy (p. A-12: "The document suggested communicating through
   'military-to-military' channels and not through the political channels
   which failed earlier this year...." etc.)
-- The article creates doubt whether Pan Am & other possible recent Libyan
   terrorism were a RESPONSE to US provocations vice autonomous actions by
   Qadhafi (p. A-1: "...some senior officials are concerned that this is in
   part a response to the administration's latest campaign against Gadhafi.")
-- Undercuts the Walters mission to Europe in early September (p. A-12
   "The administration plan specified that two US diplomatic missions be
   given an anti-Libyan spin. ... Walters' mission ... was billed as a
   briefing on the new US evidence of libyan sponsorship of terrorist acts.
   ... Walters offered no such evidence..." etc.)
-- Compromises CIA ••••••••••••••••••••••••••• (p. A-12: "One planning
   document said ... 'Libyan intelligence should be provided photography
   of Libyan dissidents meeting with Soviet officials in Paris, Baghdad,
   etc.'"
Does this help you get a start, Dave?

b1, b3
(S)

This final message in the Libya disinformation sequence contains a masterpiece of spin. Dennis Ross cooks up a nice rationalization of the lies for his bosses in the NSC Secretariat and the deputy national security adviser, Alton Keel. Ross says it was all "a policy of deterrence" meant to "keep him [Qaddafi] off balance." Lies become just a "different way of signalling."

Reagan, Speakes, Regan, Buchanan, McFarlane et. al. on Air Force One 10-10-85

pl
*** ~~Forwarding note from NSDBH~~ --CPUA   10/03/86 C9:18 ***
To: NSRBH --CPUA   ALTON G. KEEL   NSWBP --CPUA   ALTON G. KEEL
FROM: Dennis Ross
SUBJECT: Libya Follow-up

   I agree with your approach to dealing with the press. I think
we want to lay out the logic of what it is we were trying to do. We must
note that there were signs that Qadhafi was preparing to re-emerge and
become more active. That, in light of that, it was important not only to
keep him off balance, but to remind him that he wasplaying with fire if
he carried out renewed acts of terrorism. That there weredifferent ways
of signalling that to him, and that what was, in fact, involved on our part
was a policy of deterrence.

   Having said that, I'm concerned that in the current setting we not lose
sight of that policy of deterrence. If Qadhafi sees division, he'll be more
confident about acting.
██
██was a substitute for action, he'll
doubt our seriousness and credibility.

   What that means is that as we straighten out press misinformation now
and explain our position in August, we also make clear the continuity of our
objectives and sense of purpose vis-a-vis Qadhafi. At a minimum, that means
reminding everyone that we are watching Qadhafi closely; that we are determined
to ensure that those who carry-out or facilitate terrorism pay a price for
doing so; and that if we have evidence of involvement of terrorists acts we
will do what we did before.

WHITE HOUSE E-MAIL

This classic e-mail note succinctly describes the traditional practice of psychological operations, in the context of events in Yemen. Written by career navy officer James Stark (on detail to the National Security Council staff as a Middle East expert) on January 30, 1986, this note recommends that the United States capitalize on a coup attempt in the (Soviet-aligned) People's Democratic Republic of Yemen (PDRY) to score points against the Soviets through "straight propaganda" and a "carefully managed disinformation campaign." Stark doesn't rule out "altering or manufacturing evidence"; he just notes that lying is a "more dangerous course" that may be avoidable in this instance.

```
                                        01/30/86  20:11  ***
To: NSHRT    --CPUA            NSWFM    --CPUA
    NSWRP    --CPUA    DONALD  FORTIER

NOTE FROM: JAMES R. STARK
SUBJECT: PDRY opportunities
The Soviet role in the PDRY coup attempt and subsequent
fighting has given us an excellent opportunity to play up and
exploit heightened awareness of the dangers of involvement
with the Soviet Union among a number of Middle East states.
This effort ought to proceed along two tracks:
 -A straight propaganda effort to trumpet Soviet
duplicity and its attempts to undermine efforts of
states friendly to Hasani trying to provide him assistance.
 -A carefully managed disinformation campaign to
convince PDRY's neighbors that the Soviets knew of
and promoted the rebels from the beginning.  This could
be combined with indications of similarly ominous
Soviet activities in each of the target states.  Given
the nature of the Soviets, we ought to be able to find
a great deal of actual evidence which can simply be artfully
exploited, and may thus completely avoid the more dangerous
course of altering or manufacturing evidence.
   Howard, are you aware of any effort by State, USIA, or CIA
to focus on this?  If not, I think JMP ought to raise it at
a family group luncheon.
```

The most intriguing "hearts and minds" effort of all came up in the spring of 1986, with this March 26 e-mail note from NSC staffer David Wigg to Oliver North about a movie in the works called *Contras*. Wigg says "this is the kind of thing Walt R. should have been promoting for the last four years.... " "Walt R." refers to Walter Raymond, a veteran CIA psychological operations specialist, who came to the NSC staff in 1982 to run an expanded "public diplomacy" operation on issues ranging from the contra war in Nicaragua to Congressional sanctions against South Africa. Two days after this e-mail, North tells Fawn Hall to set up the requested meeting; but by early May, evidently, the moviemakers had not yet come up with the necessary $2 million to shoot. Apparently, a complete script was prepared, although the movie never reached the silver screen.

```
                                      03/26/86 10:35 ***

To: NSOLN   --CPUA

NOTE FROM: David Wigg
SUBJECT: Movie On The Contras
A friend of mine in N.Y. is leading stockholder in a movie production
company and sent one of the principals to me to help package a $2 million
budget for a feature film called:  "Contras".  It will be a credible work

about a Jewish kid who gets thrown in jail in Nicaragua, is freed by a
Contra group and eventually sides with them for the right reasons.  There is
a script currently being edited; Michael Nouri (Flashdance) will be the male
lead; Jim Brunner (Delta Force, Missing in Action) will do the screenplay and
probably direct.  They plan to shoot in the summer and release the film in
the fall.  There are a number of stupid films in the works on Central Amer.
that all come out on the wrong side.  I think we should help these people out
if possible.  I have met them and they are serious, talented and well-connected
in the industry.  Susan Moses (principal/and a sharp lady) will be in D.C. next
Tuesday (April 1).  Can you see her in the p.m. and suggest to me between now
and then who to line her up with as investors/sponsors that she could talk to
either Tuesday or Wednesday (April 2)?  Charlie Z. Wick strikes me as someone
who should be very interested both from USIA and personal perspectives.  Any
money people come to mind?  THis is the kind of thing Walt R. should have been
promoting for the last four years and I encourage you to take it seriously.
There is no better way to grab those hearts and minds we need.
```

```
To: NSDGW   --CPUA                              05/05/86 22:40:44

*** Reply to note of 05/05/86 16:31

NOTE FROM: OLIVES NORTH              -- UNCLASSIFIED
Subject: Contra Movie
Dave, will try to do what I can on this but money doesn't grow on trees.
      Contra Movie
                                                              B
```

CHAPTER 7

WORKING CAPITOL HILL

Although the Reagan administration came to office in 1981 with a Republican Senate, it faced extreme difficulties in pushing its programs through a House of Representatives controlled by the Democrats. From this conflict, and from Reagan's personal anti-Washington ideology, arose a central message of the Reagan administration—Congress-bashing. This larger theme fit well with the ideology shared by most of the National Security Council staff, firm believers as they were in the president's Constitutional powers as commander-in-chief and his right to act unilaterally in foreign affairs without interference from Congress. Thus, while all of the NSC staff took oaths of office, swearing faithfully to execute the laws passed by Congress, some of them cut corners so frequently it became habit, as in the Iran-contra affair.

But the daily White House grind of working Capitol Hill involved not so much corner-cutting as constant stroking, cajoling, head-counting, arm-twisting, and rallying outside lobbyists to bring pressure upon key votes. The White House e-mail details the actual behind-the-scenes machinations of this process, but, in the White House staff's own words, it was never intended to be published. Included are candid and sometimes devastating evaluations of key members of Congress (ranging from Senator Robert Dole of Kansas to former Senator Alan Dixon of Illinois), alongside truly remarkable revelations of the ways of lobbyists ranging from Ross Perot to the American Israel Public Affairs Committee (AIPAC).

Congressional controversy provoked some of the most revealing e-mail. For example, in the spring of 1986, the Reagan administration had agreed to sell $354 million of advanced weapons to Saudi Arabia. Attempting to head off the hard-core opposition that almost prevented the 1981 Saudi AWACS sale, White House staff won agreement from leaders of AIPAC that they would help prevent a Congressional vote of disapproval, even though they opposed the sale. The related e-mail traffic provides extraordinarily candid assessments of the American Jewish community's lobbying, as well as of key senators. Ultimately, President Reagan vetoed the Congressional resolution of disapproval, and was sustained by one vote in the Senate, allowing the sale to go through.

The White House also prevented a vote on the issue of setting up a commission to look into the Vietnam prisoner-of-war/missing-in-action (POW/MIA) issue. A series of extremely frank e-mail messages in the fall of 1986 details the arguments against such a commission (primarily that it might increase pressure for normalization of relations with Vietnam), as well as the efforts of administration supporters. Particular vitriol is reserved for Ross Perot, who makes a cameo appearance to "sandbag the entire Administration."

President Reagan, Senator Robert Dole, Senator Robert Byrd 1-4-85

This pair of e-mail messages memorializes perhaps the most vivid example of the Reagan administration's contempt for Congress. In the summer of 1985, and again in the summer of 1986, enterprising reporters such as Robert Parry and Brian Burger of the Associated Press and Joel Brinkley of the *New York Times* had identified Oliver North and the NSC staff as the generals of the contra war, who violated Congressional prohibitions on military aid. So Congress inquired. A gullible delegation from the House Intelligence Committee (HPSCI) led by Rep. Lee Hamilton (D-Indiana) and Rep. David McCurdy (D-Oklahoma) showed up at the White House Situation Room to question North; they accepted his statements of non-involvement at face value. On trial in 1989, North himself admitted his outright lies (Gen. John Singlaub's private anticommunist organization provided cover for North's contra supply operation, and Robert Owen served as North's courier to the contras). In this e-mail, NSC counsel Bob Pearson writes up the meeting and the lies for North's boss, National Security Adviser John M. Poindexter, who knows better. Note the two words that Poindexter attaches to the message—"well done"—before sending it on to North.

To: NSRBM   --CPUA   08/03/86 09:29 ***

NOTE FROM: BOB PEARSON
SUBJECT: HPSCI interview of North

Session was success - Hamilton will entertain motion soonest to
report unfavorably on Resolution of Inquiry and made clear believes HPSCI can
turn aside future offers of similar resolutions. North's remarks were thorough
and convincing. Hamilton underlined his appreciation to Admiral and to Bud for
full cooperation offered by NSC. He restated there were no facts uncovered by
or known to HPSCI to substantiate the allegations in the resolution of inquiry
or media reports on North's activities.

In response to specific questions. Ollie covered following points:

     o contact with FDN and UNO aimed to foster viable. democratic political
strategy for Nicaraguan opposition. gave no military advice. knew of no
specific military operations.

     o Singlaub - gave no advice. has had no contact in 20 months; Owen
never worked from OLN office. OLN had casual contact. never provided Owen
guidance.

     o threats/harassment - in response to question. OLN recounted incidents
of harassment/threats prior to '85 vote and again prior to '86 vote.
speculated that possibly due in part to active measures effort.

From: NSJMP   --CPUA   Date and time   28.11.86 18:44.09
To: NSOLN   --CPUA   OLLIE NORTH

                              -- SECRET --

NOTE FROM: JOHN POINDEXTER   WHITE HOUSE E-MAIL
Subject: HPSCI interview of North
Well done.

Perhaps the most controversial votes Congress faced during the 1980s involved arms sales to Saudi Arabia and the Gulf states. Until the Persian Gulf War of 1991 aligned Israel with Saudi Arabia and other erstwhile Arab foes, the latters' support of the Palestine Liberation Organization and the possibility that their military equipment might be used against Israel meant guaranteed opposition in the U.S. Congress to any arms deals. Yet the U.S.-Saudi relationship served as the linchpin of U.S. strategy in the Persian Gulf area, and in 1986, the White House intended to cement the relationship with the sale of a $354-million package of advanced weapons, including antiaircraft missiles. Attempting to head off a Congressional vote of disapproval (a two-thirds vote would be sufficient to override the president's veto and kill the deal), the White House staff found some sophisticated allies in the American Israel Public Affairs Committee (AIPAC), then headed by Thomas Dine. This March 6, 1986, e-mail from National Security Council staffer Jock Covey reveals the not-for-public-consumption rationale. AIPAC had pulled out all the stops against Reagan, but lost on the 1981 Saudi AWACs sale. Wanting to avoid a repeat, now AIPAC pursued an inside-outside strategy.

```
                                        03/06/86 11:11 ***
To: NSRBM    --CPUA    JOHN M. POINDEXTER NSWRP    --CPUA    JOHN M. POINDEXTER
NOTE FROM:  Jock Covey
SUBJECT:  AIPAC and Saudi Arms
```

Tom Dine reports that he is indeed taking a lot of heat from the likes of Cranston and Metzenbaum, who are incredulous that he would not oppose the sale flat out. At same time, Dine said he hears that certain people in the Administration are saying that AIPAC is double-dealing, talking compromise but still talking against the sale. All this makes him feel discouraged, he said.

What he has undertaken to do is to try to avoid a confrontation with the Administration, he says, and that means avoiding a vote. Personally, he still opposes the sale and so does everyone he works with. But he intends to continue working to avoid a crunch and has the support of key figures like Ken Bialken in this. He said he will stick to his guns but knows he is in for a real beating.

I told Dine we were indeed hearing grousing from some on the Hill that AIPAC was giving only lip-service to avoiding a clash but was still speaking against the sale -- but that we in the Administration recognized how complex his position is, greatly admired his efforts, and urged him to stick it out.

Bad news came within hours, as reported in this March 6, 1986, e-mail from Jock Covey through the NSC Secretariat to John Poindexter. Senator Rudy Boschwitz (R-Minnesota) had scouted out unexpected opposition, allegedly from Senators Sam Nunn (D-Georgia) and Warren Rudman (R-New Hampshire).

```
                                      03/06/86 13:52 ***
To: NSRBM    --CPUA    JOHN M. POINDEXTER NSWRP    --CPUA    JOHN M. POINDEXTER
NOTE FROM:  Jock Covey
SUBJECT: Saudi Arms and Rudy Boshwitz

Boshwitz just passed along to Shultz that he has been puzzled to find
opposition to the missile sale in places he hadn't expected it.  He
mentioned Nunn and Ruddman, specifically.  Boshwitz said he wanted
Shultz to know that he is "with Dine" on this and intended to go to work
on this.  He'll report back after he talk to Nunn and Ruddman.
```

AIPAC's stance was much appreciated by National Security Adviser John Poindexter, and this March 7, 1986, e-mail from Jock Covey details the response from Tom Dine. Covey also raises concerns about Senator Robert Dole (R-Kansas), the majority leader, and says that Ron Sable, the Congressional liaison for the NSC, was investigating.

```
To: NSJMP    --CPUA                        03/07/86 13:03:59

*** Reply to note of 03/06/86 19:22
NOTE FROM:  Jock Covey
Subject: AIPAC and Saudi Arms

Dine appreciated your appreciation.  He was quick to repeat that he personally
opposed the sale but would continue to work to avoid a vote.  Told him that is
just what you understand his position to be, and that you would be all the
more appreciative if it worked.  He was wry, saying that there is even more
resistance to the sale than he had expected.  He said he was stunned to hear
that Dole had run a whip count yesterday and had come up with only seven
Republicans in favor of the sale.  Still, he said, he will keep at it.

Ron Sable is looking in the assertion about Dole's count; it does not hang
together with Dole's go-ahead on notification late yesterday.  Ron is also
checking out the story that Nunn is against the sale.
```

WHITE HOUSE E-MAIL

President Reagan, Ron Sable & family 1-5-88

Ron Sable's report heightens the tension between the White House and Senator Dole. In this March 7, 1986, e-mail from Sable to Poindexter, Sable uses the word "disinformation" to describe Dole's pessimistic assessment of Senate chances for the arms sale.

03/07/86 14:35 ***

To: NSRBM   --CPUA   JOHN M. POINDEXTER NSWRP   --CPUA   JOHN M. POINDEXTER
NOTE FROM: Ron Sable
SUBJECT: Saudi Missile Sale
Have discussed alleged Nunn & Dole comments with Nunn(Punaro) & Pam Turner. What is clear is that Nunn has said nothing about the sale to anyone--Quite the opposite, we should be expecting him to be supportive because he is a believer in the AWAC sale and the regional need. As far as Doles alleged comment that a whip count shows only 7 Republicans would favor the sale, Pam & I came up with 12-15 without digging. As Jock Covey is beginning to suspect, this may simply be a disinformation campaign. We will confirm Doles head count(if one exists) later today.

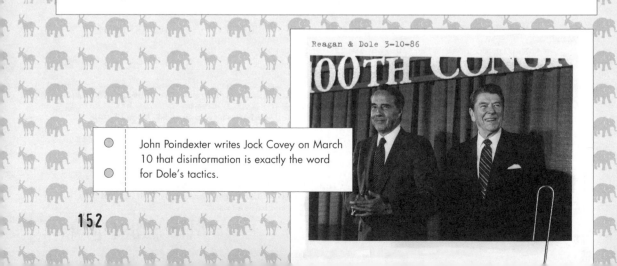

Reagan & Dole 3-10-86

John Poindexter writes Jock Covey on March 10 that disinformation is exactly the word for Dole's tactics.

152

To: NSJC   --CPUA

*** Reply to note of 03/07/86 13:03 UNCLASSIFIED

NOTE FROM: JOHN POINDEXTER
Subject: AIPAC and Saudi Arms
I AM PRETTY SURE THAT DOLE IS DELIBERATELY PUTTING OUT DISINFORMATION BUT WE
SHOULD DO NOTHING TO EXPOSE HIM. KEEP AIPAC WORKING.

But Dole wasn't that far off, as shown by this remarkable inside analysis of the ultimate
Senate vote disapproving the sale on May 6. Ron Sable gives Poindexter six reasons
for the vote, one being Dole's own presidential campaign aspirations. Among the
senators listed as either absent or protest-voting are Ted Stevens (R-Alaska), Nancy
Kassebaum (R-Kansas), Gordon Humphrey (R-New Hampshire), Paula Hawkins
(R-Florida), William Armstrong (R-Colorado), John East (R-North Carolina), Steve Symms
(R-Idaho), and Pete Wilson (R-California).

05/07/86 10:28 ***
To: NSRBM   --CPUA   JOHN M. POINDEXTER NSWRP   --CPUA   JOHN M. POINDEXTER
NOTE FROM: Ron Sable
SUBJECT: SAUDI ARMS VOTE
LAST NIGHTS VOTEIN THE SENATE ON A RESOLUTION OF DISAPPROVAL FOR THE SAUDI ARMS
 SALE(PASSED 73-22)WAS MISLEADING IN SEVERAL WAYS. FIRST,DOLE, IN OPPOSITION TO
 OUR REQUEST TO HIM, WENT AHEAD WITH THE VOTE BEFORE THE HOUSE__HAVING CUT HIS
 OWN DEAL WITH THE DEMOCRATS TO GET HIS GUN CONTROL BILL PASSED(READ PRESIDENTIA
L CANDIDATE AT WORK). SECOND, THE ABSENCE OF YOURSELF, SEC. SHULTZ AND THE PRES
IDENT LEFT SEVERAL MEMBERS SAYING THEY COULD VOTE AGAINST US AND NO ONE WOULD B
E HERE TO COMPLAIN. THIRD, WE HAD ABSENCES FROM THE VOTE_STEVENS, KASSEBAUM,LON
G, HUMPHREY, AND HAWKINS(WE WOULD EXPECT TO GET3 or 4 OF THOSE)FOURTH, OUR CONS
ERVATIVE "FRIENDS" ARE USING THIS VOTE AS A SIGNAL TO US THAT WE MUST LISTEN TO
 THEM MORE(ARMSTRONG, EAST,SYMMS, WILSON).ONE OTHER, SAM NUNN, TOLD US PRIVATEL
Y THAT HE WAS WITH US AND THEN WENT AGAINST US SAYING"I DONT THINK THE PRESIDEN
T REALLY WANTS THIS ONE.HE WILL BE A LEAD SUPPORTER OF THE AWAC SALE, SO BELIEV
E HE IS POSTURING FOR MORE WHITE HOUSE INVOLVEMENT _NOT OPPOSED TO THE MISSILE
SALE.FIFTH, ITS GETTING MORE AND MORE DIFFICULT TO PASS AN ARMS SALE ATHAT ISRA
EL OPPOSES __PARTICULARLY DURING AN ELECTION YEARAND WHEN MANY JEWISH GROUPS
WORK AGAINST THE SALE(REGARDLESS OF WHAT TOM DINE SAYS OR DOES).FINALLY, A SUMM
ARY OF THE DEBATE REFLECTS A GOOD DEAL OF "ARAB BASHING" IN GENERAL_NOT NECESSA
RILY DIRECTED AT SAUDI ARABIA. WE EXPECT A MAJORITY WILL VOTE TO STOP THE SALE
IN THE HOUSE THIS AFTERNOON,BUT ARE NOT DISCOURAGED IN OUR EFFORT TO PREVAIL. O
N THAT SCORE, SENATE PARLIMENTARIAN BELIEVES THE VETO WOULD HAVE TO BE OVERRIDE
N BY MIDNIGHT TOMORROW OR THE PRESIDENT IS FREE TO SELL.(ASKING PAUL THOMPSON T
O LOOK INTO THIS POSSIBILITY/ABE SOFAER AS WELL.

WHITE HOUSE E-MAIL

Once President Reagan vetoed the resolution of disapproval, opponents of the arms sale had to override the veto, which requires a two-thirds majority. NSC staffer James Stark relates the results of Secretary of Defense Caspar Weinberger's phone calls to some of the key Republican senators already targeted in Sable's report. Via Richard Armitage, assistant secretary of defense, the NSC hears it is dealing with quite a "group of statesmen." The reference to Percy concerns former Senator Charles Percy (R-Illinois), who lost his reelection bid to Paul Simon (D-Illinois) in 1984.

```
                                       05/09/86 07:43 ***
To: NSRKS    --CPUA            NSRBM    --CPUA      DONALD   FORTIER
    NSWRP    --CPUA    DONALD   FORTIER

NOTE FROM: JAMES R. STARK
SUBJECT: Calls to Senators on Saudi arms
Following are results of Weinberger's calls to Senators
on the arms sale as reflected in a memo from Armitage
to Pam Turner:
 Symms: Hopes we don't really need his vote.  The Israeli
lobby killed Percy and he doesn't want it to happen to him.
He's trying to build good relations with the Jewish community.
 Armstrong: He didn't know his vote was important to us.  "I'll
give it my full attention."
 Stevens: Noncommittal.  Notes the AWACS vote is coming up.  On
which ONE do we need him most.
 Humphrey:  No position taken.  Will look at carefully.
 Wilson:  Pretty far gone.  Saudis have to do everything backstage.
AIPAC is working very hard against the sale.  He will likely vote
against the sale.
 Armitage guesses we might get 1-2 votes out of this group of
statesmen.
```

As the drama progressed over the arms deal, other NSC staffers pitched in with their own running commentaries. In this May 15, 1986, e-mail, NSC senior director for politico-military affairs Howard Teicher weighs in with the kind of frank inside language —"israel right or wrong demagogues at the grass roots level," "the [Jewish] leadership's pusillanimity" (etc.)—that outsiders never hear.

*** Reply to note of 05/14/86 16:02
NOTE FROM: Howard Teicher

Declassified/Released on 4-28-94
under provisions of E.O. 12356
by D. Van Tassel, National Security Council
(F94-813)

Subject: Message

last night i learned about the proposal for the president to meet
with a group of jewish leaders to lobby them to back off their
opposition to the saudi sale. not having had an opportunity to comment
on this idea, i brought it up at the staff meeting this morning only to
have jmp practically bite my head off. don this is a bad political idea.
the jewish leaders will only see themselves being backed into a corner.
even though jmp doesn't seek a positive statement - be said the meeting
will provide senators with a figleaf - we're likely to get a lot of
negative statements which will only reinforce those senators who are
already paranoid about jewish votes in the election. moreover, whatever
one may think of the jewish leadership, the "masses" are rarely if ever
swayed by what the rational, reasonable leaders say. instead, it is
the israel right or wrong demagogues at the grass roots level that will
try to take advantage of the leadership's pusillanimity. frankly, if
the president is going to take time with jewish leaders on this issue,
quiet diplomacy has fewer downsides and the same advantages as a public
meeting. on the foreign policy side, we can also expect considerable
negative press (european and arab) about the president "groveling before
the jewish lobby". none of this will make awacs any easier, and could
make it harder as leaders who have been basically silent on missiles
will be pressed to lock into opposition early to avoid this kind of
pressure. although i recognize what the meeting would try to achieve
i cannot realistically see how the benefits will outweigh the disad
vantages.

This May 16 e-mail from James Stark describes a classic dodge by Senator Gordon Humphrey (R-New Hampshire), who plans to vote against the White House position, and uses a scheduling conflict for cover.

To: NSRBM   --CPUA   JOHN M. POINDEXTER NSWRP   --CPUA   JOHN M.
    NSRBM   --CPUA   DONALD FORTIER   NSWRP   --CPUA   DONALD
NOTE FROM: JAMES R. STARK
SUBJECT: Senator Humphrey and Saudi Arms
As directed, I contacted Ron Sable to set up a meeting
with Senator Humphrey to answer any questions he might
have. Humphrey is leaving town this morning and won't
be back until Monday evening. His office wants to wait
til he returns before they will even ask him to schedule an appointment.
With the veto override vote probably on Tuesday, I doubt
we can get to him in time, although we'll try. I suspect
he was simply looking for an excuse not to support the sale,
and used the "additional questions" as a graceful way to
do this, knowing all the time that he could put off the
follow-up meeting.

WHITE HOUSE E-MAIL

After the din of battle had died—and Reagan's veto missed being overridden by one vote—and the sale had gone through, AIPAC invited John Poindexter over for an evening. This exchange of e-mail between Poindexter, Howard Teicher, Peter Rodman, and Poindexter's secretary Florence Gantt elaborates on AIPAC's motives and the behind-the-scenes back-scratching so much a part of the Washington power game

```
                                      06/25/86 15:09 ***
To: NSRBM   --CPUA    JOHN M. POINDEXTER NSWRP   --CPUA    JOHN M. POINDEXTER
NOTE FROM: Howard Teicher
SUBJECT: dinner with the aipac senior officers
tom dine wants to know if you are interested in joining
aipac's senior officers (about 20) people for a "strictly
confidential, off-the-record" dinner on july 14. linda
would be welcome to come if you so desired. aipac hosts
this sort of dinner every few months for senators, congressmen
and cabinet secretaries. obviously, they are looking for a
free flowing exchange with you on key global issues, not only
the middle east state of play. i advised that i would query
you, though i was not aware of your policy or availability
for such a gathering. if you are free, i recommend that you
accept.
```

```
                                           06/25/86 20:31:16
To: NSPWR   --CPUA    PETER RODMAN
                                    UNCLASSIFIED
NOTE FROM: JOHN POINDEXTER
Subject: dinner with the aipac senior officers
Peter and Dennis, what do you think?  Will we need AIPAC for anything soon?
```

```
                                      06/26/86 09:08 ***
To: NSJMP   --CPUA

*** Reply to note of 06/25/86 20:31
NOTE FROM: Peter Rodman
Subject: dinner with the aipac senior officers
  In principle, it's a good idea. They probably want to size you up. A good
session with them will earn you a lot of goodwill, which is useful over the
long term even if we don't "need" anything from them in the near term.
```

```
                                           06/26/86 13:53:33
To: NSFEG   --CPUA    FLORENCE GANTT
                                    UNCLASSIFIED
NOTE FROM: JOHN POINDEXTER
Subject: dinner with the aipac senior officers
Ok, I will accept the dinner.
```

And it pays off. The next time the administration needed AIPAC—on the issue of U.S. funds for West Bank infrastructure and assistance to "moderate Palestinian[s]"— NSC staffer Dennis Ross found a receptive ear in Tom Dine. This September 10, 1986, e-mail relays their conversation to John Poindexter and refers to Senator Robert Kasten (R-Wisconsin) and Congressman David Obey (D-Wisconsin), respectively the Senate and House appropriations czars on foreign aid.

```
                                    09/10/86 15:25 ***
To: NSRBM    --CPUA    JOHN M. POINDEXTER NSWRP    --CPUA    JOHN M. POINDEXTER
FROM: Dennis Ross
SUBJECT: Tom Dine and the West Bank
     I had lunch today with Dine to discuss with him the importance
of promoting a moderate Palestinian constituency and infrastructure
on the West Bank.  I explained the importance of this from the standpoint
not only of building a moderate Palestinian leadershipbut also of pre-
empting the emergence of more radical elements on the West Bank at a time
when demographic trends may lead in that direction.
     Dine didn't need convincing.  He also didn't convincingthat this kind of
effort to generate funds for "quality of life" developments had to be handled
in a discreet way if we weren't to undermine the very forces we want to build
up.  Dine's position was that the best way to handle this is to work very
quietly with Kasten and let he and Obey figure out a way to get it done.
```

And when the Iran-contra scandal was breaking, AIPAC came to the defense of the White House again, according to this Peter Rodman e-mail from November 21, 1986.

```
NOTE FROM: Peter Rodman                            11/21/86 16:52:47
SUBJECT: AIPAC and Iran
  Max Green tells me AIPAC is working on the Hill to dampen the fires, though
they are doing it informally and do not want it advertised. It is not a
typical AIPAC campaign with talking points and mass mailings, but supposedly
the AIPAC leadership is expressing the view to all those they talk to that the
assault on the President is not good for the U.S. or for U.S.-Israeli
relations.
  This, at least, is what Max's AIPAC sources are telling Max. They have also
promised to monitor the situation for him.
  I am also aware of the reports that the Israelis are spilling their guts to
the Intelligence Committees, which is a way of covering their ass and is not
quite consistent with the above, at least in its consequences.
```

WHITE HOUSE E-MAIL

King Fahd, Prince Bandar, President Reagan 2-12-85

To: NSABF   --CPUA   02/03/87 10:45:33

FROM: Dennis Ross
SUBJECT: Arms Sales Strategy
     Alison, I'm getting a lot of disturbing noises from AIPAC
about their posture on upcoming sales; the problem here is not that
they necessarily have an interest in opposing F-16s for Bahrain, but
they think it is the tip of the iceberg. Our original strategy of
moving gradually on the items we wanted to sell made sense. Unfortunately,
in the current setting, Jewish community leaders seem to think that we
will try to compensate for our"guilt" over Iran by buying off the Arabs with
arms. Thus, they see planes for Bahrain as a harbinger of things to come and
are suddenly inclined to oppose it. I've been told that if Dine knew that
there weren't alot of big-ticket items coming down the pike--e.g., F-16s
for Jordan--then it would be much easier to move transfers that otherwise would
not be a problem. That argues for laying out what it is we are planning to
send up--demonstrating, in the process, that the current anxieties are ground-
less. What do you think? Let's talk later.

But by early 1987, the controversy was not over the arms sale to the Saudis, but F-16
jets for Bahrain. This candid February 3, 1987, e-mail from NSC staffer Dennis Ross to
legislative liaison Alison Fortier describes the inner thinking of both AIPAC and the
White House staff on the secret of winning Congressional approval for controversial
arms sales abroad.

Texas billionaire and onetime presidential candidate Ross Perot makes repeated cameo appearances in the White House e-mail lobbying for his favorite causes, especially on the missing-in-action from the Vietnam War. The following sequence of e-mail describes a particularly blatant intervention by Perot, and the dismay of the White House, over a proposal for a Congressional commission on the POW/MIA issue. The White House wanted the idea stopped (for fear it would recommend normalization of relations with Vietnam as part of settling the MIA issue) and found unlikely allies in the form of Congressman Steve Solarz (D-New York), who headed the East Asian subcommittee of House Foreign Affairs. The NSC's lead staffer on POW/MIA matters, Richard Childress, leads off on October 14, 1986, with a review of the issue and Perot's role. Among the Congressional names mentioned are former POW John McCain (R-Arizona), Jim Leach (R-Iowa), Gerald Solomon (R-New York), and then-Speaker of the House Jim Wright (D-Texas).

President Reagan & Ross Perot, circa 1987

WHITE HOUSE E-MAIL

To: NSRBM   --CPUA   JOHN M. POINDEXTER NSWRP   --CPUA   JOHN M. POINDEXTER
NOTE FROM: RICHARD T. CHILDRESS
SUBJECT: **UNCLASSIFIED** Commission of POW/MIA and Ross Perot

As the Congressional campaign has heated up, more cosponsors have
signed up for the Hendon bill in the House. They are now up to 275,
including recent signees McCain and Leach. The League of Families
have turned their guns away from Hanoi towards Congress based on
the pressure Solarz is getting to let the monster out of Committee.

They have called Leach who clearly signed up under the impression
it would not see the light of day. They also called Jim Wright to ensure
there would not be suspension of the rules. I talked with McCain,
who did not admit to signing up for political reasons, but said he
would try to stay out of it and not lend his voice in debate if it
came up. As a returned POW, he would carry weight.

Solarz with Solomon at his side has been holding the line despite
our lack of even a thank you. He said he was going to call Perot
to see if he really wanted to serve. If the answer was not, it
would kill it. I told him we would call first. Terry Mattke from VP's
office called him and told him the President was against this and
Perot acted as if this wasn't true since the President asked him
to "get to the bottom of the POW/MIA issue." This was a result of
the VP asking the President on Perot's behest to express appreciation
for his efforts.

I followed up Terry's call and told him of the President's opposition.
He did not take the same track with me but said the President should
come out front and say a commission is not needed since he has brought
Perot on board. Then he added all he would need from the Congress is
subpoena powers.

I then debriefed Solarz on the ambiguous response.

It is clear that no one in the VP's office has yet talked to Ross along
the lines of your memo. In addition, I'm spending an enormous amount of
energy ensuring his suggestions (the latest using DEA) are coordinated
with other agencies in the government.

The League is becoming increasingly restless about Perot's role, since
it is not a matter of speculation on the Hill and in the private
sector. Perot needs the talk, then we need to be prepared to respond
publicly about why he is here when it breaks in the media.

```
                                        10/15/86 11:54 ***
To: NSRBM    --CPUA    JOHN M. POINDEXTER NSWRP----CPUA    JOHN M. POINDEXTER
NOTE FROM: RICHARD T. CHILDRESS        UNCLASSIFIED
SUBJECT:  POW/MIA Commission (CO...
```

Hearing will be held today in East Asia Subcommittee. Solarz has
talked his Democratic colleagues into walking and lined up
Udall to back us. This, combined with the other Republicans, may
give us the votes to kill the commission. Solarz's fallback
is an amendment that would either ask the White House for our
view on the commission and a report on the issue by March or an
amendment to the current bill saying it was contingent on
Presidential approval since the President has provided the national
leadership on the issue.

This strategy and its implementation have been worked between us,
the League, Solarz, Solomon and Gilman. If Solarz wins for us, I
will be back for a thank you letter and we must roll Will Ball
this time.

Howard Baker, President Reagan, Ross Perot, Frank Carlucci, Colin Powell

circa 1987

WHITE HOUSE E-MAIL

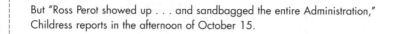

But "Ross Perot showed up . . . and sandbagged the entire Administration,"
Childress reports in the afternoon of October 15.

```
                                           10/15/86 15:11 ***
To: NSRBM    --CPUA    JOHN M. POINDEXTER NSWRP    --CPUA    JOHN M. POINDEXTER
NOTE FROM: RICHARD T. CHILDRESS
SUBJECT:  Ross Perot (CONFIDENTIAL)        UNCLASSIFIED
```

Perot showed up at the hearing and sandbagged the entire Administration.
Said VP and President asked him to get to the bottom of this. The
government was providing "bad bones" to the families, ruled out the
military option publicly for the Vietnamese to hear, slammed DIA, JCRC,
our negotiating effort, distorted the history of the issue, then went on
to say he would head a presidential commission if the President wanted
him to do so. He has been deceptive up to now, but this last caper
will have the country and the government in convulsions. He has played
into Hanoi's hands for his ego and doesn't even know it. The rest of
the government is asking me whether we are sane or not. Has he been
talked to yet?

```
                                           10/16/86 16:50:17

To: NSWRP    --CPUA

*** Reply to note of 10/15/86 16:05      UNCLASSIFIED

NOTE FROM: JOHN POINDEXTER
Subject:  Ross Perot (CONFIDENTIAL)
```
I don't know. I will talk to VP.

The next day, Childress describes the rest of the hearing, including testimony from Ann Griffiths of the League of Families (of the MIA). Robert Dornan (R-California) and Bill Hendon (R-North Carolina) were the Congressmen pushing the idea for the commission.

To: NSRBM --CPUA   JOHN M. POINDEXTER NSWRP   --CPUA   JOHN M. POINDEXTER
NOTE FROM: RICHARD T. CHILDRESS
SUBJECT: POW/MIA Commission (CONFIDENTIAL)

The Hearing yesterday was probably one of the greatest 3-ring circuses yet to take place on the Hill. Solarz gave the most eloquent defense yet of the President's commitment, our negotiating strategy, the need for facts and unity. Unfortunately for the strategy, Perot's appearance (which had to have been orchestrated with Dornan, Hendon, et al) led the Republicans for a Presidential commission (if we wanted it) to voting for the Hendon bill. They hid behind Solarz for election reasons. By making one of his colleagues walk and lining up proxies for others, Solarz secured a tie vote which killed the commission. If it had not been for him, we would have had a commission voted out that would not only write off the issue, but certainly advocate normalization or reparations publicly to gain Vietnamese cooperation. Ironically, such linkage is what Carter tried and what we inherited in 1981.

Ann Griffiths made all of the right policy points as usual. After Dornan spent 5 minutes echoing the compliments she received, he asked if she would serve on a Presidential commission depending on flattery. Ann turned it down flat and said she wouldn't participate in such a charade. BG Shufelt of DIA was also effective in putting General Tighe's assertions on proof into perspective.

We are over one hump. I heard that the VP's office spoke with Perot. I have no confirmation, but the entire IAG is waiting for another shoe to drop. Shultz and Weinberger will eventually be coming in on this unless we can keep it in bounds. Thus far, the concern is great in DOD, DIA and State, but they are depending on us to keep it rational.

The gory Perot details set off a round of phone calls to Vice President George Bush's office, since Bush was supposed to have talked with Perot and turned off the commission idea. This October 16 e-mail from Poindexter to Childress describes a conversation with Bush's chief of staff, Craig Fuller, on the subject of Perot—highly ironic in light of Perot's eventual torpedoing of the Bush presidency in 1992.

```
                                                    10/16/86 19:31:38

To: NSRTC   --CPUA     DICK CHILDRESS
                          -- UNCLASSIFIED

NOTE FROM: JOHN POINDEXTER
SUBJECT: Ross Perot
I just finsihed talking to Craig Fuller and gave him a readout on Perot's
performance on the Hill. I was rather irrate with him. He said the VP had read
your memo. I told Craig that I thought we should get Ross out of this ASAP.
Craig did not disagree. What do you think about drafting a memo for the
President that explains what Ross has come up with and what we see as the
problem and recommend that we ask Bill Clark to be a quiet private envoy as
you describe in the memo. Then Ross could turn over to him what it is that he
has learned and then Ross can step out of it. Craig said that Ross actually
proposed something like this.
```

And as late as February 1987, Perot was still angling for a lead role as official investigator of the POW/MIA issue.

```
                                                    02/19/87 16:34:53

To: NSWRP    --CPUA

*** Reply to note of 02/19/87 14:08      UNCLA
NOTE FROM: Frank C. Carlucci
Subject: House POW/MIA Task Force  (CONFIDENTIAL)
THAT PRESENTS A PROBLEM. PRESSURE IS GROWING FOR A PEROT LED MISSION. WHATT
CAN WE DO TO DEFLECT IT.
```

Other e-mail messages provide thumbnail sketches of the monster egos inhabiting Capitol Hill—the kind of personality sketches that are never reported in the press because they burn potential sources. But Senator Alan Dixon (D-Illinois) would have loved this ultimate compliment from NSC staffer Michael B. Donley (e-mail dated March 26, 1986), had Dixon only survived his primary fight with Carol Moseley-Braun in 1992.

03/26/86 11:54:01

To: NSRKS   --CPUA

NOTE FROM: Michael B. Donley
SUBJECT: USMC Tractors

None of this speaks to the political problems that Senator Dixon may continue to raise, but I would imagine they will blow over. I have watched Alan Dixon up close on the Armed Services Committee, and he is loyal Senator who faithfully and aggressively represents the interests of his constituents---- without regard for the facts, the US government, or the American people in general. It is not by accident that he is regarded by some of the staff as the Prince of Pork.He's almost good enough to be on the Appropriations Committee.

CHAPTER 8

THE HOT LINE

Throughout the 1980s, the management of the U.S. relationship with the Soviet Union took center stage at the White House, as it had in almost every post–World War II U.S. administration. The Reaganauts had come to power convinced that the détente of the 1970s had weakened the United States and emboldened the USSR, leading to Soviet advances around the world, as in Afghanistan. The first Reagan term featured a renewed Cold War and arms race, while the Soviets went through four supreme leaders in five years—Brezhnev, Andropov, Chernenko, and finally Gorbachev in early 1985. The second Reagan term saw some of the most far-reaching arms control negotiations ever undertaken, and the beginning of the end of the Cold War.

Reading the White House e-mail puts you backstage in this last act of the Cold War. The White House staff with responsibility for interpreting Soviet intentions and translating Soviet overtures produced fascinating e-mail that often reveals as much about American attitudes as it does about the Soviets. Other top-level officials anguish in the e-mail about the internal controversies—for example, pitting the National Security Council staff against the Pentagon—over U.S. proposals for arms control. And throughout the e-mail are scattered occasional rays of light illuminating the inside of the process: stories the negotiators told each other, articulated suspicions of back-stabbing and end-arounding, back-and-forth arguments over tactics and strategy, and blow-by-blow accounts of gambits, moves, and countermoves.

Sometimes the acronyms become overwhelming. SLCMs (slick-ems) and GLCMs (glick-ems), INF and SDI, MBRF and CSCE—all contribute to the priesthood effect, that is, the implied command to leave it to the experts, they're the only ones who understand what they're doing. But through the haze of high-level bureaucratic maneuvering, the e-mail highlights some fundamentals—conflicts inside the administration side by side with pressure from an increasingly Democratic Congress and constant worries about allies and proxies ranging from the NATO members to various side deals in places like Southwest Asia. No longer do we have to depend upon anonymous source accounts of this epochal era. Here in the e-mail is the history written at the time by the officials creating it.

Reagan & Gorbachev toast in Geneva 11-20-85 (Nancy & Raisa at right)

This extraordinary story of Khrushchev's impression of Eisenhower comes from an April 9, 1986, e-mail from Soviet specialist Jack Matlock through the NSC secretariat (Rod McDaniel) to the national security adviser. Matlock had been the NSC representative at a meeting between the Soviet ambassador to the U.S., Anatoly Dobrynin, and George Shultz, the secretary of state. (MFA stands for Ministry of Foreign Affairs; in this case, where Dobrynin was working in 1960.)

```
*** Forwarding note from NSJFM    --CPUA      04/09/86 14:38 ***
To: NSRBM    --CPUA      JOHN M. POINDEXTER NSWRP    --CPUA      JOHN M. POINDEXTER
NOTE FROM: Jack Matlock
SUBJECT: Shultz-Dobrynin Meeting
SECRET/SENSITIVE
```

In this regard, one of his stories was interesting. Paul Nitze asked at lunch why it was that U-2 flights did not disturb relations until one was shot down, and then it became a big issue. Dobrynin said he was in Moscow then as head of the USA Division in MFA and worked directly with Khrushchev on the issue. He said that initially Khrushchev was furious at the Soviet military because they could not shoot down the U-2. When they did, he tried to pursue the public fiction that Eisenhower was not responsible (since he wanted to continue to deal with him). He did not expect Eisenhower to disown the flights, but thought he would understand that he should not state publicly that he authorized them. When Eisenhower, however, did the latter, Khrushchev was unable to continue dealing with him because that would have meant a public loss of face. (He said that Khrushchev later commented that he would gladly entrust the education of his children to Eisenhower because he was "truly an honest man," but that he wondered if he understood the responsibilities which go with political leadership in international affairs.)

Dobrynin & Reagan 7-1-84

WHITE HOUSE E-MAIL

Some of the tension and paranoia in the U.S.-Soviet relationship during the early Reagan years comes through in this September 5, 1984, e-mail from National Security Adviser Robert McFarlane to his deputy, John Poindexter. The White House was concerned about private sector "interlocutors," whose very actions served as an implicit criticism of the administration's failure to hold constructive talks with the Soviets. Also of concern were the propaganda points that might be scored by Soviet foreign minister Andrei Gromyko on TV during his upcoming visit. McFarlane's mention of the polls refers to Reagan's commanding lead that fall over the Democratic candidate for president, Walter Mondale.

```
To: NSJMP    --CPUA                                    09/05/84 20:12:19

                            UNCLASSIFIED

NOTE FROM: ROBERT MCFARLANE
SUBJECT: Gromyko's Early Arrival??

During the Shultz meeting today, he mentioned that David Rockefeller had
mentioned to him that Dobrynin had proposed that Gromyko meet with
Rockefeller's group (he has ginned up a group--Kissinger, and one or two other
Soviet thinkers who fancy that they may be able to serve as "interlocutors')
on Sept 19 repeat 19th. That is a week before the Shultz-Gromyko meeting and
before the UNGA even starts. It suggests to me that maybe NBC has scored with
its Soviet extravaganza and will feature Gromyko on national television in a
US blast--terrific. Please ask Jack to think about this and try to see how we
can influence the presence of balanced people on the show--that will be hard.
Jack should also give his estimate of what Gromyko's strategy will be. It
seems to me that Gromyko ought to be able to read polls and that that would
seem to discount a heavy negative blast--but I could be wrong. We should also
give some thought to how we ought to try to shape the, meeting with the
Rockefeller group. many thanks.
```

Tension and paranoia were not only directed at the Soviets, as this McFarlane memo to President Reagan shows (it was saved among Poindexter's e-mail). Again, in September 1984, McFarlane warns that the Office of the Secretary of Defense (OSD), not the Joint Chiefs of Staff (JCS), is opposed "to the very concept of arms control," but predicts that the Soviets will be very interested. The implication is that if negotiations begin, they will in effect be three-way talks: Kremlin-White House-Pentagon.

```
NOTE FROM: ROBERT MCFARLANE          UNCLASSIFIED          09/17/84 09:14:48
SUBJECT: Memo to the President
```

MEMORANDUM FOR THE PRESIDENT

From: Robert C. McFarlane

Subject: Organizing for Serious Arms Control Negotiations

For a number of reasons which will be presented in a separate paper I believe
we can expect the Soviets to have a high interest in making headway on arms
control during the next four years. In order to be able to have a responsive
and imaginative process within the US government I recommend that you consider
two fundamental changes in the way your Administration handles this issue.
First, the record of the first term makes clear that there is determined
opposition within the Department of Defense (OSD not JCS) to the very concept
of arms control. In my judgment this opposition will endure unless personnel
changes are made. Secondly, this opposition and a traditionally incremental
approach to making changes to the US position within State makes it desireable
to elevate the management of the bureaucracy to the White House. Right now,
the Interdepartmental groups (IGs and SIGs) are managed by the Departments.
Unless and until these groups are chaired within the White House we will
continue to face the paralysis we ohave often faced these past four years.
What I am suggesting is that you consider naming a high level, experienced
personal representative to manage this process--a man the Soviets would
respect and who is knowledgeable on both the technical and political aspects
of arms control. There are two or three possible candidates for such a
position.

Were you to think this a sensible thing to do it would be important to discuss
it with George Shultz so that there is no appearance of his suffering a
diminution of his authority. But the truth is that your predecessors have only
been able to make breakthroughs when they have entered the process directly
from the White House. If George can be asked to think about this it could lead
to its being his idea and thus minimize the public appearance of his being
subordinated in the process. You may wish to think about this prior to your
meetings with the Secretary this week. If he comes to agree with the value of
such a change it might be possible to use it in your meeting with Gromyko and.
later, to announce this initiative which promises a more visible and active
role by the President in the next four years. Such an annoncement would show
leadership and meet persistent criticisms from the Congress and press of the
way the process has been handled these past four years. It would also be seen
by Gromyko and the Soviet leadership as indicative that you are indeed serious
about arms reductions in the coming years.I would be glad to discuss this at
your convenience.

cc: NSJMP   --CPUA

WHITE HOUSE E-MAIL

08/19/86 14:52:48

To: NSWRP   --CPUA   BOB PEARSON

NOTE FROM: JOHN POINDEXTER
SUBJECT: CAP MEMO ON INF
CAP TOLD ME THIS MORNING THAT HE HAD SENT ME A NEW MEMO ON INF. I TOLD HIM I WOULD GET IT TO THE PRESIDENT RIGHT AWAY. I TALKED TO THE PRESIDENT ON THE WAY TO CONFIRM THAT HIS POSITION WAS THAT HE WAS WILLING TO AGREE TO AN INTERIM AGREEMENT THAT TOOK US PART WAY DOWN THE PATH TO ZERO BUT DID NOT AGREE TO EXACTLY HOW WE WOULD BOTH EVENTUALLY GET TO ZERO. THE PRESIDENT SAID THAT WAS CORRECT. I HAVE REPEATEDLY TOLD CAP THAT, BUT HE WANTS TO TRY ONE LAST TIME. HE REALLY IS PERSISTENT.

08/19/86 16:27:59

To: NSREL   --CPUA   BOB LINHARD

NOTE FROM: JOHN POINDEXTER
SUBJECT: Cap's INF Memo
I just read it. He conveniently forgets the Nov. proposal. That sort of argument makes people believe that Cap is really not interested in any agreements. I will need a cover memo to the President that reminds him of my discussion with him aboard AF-1 on the way out here last Saturday. I recommend that we stick to our present interpretation.

Weinberger & Reagan 1-10-83

The key variable on the Soviet side, according to this and other e-mail, was the new attitude and energy of Mikhail Gorbachev. This excerpt from an April 9, 1986, report on the Shultz-Dobrynin meeting, written by Jack Matlock, gives some fascinating insights into the political constraints on Gorbachev, including his need for "face."

04/09/86 14:38 ***

To: NSRBM   --CPUA   JOHN M. POINDEXTER NSWRP   --CPUA   JOHN M. POINDEXTER
NOTE FROM: Jack Matlock
SUBJECT: Shultz-Dobrynin Meeting
SECRET/SENSITIVE

Shultz meeting and lunch today went smoothly. Essentially, the Secretary explained and repeated what the President had said yesterday. I detected in Dobrynin's demeanor considerably more relaxation in terms of the trend of events. In a side conversation, Bessmertnykh referred to "things being back on track again," so I believe that Dobrynin will go back with the overall report that the President is serious about moving negotiations ahead.

Dobrynin continued to stress several points: Gorbachev's desire for the summit this year; his need "as a politician" to be sure there is some minimum result; and the tendency in Moscow to read everything we do as part of a "master plan." He said specifically that Gorbachev reads every public statement made by the President, and also all speeches by Shultz and Weinberger. He often draws his own conclusions before he gets a staff analysis. (Implicit here and in much of the other discussion was the message that "face" is his most important problem at present.) When Shultz made the point that both sides would have to keep doing what they must to defend their interest, Dobrynin agreed, but observed that the way they are done and what is said about them is important. Dobrynin claimed that the reason the Black Sea transit was considered provocative was that the ship came closer than before, and precisely in an area which had been described to Nixon (when he visited the Crimea in 1973) as one of their most sensitive. Therefore, the tendency in Moscow was to treat it not as a routine FON exercise, but a deliberate effort to embarrass. (When Shultz asked if it would help if we complained about the Soviet AGI off Pearl Harbor, Dobrynin neither objected nor agreed, but obseved that "It is important for us to show that we are tending to our interests," thus implicitly confirming that it wouldn't hurt for us to complain.)As for future events, Dobrynin asked if we could do what we could to postpone routine things which might be misinterpreted and could be done as well a little later. His argument was that this is not so much a matter of substance as of "face" and political impact on the Soviet internal situation.

WHITE HOUSE E-MAIL

Reagan & Gorbachev lead their delegations at the Geneva summit 11-20-85

Another commentary from Jack Matlock (June 24, 1986) provides a candid assessment of Gorbachev's methods in the view of the White House—a "play for the public galleries."

06/24/86 16:11:32

To: NSJMP   --CPUA

*** Reply to note of 06/24/86 15:53
NOTE FROM: Jack Matlock
Subject: Chernobyl Update/IAEA Convention
This is quite possible. He certainly included powerplant safety in his letter.
Also, I think the Sovs are having their usual problem in putting together the
details of a position their leader has set out for them in general. We may
find them cooling toward some the the ideas as they work the concrete issues.
They may not have a Linhard yet to drive the interagency process.

Increasingly, one aspect of Gorbachev's style is becoming clear. In his play
for the public galleries, he puts forward broad, fine-sounding proposals
(possibly devised by Yakovlev's propaganda shop), then they get around rather
slowly to implementing them. Along the way, a lot of in-fighting occurs. Also
various potential actors trying to get a piece of the action come out of the
woodwork and start showing up on our radar screens.

Jack Matlock and staff 9-18-86

This June 25, 1986, e-mail from Peter Rodman, NSC staffer, to John Poindexter illuminates an arcane corner of the arms-race world—the controversy over whether the Strategic Defense Initiative (SDI, or "Star Wars") would violate the Anti-Ballistic Missile (ABM) Treaty. The original treaty rationale was to restrict ABM development in order to prevent further missile buildup, since the only way to overcome defensive systems was to overload them with more attacking warheads. Critics charged that an operational SDI system would kick off a new destabilizing arms race and, perversely, increase incentives for preemptive first strikes. But President Reagan was committed to the SDI notion; and here, Rodman sees an opportunity for one-upmanship versus the Russians, "legitimizing SDI" vis-à-vis the ABM Treaty.

```
                        TO: NSJMP    --CPUA              06/25/86 10:22:18

To: NSJFM    --CPUA

NOTE FROM: Peter Rodman
SUBJECT: "Clarifying" the ABM Treaty
   I notice in a cable from Geneva (NST GENEVA 5891, 241139Z JUN 86, "Reception
Conversation, June 20") a report of Hank Cooper insisting to the Soviets that
any attempt to "clarify" the ABM Treaty would have to be via the formal
amendment/ratification process.
   Is this our policy? Why do we want to be locked in on this? Why wouldn't we
want to preserve Executive flexibility? I continue to believe that the
Soviets' explicit proposal to "clarify" the activities permitted by the Treaty
-- reiterated in Gorbachev's latest letter -- is a great opening for us, in
that it implies that the Treaty needs to be adjusted to accommodate SDI. Our
public handling of this issue (even if not our letter to Gorbachev) could make
good use of this as legitimizing SDI. In any case, I would think we would
want to preserve maximum flexibility with respect to the format of any new
"understandings" reached.
```

WHITE HOUSE E-MAIL

The hard currency of the arms controllers consisted of bean-counting—the actual numbers of warheads and delivery vehicles in all their mind-numbing jargon. This July 29, 1986, e-mail from Robert Linhard to John Poindexter through Rod McDaniel includes references to ALCM (air-launched cruise missile, of which the SALT treaty limited the United States to 130), RV (re-entry vehicle), ICBMs (intercontinental ballistic missiles), and MMIIIs (the advanced Minuteman III), among many others. But the core point of the e-mail note reveals the behind-the-scenes calculations of American advantage in relation to a specific proposal originally considered to be a gimmick. The initials "RD" out to the side of the censored words indicate that the exact number of RVs carried by a Poseidon is still classified as a nuclear secret, called "Restricted Data," under the Atomic Energy Act.

08/06/86 07:54:20

*** Resending note of 07/29/86 18:27
To: NSRBM————CPUA————JOHN M. POINDEXTER NSWRP   --CPUA   JOHN M. POINDEXTER
NOTE FROM: ROBERT E. LINHARD
SUBJECT: DRAMATIC SUMMIT STEPS
ADMIRAL,

UNCLASSIFIED

    ROD ASKED ME TODAY ABOUT A PROPOSAL SUGGESTED BY NIXON TO THE PRESIDENT PRIOR TO THE LAST SUMMIT INVOLVING BOTH SIDES TAKING DOWN 1000 WEAPONS. I TOLD ROD THAT I DIDN'T REMEMBER SUCH A PROPOSAL -- AND THAT BUD MAY HAVE HANDLED THAT DIRECTLY. I COULD UNDERSTAND SUCH AN ACTION, SINCE IT SOUNDS VERY MUCH LIKE A GIMMICK TO ME.

    I GUESS IF ASKED TO EVALUATE SUCH A PROPOSAL TODAY, I WOULD LIKELY TAKE A MUCH LONGER LOOK AT IT. THE REASON IS THAT IF THE SOVIETS WERE PREPARED TO TAKE 1,000 BALLISTIC MISSILE WARHEADS DOWN, BEGINNING IMMEDIATELY, WE COULD USE THIS TO DRIVE THE RETIREMENT OF ●● OLDER POSEIDON SSBNs -- THUS SIDESTEPPING THE ISSUE OF THE 131ST ALCM (AND OTHER SALT CONSTRAINTS) FOR THE REMAINDER OF THE ADMINISTRATION. THE KEY WOULD HAVE TO BE THAT WE COULD USE THE OLDER POSEIDON FORCE ●●●●●●●●●●●●●●●●●● TO "PAY FOR" OUR REDUCTIONS (1 POSEIDON ●●●●● RVs) WHILE THE SOVIETS WOULD LIKELY HAVE TO TAKE DOWN ICBMS, AND PROBABLY MORE SNDVs THAN WE (UNLESS THEY PLAY WITH THEIR SS-18s WHICH I DOUBT THEY WOULD).

b (i)
(C/RD)

I THINK THAT WE SHOULD TAKE A CLOSER LOOK AT THIS. I WOULD ALSO LIKE YOUR OK TO TALK TO BUD AND SEE IF HE REMEMBERS THIS IDEA -- AND WHAT DROVE OUR THINKING ON THIS LAST TIME.

YOU SHOULD NOTE THAT IF WE BEGIN PLAYING THIS GAME, THE SOVIETS WILL TRY TO CHANGE THE RULES TO THEIR FAVOR. THEY DID OFFER THE "QUICK MEASURE" OF PULLING DOWN 200-300 ICBMs AS AN AGREEMENT AT THE SUMMIT. WE REJECTED AS A GIMMICK -- BUT BECAUSE WE DIDN'T THINK WE COULD AFFORD TO TRADE AWAY OUR MMIIIs FOR OLDER SOVIET ICBMs. IF WE COULD HOLD THE DEAL TO BALLISTIC MISSILE WARHEADS, AND THEN USE OLDER SSBNs, IT COULD BE INTERESTING.

Reagan, Powell, Linhard 8-4-88

Baker, Reagan, Bush & Matlock 7-14-87

Reagan & Gorbachev after Reykjavik summit breaks down 10-12-86

Reagan & Gorbachev at Reykjavik before the breakdown

Sometimes Gorbachev grabbed the initiative in arms control proposals, and the White House scrambled to respond. On March 13, 1986, for example, Gorbachev announced that the Soviet Union would continue its nuclear testing moratorium indefinitely if the United States would also refrain. As evidenced in this March 14 e-mail to all the White House Soviet specialists and NSC higher-ups, Robert Linhard and his crew raced into action, announcing President Reagan's rejection of Gorbachev's proposal and a new U.S. initiative for improving verification of nuclear tests. This note provides a snapshot of White House instant reaction work.

NOTE FROM: ROBERT E. LINHARD
Subject: NUCLEAR TESTING

UNCLASSIFIED

THIS IS A RETRANSMISSION OF A NOTE I WAS BUSY WRITING AND SENT INADVERTENTLY
BEFORE I COMPLETED THE TEXT.   SORRY FOR ANY CONFUSION.

*** Forwarding note from NSREL   --CPUA   03/14/86 09:17 ***

To: NSWHW   --CPUA   NSSES   --CPUA
    NSSFK   --CPUA   NSLSS   --CPUA
    NSRKS   --CPUA   NSRBM   --CPUA
    NSJFM   --CPUA   NSPRS   --CPUA

NOTE FROM: ROBERT E. LINHARD
SUBJECT: NUCLEAR TESTING

UNCLASSIFIED

THIS IS JUST TO REVIEW THE BIDDING SO THAT WE CAN ENSURE WE ARE ALL ON THE SAME
WAVELENGTH ON NEXT STEPS ON THE NUCLEAR TESTING ACTION.

ASSUMING A GO AT 09:30-10:00 THIS MORNING, STATE WOULD RELEASE THE MESSAGES TO
GORBACHEV, ALLIED LEADERS AND THE DELHI SIX ASAP.   STATE HAS A COPY OF THE
LATEST VERSION TO KEYBOARD THIS MORNING.   WE WILL NEED ROD'S HELP TO ENSURE
STATE SS EXPEDITES THE TASK.

SVEN/STEVE -- WE NEED A WHITE HOUSE STATEMENT SOONEST. WE CAN TALK ABOUT WHEN
AND HOW IT COULD BE USED AFTER WE HAVE THE BASIC TEXT IN OUR POCKET.   I THINK
IT SHOULD BE A COMBINATION OF THE DOLE LETTER RATIONALE ON CTB, MORATORIA AND
TESTING PLUS THE ALLIED LEADERS LETTER'S TREATMENT OF THE NEW INITIATIVE.   LETS
SHOOT FOR 11:30 FOR A DRAFT.

BILL -- PER OUR AGREEMENT, YOU WILL CONTACT LYNN SACHS AND WORK UP A QUICK
CONGRESSIONAL NOTIFICATION PLAN AND TALKING POINTS FOR MAKING THE CALLS.
WE ARE AGREED THIS WE NEED THIS ALSO THIS MORNING SOONEST (BY ABOUT 11:30).

Q&AS -- WE HAVE ASKED STATE PM TO WORK UP A QUICK DRAFT Q&A PACKAGE FOR OUR
REVIEW LATER TODAY. STEVE/SVEN -- WHEN WE SURFACE FROM THE STATEMENT, NEED TO
LOOK AT THIS.   SHOULD HAVE SOME THING BY COB TODAY.

CABLE TO POSTS. FINALLY, WE WILL NEED TO SEND A CABLE TO POSTS INFORMING
THEM OF THIS INITIATIVE AND PROVIDING THE STATEMENT AND Q&AS.   THIS WILL
NEED TO GO THIS PM AT COB.   WE CAN REGROUP AT NOON TO DECIDE HOW TO MAKE
THIS LAST PIECE COME TRUE.

HOW DOES THIS SOUND? ANY SUGGESTED CHANGES?   IF NOT, LETS EXECUTE THE PREP
WORK -- BUT REMEMBER, WE STILL NEED A FINAL GO ON THE INITIATIVE FROM JMP AND
THE PRESIDENT BEFORE WE LET ANY OF THIS GET OUT OF OUR DIRECT CONTROL.   HOPEFUL
THAT WE WILL GET A GO BY MID-MORNING.

```
                           09/20/86 17:19 ***
           JOHN M. POINDEXTER NSWRP    --CPUA    JOHN M. POINDEXTER
NOTE FROM: ROBERT E. LINHARD
SUBJECT: DEBRIEFING SHULTZ-SHEVARDNADZE
ADMIRAL,
   THIS FOLLOWS-UP ON OUR CONVERSATION IN THE CAR.  WE NEED TO DEBRIEF
THE FOLLOWING ELEMENTS:  (1) THE SHULTZ-SHEVARDNADZE MEETINGS
                         (2) THE BASIC LETTER FROM GORBACHEV
                         (3) ANY ADDITIONAL SENSITIVE MATERIAL YOU CHOOSE.
AT THE SAME TIME, WE NEED TO DEBRIEF THE FOLLOWING GROUPS OF PEOPLE:
     (A)  KEY ALLIED HEADS OF STATE (UK, FRG, ITALY, FRANCE, JAPAN, CANADA)
     (B)  ALLIED GOVERNMENTS (NATO, JAPAN, AUSTRAILIA, KOREA, ISREAL)
     (C)  NSC PRINCIPALS (DCI, CJCS, SECDEF)
     (D)  OTHER SENIOR OFFICIALS (ADELMAN, ROWNY, NEGOTIATORS)
     (E)  KEY OFFICIALS IN ADMIN (SACG, ACSG, IG CHAIRMEN)
     (F)  CONGRESSIONAL LEADERSHIP
     (G)  CONGRESSIONAL OBSERVERS GROUP
WHILE THE ACCESS TO MORE INFORMATION MAY BE NECESSARY LATER, EARLY NEXT WEEK
I THINK THE FOLLOWING GROUPS NEED ACCESS TO THE FOLLOWING INFO.
  (A) KEY ALLIED LEADERS -- NEED ITEMS 1-3 AND SHOULD BE TRANSMITTED VIA
                            A PRESIDENTIAL BACK CHANNEL MESSAGE
  (B) ALLIED GOVERNMENTS -- NEED ITEMS 1 & 2 TRANSMITTED VIA A NORMAL
                            HEAD-OF-STATE LETTER (THIS WILL COVER ANY
                            LEAKS OF OTHER MORE PRIVATE PRESIDENTIAL
                            MESSAGE TO GROUP A.
  (C) NSC PRINCIPALS     -- NEED ITEMS 1-3.  KEY STAFF CAN BE BRIEFED ON
                            DETAILS OF 1&2 AS INDICATED BELOW.  ITEM 3
                            SHOULD BE DONE BY SECURE PHONE BY YOU.
  (D) OTHER SENIORS      -- NEED ITEMS 1&2.  CAN GET THIS FROM THEIR
                            STAFF WHICH WILL BE BRIEFED AS INDICATED
                            BELOW.  ITEM 3 ON CASE-BY-CASE BASIS.  FOR
                            EXAMPLE, YOU MAY WISH TO TELL ADELMAN ABOUT
                            THE ITEM 3.
  (E) KEY STAFF          -- NEED ITEMS 1&2 ONLY.  WE CAN SET UP A SPECIAL
                            DEBREIF ON EARLY MONDAY PM HERE IN OEOB.
                            FOLLOWING THAT, CABLES TO NEGOTIATORS.
  (F) CONGRESSIONAL LEAD -- ITEMS 1&2.  CAN BUILD TALKING POINTS FOR
                            USE IN CALLS.  ITEM 3 ON CASE-BY-CASE BASIS.
                            THINK YOU SHOULD CALL LEADERSHIP ON THIS.
  (G) OBSERVERS          -- ITEMS 1&2.  SCHEDULE NITZE TO DEBRIEF.
```

IF YOU AGREE WITH THE ABOVE, WE WILL DO THE FOLLOWING ON MONDAY MORNING:
    STEP 1.   INSTRUCT STATE TO DRAFT A PRESIDENTIAL HEAD-OF-STATE LETTER
                IN MESSAGE FORM FOR NATO, JAPAN, KOREA, AUSTRAILIA -- INFO
                NEGOTIATORS -- WHICH LAYS OUT ITEMS 1 AND 2.
    STEP 2.   DRAFT HERE A SHORT PRIVACY CHANNEL MESSAGE WITH ANY ITEM 3
                MATERIAL EYES ONLY FOR LEADERS OF UK, FRANCE, FRG, ITALY,
                JAPAN, CANADA.
    STEP 3.   SCHEDULE A DEBRIEF SESSION FOR SACG (LESS YOU) FOR MONDAY
                EARLY AFTERNOON TO DEBRIEF KEY PLAYERS (BELOW CABINET) ON
                ITEMS 1 AND 2.   HOLD THAT SESSION MONDAY AT 12 OR 1PM.
    STEP 4.   INSTRUCT STATE TO DRAFT TALKING POINTS ON ITEMS 1 AND 2 FOR
                USE IN CALLS TO CONGRESSIONAL LEADERSHIP. YOU WOULD ADD ANY
                INFO ON ITEM 3 TO THOSE YOU SEE FIT TO CALL. NEED SOME
                NOTIFICATION OF CONGRESS FOR THE PECORD.
    STEP 5.   YOU CALL SENIOR CABINET OFFICIALS ON ITEM 3.
    STEP 6.   ASK PAUL TO SCHEDULE A DEBRIEF ON ITEMS 1 AND 2 WITH CONGRESSIONAL
                OBSERVERS.
THEN ON MONDAY, THE FOLLOWING WOULD OCCUR:
    EVENT 1. YOU CALL THE CABINET LEVEL ON ITEM 3.
    EVENT 2. WE HOLD DEBRIEF OF SACG (LESS YOU) ON ITEMS 1 AND 2. THEY DEBRIEF
                THEIR PRINCIPALS ON THIS MATERIAL.
    EVENT 3. YOU CALL CONGRESSIONAL LEADERSHIP ON ITEMS 1 AND 2, AND
                SELECTIVELY ON ITEM 3.
    EVENT 4. BY COB, YOU RELEASE FRONT CHANNEL MESSAGE TO HEADS-OF-STATE
                ON ITEMS 1 AND 2, AND A BACK CHANNEL TO UK, FRG, FR, CANADA,
                ITALY, JAPAN ON ITEM 3.
    EVENT 5. WE SCHED NITZE TO BRIEF OBSERVERS ON TUES/WED.

PLEASE GIVE ME YOUR APPROVAL OF THE ABOVE IF ACCEPTABLE TO YOU. IF
INDIVIDUALS STEPS OR EVENTS ARE NOT ACCEPTABLE, IDENTIFY AND WE WILL
MODIFY. I WILL NOT IMPLEMENT THIS PLAN WITHOUT YOUR EXPRESSED APPROVAL
SINCE EVENTS MAY CHANGE BEFORE MONDAY AND BEFORE I CAN TALK TO YOU.

To: NSJMP   --CPUA   JOHN M. POINDEXTER   11/08/86 11:27:54

NOTE FROM: ROBERT MCFARLANE
SUBJECT: George

George's comments are a little dissappointing. Not that I would expect him to be enthusiastic in support but there is a fundamental issue of the relationship with Iran that ought to have some clear importance and which would warrant at least comments such as, "...there's far more to this than meets the eye..." or something.

But I can understand how it is hard to broker that. If you wish, I will call him and try to create some understanding. I assume that he has been kept informed.

Were his talks in Vienna as dissappointing as headlines made them appear? I was encouraged by the news of the all-night session and by the separate introduction of a position at Geneva by the Russians. But that too may be posturing. I hope to meet with Steve Steiner and a Pentagon briefer for an update on SDI next week so as to be better able to reign in my group studying this matter. But I remain optimistic that Goprbachev will come around to accept a very vigroous R&D and testing program and the 50% part of the Iceland outcome. Hang in there.

Shultz & Reagan at Camp David 8-14-82

To: NSRCM   --CPUA

*** Reply to note of 11/08/86 11:27   --UNCLASSIFIED

NOTE FROM: JOHN POINDEXTER
Subject: George

As you know George is too damn emotional and he lets it show through. Linhard
said he was ready to go out after the Vienna meeting and be very negative
about ever reaching an agreement with the Soviets. Bob talked him out of that
approach. George is just not very patient. As you and I have always said the
only way we are going to get an agreement with the Soviets is through private
channels. The Soviets have just shifted to a propaganda mode for awhile. I
think your objective is still attainable.

On Iran I agree with you. I am terribly disappointed with the way George has
handled this. I sent him a rather scorching message yesterday about his
department and the way people are talking. Of course he isn't helping but I
didn't say that. Let's talk at 2:00 about whether you should talk to him.

WHITE HOUSE E-MAIL

Sometimes posturing was the order of the day in U.S.-Soviet relations. After the United States bombed Tripoli in April 1986, in retaliation for Libyan sponsorship of a bombing in Germany that killed an American soldier, the Soviets postponed a scheduled foreign ministers' meeting. Here, Peter Rodman postulates an explanation wrapping these events up with visits to Moscow by top Libyan and Syrian officials.

05/28/86 15:20:49

NOTE FROM: Peter Rodman
SUBJECT: Jallud and Khaddam in Moscow
   I have a somewhat off-the-wall theory about the simultaneous Moscow visits of Jallud and Khaddam: By postponing the Shultz-Shevardnadze meeting over Libya, the Soviets put themselves into a corner which it has been somewhat tricky to get out of. Thus a visible, dramatic, fist-waving display of "solidarity" with their Libyan and Syrian friends may be the necessary precondition -- and thus the precursor -- of the resumption of the US-Soviet dialogue.Putting this together with other signs, including the divided families move, I would expect them soon to move to reschedule the Shultz-Shevardnadze meeting. The conciliatory tone cf the President's letter should help, and the Interim Restraints decision was sufficiently ambiguous so as not to hurt too much.

Reagan & Shultz with Gorbachev & Shevardnadze plus translators and notetakers, Reykjavik, Iceland 10-12-86

Libya and Syria were hardly the most important third parties that kept interfering in U.S.-Soviet relations. Events in Southwest Asia created a complex dance of interests involving strong U.S. support for Pakistan (which in turn cultivated ties with China) facing off with Soviet troops in Afghanistan and close Soviet ties to India. But when the Soviets got serious in U.N.-sponsored talks in Geneva seeking an Afghan settlement, all kind of back-channels ensued. This May 15, 1986, e-mail from NSC Soviet specialist Steve Sestanovich describes "hysteria" in a cable from Undersecretary of State Michael Armacost to Deane Hinton, the U.S. ambassador to Pakistan, because "the Paks just spent long hours with him lying to him." (Bud refers to Robert McFarlane, and Junejo was the Pakistani prime minister at the time.)

05/15/86 16:50:48

To: NSDRF   --CPUA   DONALD FORTIER

NOTE FROM: Steve Sestanovich
SUBJECT: Afghanistan
Shirin and I have just finished looking at an astonishing cable
from Armacost to Hinton expressing his panic at the state of the
Geneva negotiations. He has realized that the Paks are not leveling
with us, and the text of the cable is about as extreme as you could
imagine from him. He says in so many words that the draft agreement
is not a plausible basis for a settlement, and that the Paks and Soviets
seem to be conducting the real talks in a channel we know nothing about.
Armacost is "asking for Hinton's thoughts", but obviously the real
question is what to do if this dire view of the situation has really
taken hold at State. We think the view is probably correct -- with
a little late-in-the-day hysteria that may overdo things -- but if
the next step is merely to send Mike Armacost out for another round
of talks we aren't going to make any progress. The Paks just spent
long hours with him lying to him. We need a different channel. Our
idea, which only you may be able to promote, is Bud. Not only would
this show we were moving the dialogue to a higher level (White House
vis, etc.), but he could do a bit of nuclear talk before Junejo comes.
I'm leaving in just minutes, but if you think this is at all a good
idea you might follow up with Shirin or Peter. If you don't think
it's a good idea, do you have another inspiration? I am inclined to
think that it would not be an overreaction to have John go (especially
if it could be secret).
The cable looks from its markings as tho it will come to you, but Shirin
will check with the sit rm to make sure. It's worth getting to right
away.

WHITE HOUSE E-MAIL

10-Feb-1987 06:49 EST

MEMORANDUM FOR: SEE BELOW

FROM: Fritz W. Ermarth
              (ERMARTH)

Declassified/Released on ___8-22-94___
by NARA on the recommendation of the NSC.

SUBJECT: Star Chernobyl

CONFIDENTIAL

CHERNOBYL' MEANS DARK SAGA OR LEGEND. IT IS ALSO THE FOLK NAME FOR A VARIETY OF WORMWOOD. REVELATIONS (8/10,11) READS AS FOLLOWS: "THE THIRD ANGEL BLEW HIS TRUMPET; AND A GREAT STAR SHOT FROM THE SKY, FLAMING LIKE A TORCH; AND IT FELL ON A THIRD OF THE RIVERS AND THE SPRINGS. THE NAME OF THE STAR WAS WORMWOOD; AND A THIRD OF THE WATER TURNED TO WORMWOOD, AND MEN IN GREAT NUMBERS DIED OF THE WATER BECAUSE IT HAD BEEN POISONED." UKRAINIAN COUNTRY PEOPLE HAVE NOTICED THIS ASSOCIATION AND CONNECT IT WITH THE DISASTER AT THE CHERNOBYL' NUCLEAR POWER PLANT. IT IS NOT KNOWN AT THE MOMENT HOW WIDELY THIS CONNECTION IS KNOWN IN THE USSR; BUT UKRAINIANS AND RUSSIANS ARE BOTH RELIGIOUS AND SUPERSTITIOUS. THE CONNECTION IS WIDELY APPRECIATED IN THE SOVIET EMIGRE COMMUNITY.

Distribution:

FOR: Frank C. Carlucci   (CARLUCCI)
FOR: Colin L. Powell   (POWELL)
FOR: Grant S. Green   (GREEN)
FOR: W. Robert Pearson   (PEARSON)
FOR: Paul B. Thompson   (THOMPSON)

CC: Baerbel K. Houck   (HOUCK)

Summits make a lot of work for everybody, even long after they've faded from the front pages. This February 4, 1987, e-mail from NSC staffer Linton Brooks gives legislative liaison Alison Fortier a heads-up about some potential heat from Capitol Hill, in the wake of the failed Reykjavík summit between Reagan and Gorbachev. Aspin refers to then-chair of the House Armed Services Committee, Les Aspin (D-Wisconsin). JCS is the Joint Chiefs of Staff. Note especially the reference to "file and forget" drills.

02/04/87 21:06:19

To: NSABF   --CPUA   Allison Fortier

NOTE FROM: LINTON BROOKS
SUBJECT: NSDD 250
After Reykjavik we took a LOT of flack in Congress for the suggestion on eliminating ballistic missiles. Aspin was a prime mover. One issue was JCS involvement.

To attempt to kick that can downstream, we wrote NSDD 250, a long NSDD that:
   (1) Set forth the rationale why a ballistic missile-free world is good.
   (2) Asked JCS for a plan of how to (NOTE: "how to," not "whether to") safely transition to such a world by 1996.
   (3) Gave them some guidelines, including fiscal.

JCS response will be here next week. It will not repudiate the President's Reykjavik offer, but it isn't a ringing endorsement. Says you can move to zero ballistic missiles safely by 1996 OR you can meet our fiscal guidelines, but you can't do both. Implies hundreds of billions in extra spending might be needed if ballistic missiles are eliminated.

Problem is that some on the Hill know this drill is going on. While we will probably treat this input as a "file and forget" drill (PLEASE don't use that characterization with DOD; there has been a huge amount of effort expended on this), IF Aspin picks up on this and holds hearings, we have the potential for another "beat up on the President" session.

I don't think we need to do anything, but you asked for potential problems and here's one. If this is a problem at all, it will be a problem in the next 3-5 weeks; after that no one will remember. On the other hand, we may skate by this w/o anything happening; no one is talking about zero ballistic missiles much any more.

WHITE HOUSE E-MAIL

When waltzing with the Soviets, the White House also had to watch out for the allies' sensitivities. This December 30, 1988, memo (sent through e-mail) from Nelson Ledsky to National Security Adviser Colin Powell (who was in California with President Reagan for the holidays) goes into detail blasting a State Department plan for a Shultz-Shevardnadze letter on the grounds that it would annoy three important allies: "the British, the Canadians and the Congress."

SECRET

30-Dec-1988 14:17 EDT

MEMORANDUM FOR: SEE BELOW

FROM: Nelson C. Ledsky
(LEDSKY)

SUBJECT: Moscow Human Rights Conference

2. I do not want to argue the issue of whether or not the Soviets have complied fully enough with our criteria to warrant U.S. agreement to go to a Human Rights Meeting in Moscow in 1991. I also do not wish to object to a policy which aims at ending the Vienna meeting before the end of the Administration,although it is clear that countries that want to move quickly mayhave to pay a higher price in CSCE.

-- 2. The presidential letter to Mrs. Thatcher should be sent first and well in advance of any letter sent to the Soviets. Indeed, we should tell the British what we plan to do and ask for their views and support. We owe this much to Mrs. Thatcher. We should not take a decision which essentially isolates her and gives her no maneuver room. Mrs. Thatcher deserves better from us. Moreover, she deserves to have the question she put to the President about "conditionality" in our decision dealt with in a satisfactory manner. All this suggests that the draft letter to Mrs. Thatcher needs substantial editing.

-- 4. I think the rush to get the Moscow Human Rights issue settled before the Secretary sees Shevardnadze in Paris is unwarranted. After the President reaches his decision, we should write to the British, consult the Canadians, and the Congress. This task should be completed on or about January 6, which would let the Secretary pass to the Soviets oral approval of our decision. Thus I believe the letter to Shevardnaze should not be sent. Saving a few days between now and January 6 but in so doing annoying the British, the Canadians and the Congress is not wise policy.

Let us know back here in Washington how it all turns out.

Distribution:

FOR: Colin L. Powell   (POWELL)   CC: Lisa R. Jameson   (JAMESON)
FOR: Paul S. Stevens   (STEVENS)   CC: Peter Rodman   (RODMAN)
FOR: Marybel Batjer   (BATJER)   CC: Rudolf V. Perina   (PERINA)
                                      CC: Baerbel K. Houck   (HOUCK)

Sometimes the White House e-mail serves as a corrective to after-the-fact memoirs of top officials. For example, in his 1994 book *Special Trust*, Robert McFarlane argues that the Reagan administration strategy with the Soviets was meant to bankrupt them and mount sufficient pressures on the Soviet system to cause its collapse. While he worked in the White House, however, e-mail like this September 9, 1985, note to Bob Pearson shows that McFarlane did not envision the fall of the Soviet Union (after all, who did?). Rather, in his own words, "it iwll [sic] not change ideologically and therefore our task is to establish a basis for peaceful competition with them"—"a policy of steady prolonged peaceful competition." This high-level strategy memo is certainly a far stretch from the original notion of the White House e-mail system as simply replacing telephone message slips.

09/09/85 13:20 ***

*** Reply to note of 09/09/85 11:33

UNCLASSIFIED

NOTE FROM: ROBERT MCFARLANE
Subject: SACG & NSC

On the NSC meeting, I have reflected on this over the weekend and believe we can serve a larger purpose of establishing the President as driving/leading the preparatory process by having him convene his principals as a family in the residence to talk conceptually about the context of the Geneva meeting historically. Where is the United States in the late 20th centruy; isolationism behind us, the public willing to spend 6+% of its GNP on defense; defense modernization underway; the alliances in basically good shape; the economy recovering--in short, we are country that is politically, economically and militarily strong. The question before us is how we engage with the leading threat to peace--the Soviet Union-- so as to establish a more stable international climate for peace. He should turn to the state of the Soviet Union--a country that is strong militarily but in substantial decline in virtually every other measure. But it iwll not change ideologically and therefore our task is to establish a basis for peaceful competition with them. We must eschew the errors of the past in which we have oscillated between extremes of euphoria (detente) in which we based our hopes on the expectation that the Soviet Union would turn away from the global revolution and the other extreme of confrontation. We must adopt instead a policy of steady prolonged peaceful competition.

CHAPTER 9

TURF WARS &
BUREAUCRATIC OPS

The White House e-mail details hundreds of pitched battles between the National Security Council staff and their erstwhile colleagues at the State Department, the Pentagon, and other agencies over who was to chair meetings, task actions, draft documents, and generally be in the loop. White House staff also were called on to referee fights between other agencies, or in cases where the argument had reached the status of a duel, as seconds to hold the pistols.

During the Reagan administration, personal animosities added a major complicating factor. For example, despite coming from the same corporate environment (Bechtel Inc.), Secretary of State George Shultz and Secretary of Defense Caspar Weinberger despised each other. In dictated notes taken by Charles Hill, Shultz's top aide, Shultz went so far as to describe Weinberger as "either stupid or dishonest, one or the other" (Hill note, 12/28/86).

Life at the White House not only featured turf wars with agencies of the federal government, but also constant bureaucratic battling internally. For example, National Security Adviser Robert McFarlane resigned in December 1985 largely because of conflicts with White House Chief of Staff Donald Regan. The White House e-mail contains classic examples of the various tools employed by veteran infighters on the White House staff, ranging from the usual jockeying for position on trips and in meetings, all the way to the consummation most devoutly to be wished, a private back-channel to the top.

The umpires of this game and the guardians of process, the National Security Council Secretariat, tried to infiltrate the back-channels and route all high-level notes and tasking traffic through their central office. It was a losing struggle. The e-mail system featured a unique response mechanism: If a recipient saved a note from someone else, simply using the same subject line with a reversed "to" and "from" ensured a direct response, out of view of the secretariat.

Other tricks illustrated in the e-mail are not so technical. The e-mail features such time-honored pre-computer ploys as restricting information flows, disinviting rivals from scheduled meetings, setting up special bureaucratic structures and volunteering to staff them, covering one's flanks with memos to the file, monopolizing intelligence, and being solicitous of superiors, among others. As this chapter shows, winning turf battles via e-mail does not require different skills than those of traditional bureaucratic operators, just a more rapid response time.

President Reagan & the senior National Security Council staff,

Oval Office, 3-24-88

The highest-level turf wars the White House worried about in the 1980s involved the secretary of state versus the secretary of defense, with the White House staff as referees and sitters, on occasion. This June 12, 1986, e-mail from senior National Security Council official Peter Rodman to his boss, National Security Adviser John Poindexter, reporting on a lunch with top Pentagon official Fred Ikle, suggests that the regular high-level breakfast meetings between Poindexter, Shultz, and Weinberger ("S-W-P") had, on occasion, degenerated into "slugfests." Dubinin refers to the new Soviet ambassador in Washington.

```
FROM: NSPWR   --CPUA      TO: NSJMP   --CPUA                06/12/86 17:01:36
To: NSJMP   --CPUA      JOHN M. POINDEXTER

NOTE FROM: Peter Rodman
SUBJECT: Lunch with Fred Ikle
    I had lunch with Fred Ikle today. We compared notes on a lot of substantive
issues, mainly regional issues, in a friendly way. Nothing really significant.
However, he volunteered his hope that we could keep future S-W-P breakfasts
from degenerating into slugfests. We agreed it wasn't really productive to get
into these big debates over basic principles when neither side was going to
convince the other. The trick was to use the breakfasts to discuss issues that
were (1) soluble and yet (2) not so trivial as to waste the principals' time,
or to keep each other informed of interesting things (e.g., Shultz's
impressions of Dubinin).We pledged to try to think of topics that made
constructive use of the forum.
```

Some forty-five minutes later, Poindexter responds with the suspicion that Ikle had "put Cap [Weinberger] up to those complaints," but suggests that his so-called family group meetings, which added CIA director William Casey to the mix, also needed fixing.

```
To: NSPWR   --CPUA                                         06/12/86 17:47

*** Reply to note of 06/12/86 17:01     UNCLASSIFIED
                                        -- SECRET --

NOTE FROM: JOHN POINDEXTER
Subject: Lunch with Fred Ikle
THAT WAS A VERY WORTHWHILE LUNCH. I APPRECIATE YOUR DOING IT. OF COURSE I
THINK FRED PUT CAP UP TO THOSE COMPLAINTS. IF YOU CAN WORK TO IMPROVE THE
BREAKFASTS, THAT WOULD BE VERY HELPFUL. ALSO A LONG RANGE AGENDA FOR THE
FAMILY GROUP LUNCHES THAT GEORGE, CAP, BILL AND I HAVE IS ALSO DESIREABLE. IF
WE COULD HAVE ONE MEATY ITEM PER LUNCH, I THINK IT WOULD BE ABOUT RIGHT.
```

WHITE HOUSE E-MAIL

Less than a week later, Rodman writes up an S-W-P breakfast with the new focus on the security assistance budget; but the subtext reflects—if not a "slugfest"—certainly continuing disagreement between Shultz and Weinberger.

The issue is whether to seek a "supplemental" appropriation from Congress to underwrite security assistance or just make sure the likely "CR" (a continuing resolution that authorizes spending in the next fiscal year

in the absence of an approved budget) includes the necessary amounts for security assistance. Interestingly, Rodman notes he left Weinberger in the dark about possible "off-budget" help to Israel.

Partially Declassified/Released on 11-18-93 under provisions of E.O. 12356 by N. Menan, National Security Council

FROM: NSPKR   --CPU;   TO: NSHP1   --CPU;   06/13/86 09:51:0
NSPPF   --CPU;

FROM: Peter Rodman
SUBJ: S-W-P Breakfast: Security Assistance Budget

This subject dominated the breakfast. Among the highlights:

- Shultz said Jim Baker predicted there would be no Congressional budget resolution; the appropriations committees wouldn't get very far; so we would end up with a big CR by September. Therefore, said Shultz, we should continue a sustained high-pressure campaign for all our programs and watch the details closely. Shultz thought we should develop a campaign plan for the national security accounts, working with OMB, and take it to the President.

-- Weinberger thought we should try for a supplemental and put the anti-defense crowd on the defensive. If the President put all his weight behind it . . . . Shultz demurred, saying the deficit was a real problem; it even had national security implications because it helped fuel the trade deficit which fueled disastrous protectionist measures which would brutalize our allies and wreck the world economy. Cap backed off somewhat, saying a supplemental was "not the only option."

-- Then there was some discussion of the pressures on the President to agree to new taxes or other "revenue enhancement" measures.

- There was only a brief discussion of going after the Israel and Egypt earmarks. Shultz pointed out that AIPAC was usually very supportive of the overall aid budget and we should go to them for help at the appropriate stage. (I did not mention the informal group we had working on the off-budget measures for Israel; I figured they were things that Cap didn't like. Also, John suggested to me that these are things to do at a later stage when we are forced to work within aggregates that are more firmly set.)

```
                                                        01/15/86 12:04:22

   To: NSJMP   --CPU1

   *** Reply to note of 08/31/85 13:26

                                     -- SECR: _ =-

   NOTE FROM: OLIVER NORTH
   Subject: PRIVATE BLANK CHECK
   IAW yr direction, met w/ Casey last night after W'bgr speech at Ft.McNair.
   Casey then tried to contact Cap but he had already departed.  Casey has
   called urging that you convene a mtg w/ he and Cap ASAP so that we can
   move on.  Casey's view is that Cap will continue to create roadblocks
        V  PRIVATE BLANK CHECK                                         R
   MSG FROM: NSOLN   --CPUA     IO: NSJMP   --CPUA       01/15/86 13:01:06
   To: NSJMP   --CPU1

   *** Reply to note of 08/31/85 13:26
```

Cap Weinberger himself played a tough bureaucratic game. When President Reagan overruled Weinberger and Shultz and ordered the arms-for-hostages deals with Iran to continue in January 1986, neither man resigned on principle. Instead, the defense secretary dragged his feet on the Pentagon's supply of the necessary TOW missiles (tube-launched, wire-guided anti-tank weapons).

This January 15, 1986, e-mail from Oliver North to John Poindexter explains how CIA director William Casey is conspiring to push Weinberger ("W'bgr") into line. Internal references include "Copp," the code name for Iran-contra entrepreneur Richard Secord; "Nir," North's Israeli counterpart; "Karubi," an Iranian middleman; and "Brt" meaning Beirut, where the hostages were held. The message concludes with a fascinating conversation between North and Colin Powell, then serving as Weinberger's military aide, and, therefore, the coordinator of the Pentagon's role in the arms supply. While North lied to Powell in his first answer (the United States was dealing directly with the Iranians, not at arms-length through the Israelis), Powell's questions indicate the degree to which, despite later disavowals, Weinberger and Powell were intimately familiar with the arms-for-hostage deals.

WHITE HOUSE E-MAIL

`-- SECRET --`

`NOTE FROM: OLIVER NORTH`
`Subject: PRIVATE BLANK CHECK`

Continuation of last note (hit SEND when I meant to hit ADD LINES) ...
Casey believes that Cap will continue to create roadblocks until he is
told by you that the President wants this to move NOW and that Cap will
have to make it work. Casey points out that we have now gone through
three different methodologies in an effort to satisfy Cap's concerns
and that no matter what we do there is always a new objection. As far
as Casey is concerned our earlier method of having Copp deal directly with
the DoD as a purchasing agent was fine. He did not see any particular problem w/ making Copp an agent for the CIA in this endeavor but he is concerned
that Cap will find some new objection unless he is told to proceed. Colin
Powell, who sat next to me during Cap's speech asked the following questions
(my answers are indicated):

Q. Does Copp deal w/ Iranians or Israelis?
A. With the Israelis.

Q. Is the intelligence a prerequisite?
A. It is probably something that can be negotiated but in any event it
is not a DoD matter. It is covered in the finding and is in fact one
of the few means we have to make a long term penetration in Iran.
Our ultimate objective of changing/moderating the govt. is served by this.

Q. What cost are the Israelis willing to pay for the basic TOWs?
A. They (thru Copp) have funds to pay Fair Market Value (FMV should
be about $4900-$5400 ea. depending on age) and to cover the cost of
transportation. They do not have enough to pay for I TOW (about
$9500 ea or TOW II (about $15000 ea.). We have frequently sold
the Israelis weaps/materiel at FMV vice the replacement cost to the
U.S. Since we have over 100K of the basic TOW in our inventory and
cannot even use it in training due to its age, we ought to look at this as
an opportunity to collect on a weapon which we aren't using (all are in
PWR according to Koch) and will eventually have to dispose of because
we cannot sell them off otherwise. (I'm told that Hughes Acft, the mfgr.
has an agreement w/ DoD that all normal FMS transactions will be handled
as a producer sale in order to keep DoD fm undercutting the production
line by selling off old stocks).

The most recent proposal (Copp as agent for the CIA and sales to the
Israelis who then deliver weaps to the Iranians) can only work if
we can get the Israelis to come up on their price. I have been
unable to contact NIR who is in Europe for a meeting w/ Karubi. He
still does not know that we are aware that the Iranians have offered
$10K per TOW. He has however left a message that we must have a go/
no go decision today and that conditions in Brt. continue to deteriorate.

Sometimes the turf problem was not just the Pentagon but within the White House as well. This August 6, 1986, note to Poindexter from Robert Linhard, the NSC's senior arms control and Star Wars specialist, complains that the head of the Star Wars program at the Pentagon, Lt. Gen. James A. Abrahamson, had left Linhard out of the loop on a briefing for White House communications director Patrick Buchanan and his public affairs staff. Linhard's real worry is that Buchanan is pushing his own agenda for "early deployment" of Star Wars weaponry. Interestingly, Linhard considers the fact of the briefing worthy of a "damage assessment."

```
*** Resending note of 08/01/86 19:36
To: NSRBM    --CPUA    JOHN M. POINDEXTER NSWRP    --CPUA    JOHN M. POINDEXTER
NOTE FROM: ROBERT E. LINHARD
SUBJECT: SDI AND PAT BUCHANAN
ADMIRAL,
     HAD AN INTERESTING DEVELOPMENT TODAY.  WHILE WE (NSC) WERE NOT INVITED
OR FORMALLY NOTIFIED, GEN. ABRAHAMSON PROVIDED A BRIEFING ON SDI FOR THE
WHITE HOUSE PUBLIC AFFAIRS STAFF (PAT + ABOUT 25-30 PEOPLE) IN THE
ROOSEVELT ROOM.  I FOUND OUT ABOUT THIS JUST PEFORE THE PITCH, AND HAD
WILL TOBEY SIT IN.
     CALLED GEN ABE ON THIS.  HE CLAIMS HE THOUGHT THAT WE WERE INVITED AND
THAT IT WAS SIMPLY TO GO OVER THE PA PLAN.  WHAT ENSUED WAS A RATHER
DETAILED QUESTIONING OF GEN ABE BY PAT ABOUT EARLY DEPLOYMENT OPTIONS --
WITH THE FIRST QUESTION BEING WHAT COULD BE DONE TO PROVIDE AN EARLY
DEFENSE FOR US AND FOR OUR ALLIES, SPECIFICALLY ISREAL!
     I WILL HAVE WILL DO AN MFR AND, FROM IT, SEND YOU A LIKELY DAMAGE
ASSESSMENT.  HAVING PAT ENTER THE FRAY AT THIS POINT IS NOT USEFUL.  IF
YOU REMEMBER THE RECENT NATIONAL REVIEW ARTICLE WRITTEN BY BOB JASTROW
(FRIEND OF PAT) THE THRUST WAS "PRESIDENT IS NOT GETTING ALL THE FACTS ON
EARLY DEPLOYMENT" AND THEREFORE WOULD MAKE A MISGUIDED DECISION IF HE AGREED
TO DELAY SDI DEPLOYMENT OPPORTUNITIES.
     WILL SEND YOU MORE AS SITUATION UNFOLDS.  HAVE EXPRESSED MY DISAPPOINTMENT
TO GEN ABE ABOUT THE BRIEFING.
```

This e-mail combination presents a four-way gambit by NSC Middle East specialist Howard Teicher to get himself invited to a meeting in August 1985 between National Security Adviser McFarlane, Richard Murphy (assistant secretary of state for the Middle East), Thomas Pickering (ambassador to Israel), and Jock Covey (another NSC Middle East staffer). First, Teicher first appeals to McFarlane's secretary, Joan Yonaitis. She then e-mails Bud about Teicher's feelings. While she's writing, NSC deputy executive secretary Robert Pearson sees the note "over [her] shoulder." Then Yonaitis lets Teicher know the upshot.

```
To: NSRCM    --CPUA    ROBERT C. MCFARLAN        08/24/85 10:52 ***

NOTE FROM: Joan Yonaitis
SUBJECT: Noon mtg w/Murphy, Pickering and Covey
Howard Teicher stopped by the Sit Room this morning, saw your
schedule, and has asked to sit in on the meeting.  I asked
Howard if he had been in touch w/Covey -- answer was "no".
Mr. McFarlane, I've been made privy to the fact that Howard
feels "left out of things," and hasexpressed this sentiment
to both you and JMP.  I have not encouraged Howard either way.
Decision is up to you.
```

```
To: NSHRT    --CPUA                              08/24/85 11:04:07

NOTE FROM: Joan Yonaitis
Subject: Noon mtg w/Murphy, Pickering and Covey
Heads up.  Pearson stood behind me and read subject note over my
shoulder -- WITHOUT INVITATION.  Might be a blessing in disguise.
*** Forwarding note from NSJJY
```

198

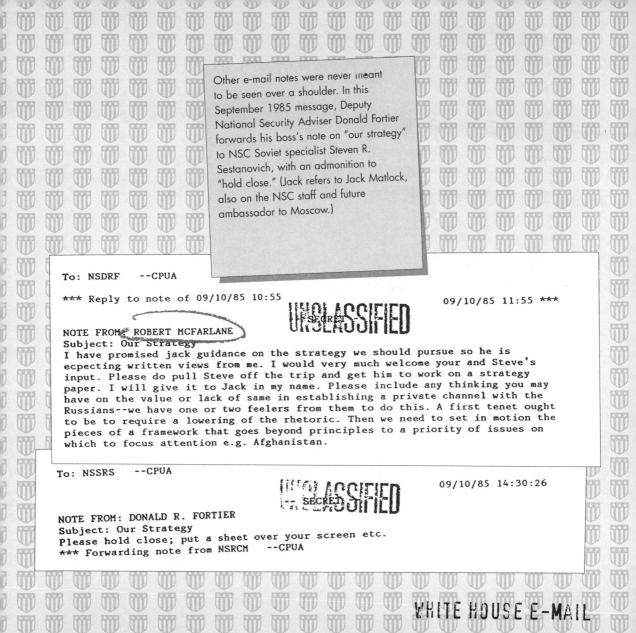

Other e-mail notes were never meant to be seen over a shoulder. In this September 1985 message, Deputy National Security Adviser Donald Fortier forwards his boss's note on "our strategy" to NSC Soviet specialist Steven R. Sestanovich, with an admonition to "hold close." (Jack refers to Jack Matlock, also on the NSC staff and future ambassador to Moscow.)

To: NSDRF   --CPUA

*** Reply to note of 09/10/85 10:55   09/10/85 11:55 ***

UNCLASSIFIED
SECRET

NOTE FROM: ROBERT MCFARLANE
Subject: Our Strategy
I have promised jack guidance on the strategy we should pursue so he is
ecpecting written views from me. I would very much welcome your and Steve's
input. Please do pull Steve off the trip and get him to work on a strategy
paper. I will give it to Jack in my name. Please include any thinking you may
have on the value or lack of same in establishing a private channel with the
Russians--we have one or two feelers from them to do this. A first tenet ought
to be to require a lowering of the rhetoric. Then we need to set in motion the
pieces of a framework that goes beyond principles to a priority of issues on
which to focus attention e.g. Afghanistan.

To: NSSRS   --CPUA   09/10/85 14:30:26

UNCLASSIFIED
SECRET

NOTE FROM: DONALD R. FORTIER
Subject: Our Strategy
Please hold close; put a sheet over your screen etc.
*** Forwarding note from NSRCM   --CPUA

WHITE HOUSE E-MAIL

President Reagan & Peter Rodman 3-24-88

This e-mail represents classic jockeying for position on an overseas trip, in this case, between NSC Middle East specialists Dennis Ross and Peter Rodman. Charlie Hill was the top aide to Secretary of State Shultz.

```
                                    07/03/86 13:41 ***
To: NSRBM   --CPUA    JOHN M. POINDEXTER NSWRP   --CPUA    JOHN M. POINDEXTER
FROM: Dennis Ross
SUBJECT: Shultz Trip to Middle East
     Peter mentioned to me after our meeting that Charlie
Hill had asked if he would be available to go on the trip.
As I told Peter, I have no problem with Peter going, provided
it doesn't send a signal to the bureau and people in the area
that they don't have to take me seriously.  Right now, I'm
taken very seriously, and I wouldn't want my absence from the
trip to change that.
```

Dennis Ross got to go on his own trip with Vice President George Bush a month later. This remarkable e-mail from Rodman to Poindexter, with the inevitable subtext of Rodman-Ross issues, provides a starkly candid description of the motivations on all sides of the Middle East problem—including those of Vice President Bush himself, Israeli prime minister Shimon Peres, Egyptian president Hosni Mubarak, the State Department, and the NSC. The e-mail also describes the extraordinary bureaucratic maneuvering necessary to water down a possibly controversial "7-Point Mideast Peace Plan" into a "general, upbeat description."

To: NSRBM   --CPUA

08/01/86 17:11:07

NOTE FROM: Peter Rodman
SUBJECT: VP's 7-Point Mideast Peace Plan
   I spoke to Dennis over the secure phone. In a nutshell, it's something that Peres urged on the VP and that Dennis supported -- and drafted. Murphy was on board in a general way but had no hand in drafting. The theory is:
   -- The VP obviously wants to have something "substantive" to point to;
   -- Peres, as well as other Mideast interlocutors, are eager for the US
      to "breathe new life into the peace process" (driven by fear of
      rotation);
   -- It would help Mubarak if he doesn't seem to be moving all alone
      toward Israel while Palestinian interests are neglected;
   -- There is a genuine sense of common ground on some issues.
   I gave him the preliminary (skeptical) reaction back here, saying that:
   -- The points may have Peres's blessing but they would run aground on the
      Arab side, embarrassing the VP;
   -- The formulations may look innocuous but they deviated from long-standing
      formulations (especially Sept. 1) and were asking for trouble;
   -- Shultz felt strongly that a "7-point" statement looked like a new peace
      plan and that that kind of statement was a big mistake;
   -- The Admiral was uneasy about a new initiative being floated without
      adequate spadework and deliberation back here.
   Dennis said that a possible fall-back option was to drop the part "calling
on the parties to accept these principles" and to dismantle the 7-point
structure, turning it into a general, upbeat description of common ground and
new possibilities for peace. I thought this was the right direction to go, and
I said I would call State and factor this into the substitute language they
were drafting.
   I have since spoken to Arnie Raphel along these lines. He said this was
exactly the approach they were taking. He promised us a copy of their proposed
substitute language by fax ASAP.

WHITE HOUSE E-MAIL

July 25, 1985

~~SECRET~~

ACTION

MEMORANDUM FOR ROBERT C. McFARLANE

FROM: BOB LINHARD / GIL RYE

SUBJECT: Request for Office Visit by Edward Teller

You had asked for a staff recommendation whether you'd schedule an office visit requested by Edward Teller. Edward gets into town this Saturday. He wishes to talk to you about three main topics:
(1) level of funding support for the Livermore ▓▓▓▓▓▓▓ X-ray laser;   (b)(1)(c)
(2) SDI in the context of the NST talks; and
(3) the Reagan/Gorbachev meeting.

On the first of these subjects, Edward feels that a commitment was made to increase the funding for his project during the meeting he had with the President (and yourself) on June 11. Our G-2 is that he wants to complain about the follow-through on this. I must admit that I thought while you did give appropriate praise to the effort, I did not think that any commitment to increase the funding was explicitly made. Any light that you could shed on such a commitment would be helpful.

We have no idea what Edward has in mind on the second and third items on his agenda.

If such a meeting with Teller were scheduled, we would recommend that you have your own agenda -- to include a discussion of a conference in Sicily that is scheduled to occur in August. This is a yearly event in which the scientific community gets together at Erice and largely discusses non-scientific issues (i.e., SDI and nuclear winter). If you decide to spend the time with him, we might as well frame some of the conversation.

Overall, however, NSC staff see little real return from this meeting. We would suggest that if you can gracefully avoid this meeting you do so.

Recommendation

That if you can avoid this meeting that you do so.

Approve _____   Disapprove _____

That you provide any feedback to us that you can on any commitments made to Teller with respect to additional funding for the Livermore ▓▓▓▓▓▓▓ laser work.   (b)(1)(c)

Approve _____   Disapprove _____

```
To: NSSRS    --CPUA        06/06/86 08:16:40

NOTE FROM: Walter Raymond
SUBJECT: Afghanistan
```

I am a bit confused as to who is on first re Afghanistan. The SIG report (NSC #4371) is a case in point. It covers aspects that you and Peter have been involved in (Negotiating strategy with the Soviets and Alliance politics) and items I have agonized over (CBA and Media). You have been conscious of the issues I am working and I have been conscious of the Alliance question. I had been developing (in my mind) an extremely aggressive statement for JMP to send to State/AID re CBA I still want to do that. I have worked directly with USIA to break loose the media question. I do not agree with the syrup that is served up by the SIG report on these items.

The nitty gritty questions: We should decide (not ExexSec) if this needs to go to the President. I do not think it should go. Secondly, it would seem to me that you and I, with suitable coordinations with Peter and Shirin, would be the logical drafters on this monster. I would be happy to produce the pertinent paragraphs for a JMP to Shultz for the CBA and Media sections. In the future if Shirin is going to dig in deep and wants to take on the CBA question, fine, but right now I have thefacts. What do you recommend? NB: This is not a turf question; it is being raised by me now so we can sort this thing out and not have us all duplicating our efforts. Possibly, you should get Peter's proxy and then you, me, Shirin and Vince should meet briefly to develop a joint drafting and operating strategy. Pls advise.

Shultz, Poindexter & Reagan 5-5-86

WHITE HOUSE E-MAIL

This exchange of e-mail illustrates the phone tag that the White House system was designed to eliminate, as well as the usual State Department versus White House tension. Here, the phone tag revolves around a State official's request in October 1986 for a meeting with Oliver North and his counterterrorism staff, Robert Earl (RLE) and Craig Coy (CPC). North's secretary, Fawn Hall, tells them that the meeting is on; North asks what about; Coy asks "anything new"; and Fawn responds with the details of the tag, while Earl follows up and says let's do it.

```
                                    10/08/86 15:51 ***
To: NSOLN    --CPUA            NSRLE    --CPUA
    NSCPC    --CPUA

NOTE FROM: FAWN HALL
SUBJECT: Meeting with Mr. Lou Schwartz

Mr. Schwartz, Director Diplomatic Security Services at the Department
of State, called to arrange a meeting with OLN, RLE, and CPC.  I have
set the appointment for Wednesday, October 22, at 10:30 a.m.
```

```
To: NSFH     --CPUA                       10/09/86 15:53:48

NOTE FROM: Craig P. Coy
Subject: Meeting with Mr. Lou Schwartz
any thing new on this?
*** Forwarding note from NSFH     --CPUA
```

```
                                          10/09/86 10:02 ***
To: NSFH    --CPUA

*** Reply to note of 10/08/86 16:10
NOTE FROM: OLIVER NORTH
Subject: Meeting with Mr. Lou Schwartz
What does he want to talk about?
```

```
                                  10/09/86 19:29 ***
To: NSOLN   --CPUA          NSRLE    --CPUA
    NSCPC   --CPUA

NOTE FROM: FAWN HALL
Subject: Meeting with Mr. Lou Schwartz

Schwartz had called last week for OLN and RLE was kind enough to return
the call.  But when he did apparently Mr. Schwartz claimed he never called.
In the meantime, his office called to set up this appt w/OLN RLE CPC
(I not knowing what happened when RLE returned the call -- assumed that
it was a follow-on to RLE's conversation with him and didn't ask for the
subject).  CPC says he met with Schwartz and he'd talk to him and find out.
I called his secretary Joanne to see if she knew -- she didn't.  So, I
asked if he was in to speak with Craig.  She said he was on travel and
added that she was sure that it was a "get aquainted" meeting.  (Sounds
funny to me, but there you go).  Any comments?  Mtg Wed, Oct 22 1600
*** Forwarding note from NSOLN   --CPUA
```

```
                                          10/09/86 20:55:48
To: NSFH    --CPUA

*** Reply to note of 10/09/86 19:29
NOTE FROM: Robert L. Earl
Subject: Meeting with Mr. Lou Schwartz
I think the guy genuinely wants a "get acquainted" meeting w/ the CT gang
at the NSC....  Having met the guy briefly, I think he's a straight shooter.
It won't hurt to have a half hour meeting w/ him when we can fit it in.
```

WHITE HOUSE E-MAIL

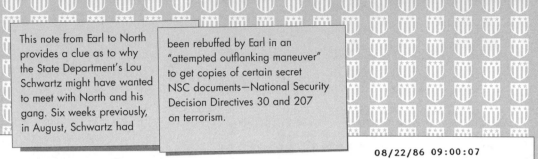

This note from Earl to North provides a clue as to why the State Department's Lou Schwartz might have wanted to meet with North and his gang. Six weeks previously, in August, Schwartz had been rebuffed by Earl in an "attempted outflanking maneuver" to get copies of certain secret NSC documents—National Security Decision Directives 30 and 207 on terrorism.

```
                                                   08/22/86  09:00:07
To: NSOLN    --CPUA              NSCPC    --CPUA
NOTE FROM: Robert L. Earl
SUBJECT: Diplomatic Security Request for NSDDs
Stephanie Stauffer called from SY w/ a request for Lou Schwartz and Bob
Lamb to be given their own copies of NSDD 30 and 207.  I tried to deflect
her request by telling her she could go to Oakley's office anytime she
needed to refer to the NSDDs on terrorism, but she insisted that Lamb
wants his own copy.  I'll call Oakley to give him a heads up of this
attempted outflanking maneuver by SY and then tell Stephanie that the
White House made distribution to the Secretary of State and that internal
distribution w/in the Dept of State is a Shultz decision, not a White House
decision.  Why is State so fucked up?
```

```
                                                   08/31/85  13:26:58
To: NSOLN    --CPUA     OLLIE NORTH

                       UNCLASSIFIED

NOTE FROM: JOHN POINDEXTER
SUBJECT: PRIVATE BLANK CHECK
If you save this note in your files, I believe that you can always reply
direct to me when you have sensitive info.
```

This note established probably the most infamous of all the back-channels at the National Security Council in the 1980s —Oliver North's direct e-mail link to his boss, Admiral John Poindexter. The subject line, "Private Blank Check," captures in a single phrase the extraordinary leeway given North by his superiors. This note was the only one remaining in North's user area after he finished his electronic "shredding" on the weekend of November 22–25, 1986, his last weekend on the White House staff before the Iran-contra scandal broke.

The North-Poindexter loop did not go unnoticed within the NSC staff. In this case, the issue was intelligence on the Iran arms deals, which North was treating as his own private property, much to the dismay of the NSC Secretariat. Here, NSC staff legal counsel Paul Thompson responds to a note from NSC executive secretary Rod McDaniel and suggests the Situation Room ("sit rm") as the proper switchboard for intelligence. North's sources were evidently participants in the arms deals, but not Israeli prime minister Shimon Peres, with whom North had met.

To: NSRBM   --CPUA

*** Reply to note of 02/04/86 11:48   02/04/86 12:26:12

NOTE FROM: PAUL THOMPSON
Subject: Ollie
i believe it should. it should also be provided somehow to the sit rm
as a central point of intelligence. Of course, Ollie will feel that in this instant he is working
the classified portfolio concerning hostages and since his info came from
one of those sources(and not from the Peres by the way)that he needed to
talk only to JMP. There are about 15 to 20 staff officers who frequently
reach the same conclusion.

WHITE HOUSE E-MAIL

North's deputy, Robert Earl, complains in this September 1986 e-mail about too much info-sharing of the CIA's first Terrorist Debriefing (TD) document. Earl notes that the CIA's Charles Allen will tighten the loop. The NSC's own method for limiting access was to make documents part of "System IV," a hand-delivered and guarded channel illustrated by a January 1987 note from NSC staff assistant Brian Merchant (in the intelligence section) to NSC Middle East specialist Dennis Ross.

```
                                                        09/08/86 20:54:15
To: NSOLN    --CPUA
NOTE FROM: Robert L. Earl
SUBJECT: TERRORIST DEBRIEFINGS
The first TD is in w/ preliminary results (CIA 081638Z Sep 86).  Guess
how many NSC staffers received this cable? Would you believe 30?   I
complained to Charlie Allen that there were no dissemination restrictions
on the TD -- that it didn't matter too much w/ this first cable (not much
sensitive there), but that it could be extremely sensitive in future!
He agreed and is taking steps immediately to put distribution controls on
future bebriefing reports.
```

```
FROM: NSBTM    --CPUA      TO: NSDBR    --CPUA         01/05/87 19:47:32
To: NSDBR    --CPUA

  . . . . . .
. . . . . . . . . . . . . . . . . . . . . . . . . . . . .  UNCLASSIFIED
NOTE FROM: BRIAN T MERCHANT
SUBJECT: SYSTEM IV DOCUMENTS

The CIA cables which I send to you FYI must be returned to me in SEALED
ENVELOPES.  Do not return them any other way.  Thanks.
THANK YOU.  HAVE A GOOD DAY.
```

Much of Oliver North's bureaucratic clout arose from a bewildering array of interagency structures he chaired, coordinated, or staffed. In this note, he lists them for Robert Pearson of the secretariat. Some translations: IG is Interagency Group; SIG is Senior IG; C/T is counterterrorism; TIWG is Terrorist Incident Working Group. Note especially North's use of the third person when writing about himself.

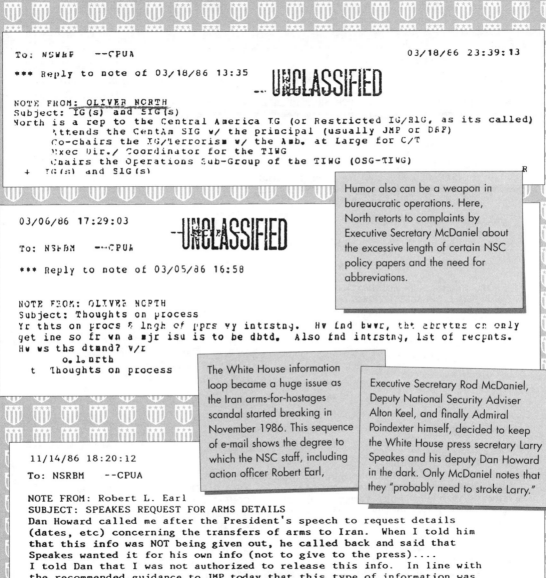

To: NSWBF --CPUA   03/18/86 23:39:13

*** Reply to note of 03/18/86 13:35   -- UNCLASSIFIED

NOTE FROM: OLIVER NORTH
Subject: IG(s) and SIG(s)
North is a rep to the Central America IG (or Restricted IG/SIG, as its called)
        Attends the CentAm SIG w/ the principal (usually JMP or DBF)
        Co-chairs the IG/Terrorism w/ the Amb. at Large for C/T
        Exec Dir./ Coordinator for the TIWG
        Chairs the Operations Sub-Group of the TIWG (OSG-TIWG)
    +   IG(s) and SIG(s)

Humor also can be a weapon in bureaucratic operations. Here, North retorts to complaints by Executive Secretary McDaniel about the excessive length of certain NSC policy papers and the need for abbreviations.

03/06/86 17:29:03   -- UNCLASSIFIED

To: NSRBM --CPUA

*** Reply to note of 03/05/86 16:58

NOTE FROM: OLIVER NORTH
Subject: Thoughts on process
Yr thts on procs & lngh of pprs vy intrstng. Hv fnd hwvr, tht abrvtns cn only
get me so fr wn a mjr isu is to be dbtd. Also fnd intrstng, lst of recpnts.
Hw ws ths dtmnd? v/r
        o. l. nrth
    t   Thoughts on process

The White House information loop became a huge issue as the Iran arms-for-hostages scandal started breaking in November 1986. This sequence of e-mail shows the degree to which the NSC staff, including action officer Robert Earl,

---

Executive Secretary Rod McDaniel, Deputy National Security Adviser Alton Keel, and finally Admiral Poindexter himself, decided to keep the White House press secretary Larry Speakes and his deputy Dan Howard in the dark. Only McDaniel notes that they "probably need to stroke Larry."

11/14/86 18:20:12

To: NSRBM --CPUA

NOTE FROM: Robert L. Earl
SUBJECT: SPEAKES REQUEST FOR ARMS DETAILS
Dan Howard called me after the President's speech to request details
(dates, etc) concerning the transfers of arms to Iran. When I told him
that this info was NOT being given out, he called back and said that
Speakes wanted it for his own info (not to give to the press)....
I told Dan that I was not authorized to release this info. In line with
the recommended guidance to JMP today that this type of information was
one of those that must remain classified and sensitive, I recommend that
we do NOT give those details to anyone who is not in the operational
compartment.

WHITE HOUSE E-MAIL

```
11/14/86 08:51 ***

To: NSAGK    --CPUA    ALTON G. KEEL    NSJMP    --CPUA    JOHN M. POINDEXTE
NOTE FROM: ROD B. MCDANIEL
Subject: SPEAKES REQUEST FOR ARMS DETAILS
fyi--presume you concur--probably need to stroke Larry.
*** Forwarding note from NSRLE    --CPUA
```

```
To: NSRBM    --CPUA    11/14/86 18:20:12    NSJMP    --CPUA    JOHN M. POINDEXTER
NOTE FROM: Alton G.
Subject: SPEAKES REQUEST FOR ARMS DETAILS
Agree. John can talk to Larry if necessary.
*** Forwarding note from NSRBM    --CPUA
```

```
To: NSRBM    --CPUA    11/14/86 20:42:33

*** Reply to note of 11/14/86 08:51    -- SECRET--    UNCLASSIFIED

NOTE FROM: JOHN POINDEXTER
Subject: SPEAKES REQUEST FOR ARMS DETAILS
I agree with Bob Earl's position.  Hold the info.
```

Cutting people out of the loop often meant lying to them as well. In this case, the NSC counter-intelligence specialist David Major, an FBI veteran who was used to seeing the most sensitive products of the intelligence community, protests North's internal deceptions via e-mail. North's response to Major's protest only continues the lie.

```
11/14/86 17:27 ***

To: NSOLN    --CPUA

NOTE FROM: David Major
SUBJECT: DISINFORMATION
AS THE IRANIAN MATTER UNFOLDS, MAYBE YOU CAN ANSWER A QUESTIONS FOR ME.
SINCE WE ARE PROFESSIONAL ASSOCIATES IN THE INTEL BUSINESS, THERE ARE
A FEW PEOPLE YOU MUST TRUST. YOU AND  I COME FROM THAT WORLD. BOTH
VETS, BOTH TRUSTWORTHY. I HAVE NOT BEEN ABLE TO UNDERSTAND WHY YOU FELT
IN NECESSARY TO RUN A DISINFORMATION OPERATION AGAINST ME. YOU WILL
RECALL OUR CONVERSATION IN MY OFFICE THE DAY THE IRAN ARMS DEAL BEGAN TO
BREAK AND YOU WERE TELLING ME AND KED THAT PETER RODMAN WAS LEAKING
THE OPERATION AND THAT THE ARMS WERE NOT BEING SHIPPED BUT IRANIANS
WERE BEING GRAPPED IN EUROPE AND TRADED FOR THEHOSTAGES.
WHY DID YOU FEEL OBLIGATED TO BULL SHIT ME!!!!!!
```

To: NSDGM   --CPUA

*** Reply to note of 11/14/86 17:27   11/14/86 19:53:27
NOTE FROM: OLIVER NORTH
Subject: DISINFORMATION
You possibly are the only one who doesn't leak since that particular item has
not yet become public. If you wish, I can show you from the pattern of the six
deliveries, that they don not coincide w/ hostages. The question being asked
then - as now - is did we trade weaps for people. The answer is still no. Nos
shit. V/R, yur friend
        DISINFORMATION

To: NSPSS   --CPUA   12/21/87 18:52:48

*** Reply to note of 12/21/87 14:48
NOTE FROM: Colin L. Powell
Subject: General Powell's Schedule   CONFIDENTIAL
   Thanks for your concerns. I feel quite safe on post and in quarters. I will
vary the route; that's easy to do because there are multiple routes off of Ft
yer. My days in Frankfurt made me quite security conscious. I feel safe on
post because I doubt terrorists would risk targetting the house. They don't
have a good opportunity to recon it and the constant MP patrolling makes it
silly for them to do so. My vulnerablility is just after leaving post in the
morning.)It's too hard to vary the time much in the morning but varying the
route covers that threat. I had an alarmed house when I lived at Ft McNair
earlier this year. Pain in the neck. Scared hell out of the family initially
and then became amusing when the MPs assaulted the house every time the alarm
misfired.

Kenneth Duberstein, Howard Baker, President Reagan,
Colin Powell 4-18-88

Subordinates always get points for
inquiring about the welfare of their
bosses. In this December 1987
instance, NSC executive secretary
Paul Schott Stevens e-mailed
National Security Adviser Colin
Powell about his security arrangements, and got a nice note back.

WHITE HOUSE E-MAIL

CHAPTER 10

SPOOKS

The world of spies and counterspies, surveillance satellites and covert operations, remains the most closed area of the U.S. government. "We steal information for a living," sums up R. James Woolsey, who, until recently, was the Clinton administration's director of central intelligence. But the CIA directly, and the rest of the intelligence community generally, still reports to the White House—the ultimate consumer of the stolen goods. In fact, President Harry Truman established the CIA "under" the National Security Council in 1947; and to this day, senior members of the NSC staff, who are often intelligence officers themselves, devote their days solely to coordinating, overseeing, tasking, and checking on the spooks.

As a window on the intelligence world, the White House e-mail is unprecedented. Here are the president's top national security advisers in the 1980s chatting informally by computer about the innermost secrets of the spies. Here we see the personnel and personality gossip, running commentaries on who's up and who's down, early retirements and late promotions, back-scratching and back-stabbing alike—normal behavior for most bureaucracies, but practically unknown to the public until now. In the e-mail we find jokes about the CIA director, detailed TOP SECRET updates on espionage cases, references to the most sensitive sources and methods of intelligence collection, operational plans for covert airlifts, and candid discussion of intelligence successes and failures.

Looming over the intelligence operations of the 1980s, at least until his death in 1987, was the almost mythic figure of William Casey, director of central intelligence. OSS veteran of World War II, lawyer and author, Wall Street speculator, Reagan campaign director in 1980, Casey was renowned for his lack of oral clarity—a garbled manner of speech most people found impossible to understand. This White House e-mail of September 22, 1986, from Oliver North to John Poindexter, gives a half-joking Casey anecdote about his mumbling to Secretary of State George Shultz and, previously, to Senate Intelligence Committee chair Barry Goldwater (R-Arizona). The context is a trip arranged by North for Ali Bahrameni, the nephew of Iranian leader Hashemi Rafsanjani, to the White House in September 1986, including a midnight tour of 1600 Pennsylvania Avenue. The mining of Nicaraguan harbors in early 1984, about which Goldwater publicly exploded that he hadn't been told and was "pissed off," ultimately resulted in a World Court judgment against the United States for violating international law.

```
        Re the Casey/Shultz discussions: Casey informs that he told Shultz,
alone, that the CIA was assisting in bringing Ali into and out of the U.S. for
talks and that he (Casey) wd get back to Shultz at some point in the future on
what had transpired. According to Bill, Shultz simply said "OK." Hope this is
not another example of "mumbles" being misunderstood. The last time he told Go
ldwater we were going to "lay some mines in Nicaragua," Goldwater thought he
said we were going to "pay some fines for some joggers.
```

Reagan, Casey, McFarlane et. al., Situation Room 6-20-85

Some of the most fascinating White House e-mail references to the CIA come in the form of play-by-play commentary on internal agency matters that are never discussed in public, such as the unhappy retirement of the number-

two covert operator referred to in this April 4, 1986, e-mail from Ken DeGraffenreid to John Poindexter. ADDO stands for Associate Deputy Director (of the CIA) for Operations, that is, the clandestine service. DDO at the time was Clair

George, later of Iran-contra fame, while CT refers to counterterrorism, the office headed by noted cowboy and Casey protégé Dewey Clarridge.

04/04/86 17:19
JOHN M. POINDEXTER NSRR CFUA

UNCLASSIFIED
SECRET

NOTE FROM: Ken DeGraffenreid

SUBJECT: Retiring ADDO
FYI: ADDO Ed Juchniewicz is retiring April 30, basically over frustration over the accession of Bob Gates as DDCI and the feared subordination of the DDO ("the DDO is no longer master of its own house"). Believe we should promote Dewey Clarridge as his replacement based on the fact that despite Dewey's new role, the new offices effectiveness is beING thwarted by lack of DDO front office support. As ADDO, he WOULD WIELD the needed clout to ensure success of the CT operation, as well as bring needed reform to the DO across the board. And we can ensure a worthy officer to run the CT operation under Dewey. What do you think?

UNCLASSIFIED
SECRET

Casey and Reagan, Oval Office 10-22-85

```
                                          05/06/86 11:23 ***
To: NSRBM    --CPUA     JOHN M. POINDEXTER NSWRP
NOTE FROM: Vincent Cannistraro
SUBJECT: CIA C/T Actions
Dewey Clarridge (pls protect) told me that he is being frustrated in
carrying out the new counterterrorist program by Clair.  Specifically
Clair is refusing to sign off on command cables setting up ops to
apprehend terrorists abroad for return to U.S. where they will be
subject to legal process. ••••••••••••••••••••••••••••••••••••••••••
•••••••••••••••••••••••••••••••••••••••••••••••••••• Clair is telling
Casey that the Administration is not of one mind on the c/t program,
and therefore the operations should proceed in modest fashion.  This
characterization of Administration attitude is false.  In coordinating
the new C/T Finding among NSPG, there was solid agreement on the
objectives and intent and the only contentious point was legal language
which CIA wanted and State and White House counsel insisted be deleted.
(It is deleted in the final version).  Thus appears Clair's objections
to aggressively pursuing program are disingenuous- he really doesnt
want CIA to get into the proactive counterterrorist mode. I discussed
above with Ollie before he left on his trip and he agrees. I think you
should raise directly with Casey.  If you agree, I will do this as
DCI/JMP agenda item or as T.P.'s for a secure line call.
```

b1
(S)

When cowboys don't get what they
want, they call for the cavalry, as in
this remarkable e-mail from the
CIA's liaison officer at the National
Security Council, Vincent Cannistraro,
to Poindexter. Clarridge appeals to
the White House to intervene in a
dispute between him and his boss,

the regular meetings between Director
of Central Intelligence Casey and
National Security Adviser John
Poindexter; and T.P.'s refers to
talking points.

Clair George. The deleted sentence
probably refers to a planned kidnap
operation that George had refused
to sign off on. C/T refers to counterterrorism; NSPG is National Security
Planning Group, a special meeting of
principals and staff of the NSC focused
on a single topic; DCI/JMP refers to

Cannistraro & Poindexter 12-4-86

NOTE FROM: David Major
SUBJECT: MEMO FOR FCC FROM DGM, NEED SOONEST TODAY-TOP SECRET
please tpye for fcc meeting with Gates tonight. thanks

TO:FCC
FROM DGM
SUBJECT LONGTREE ESPIONAGE CASE

AS YOU WILL RECALL MARINE SGT LONGTREE HAS BEEN ARREST BY THE NAVAL
INVESTIGATIVE SERVICE AND CHARGES WITH BEING A KGB AGENT WHILE A MARINE
GUARD IN MOSCOW AND VIENNA. THE FOLLOWING IS AN ASSESSMENT OF WHAT WE KNOW
ABOUT THIS CASE TO DATE AND THE POLICY IMPLICATIONS:

DAMAGE ASSESSMENT
IT APPEARS LONGTREE WAS RECRUITED BY THE KGB IN MOSCOW IN FEBRUARY 1986
AND CONTINUED TO WORK FOR THE KGB WHEN HE WAS TRANSFERED FROM MOSCOW IN
MARCH 1986 VIENNA. HE CONTINUED TO WORK FOR THE KGB WHILE IN VIENNA, UNTIL
HIS LAST KNOWN MEETING WITH THE KGB IN VIENNA on 12/14/86.

THE AMOUNT OF DAMAGE TO NATIONAL SECURITY HE DID IS STILL BEING EVALUATED
AT A MINIMUM IT IS SERIOUS BUT COULD BE VERY DAMAGING BUT NOT ANY WHERE
COMPARED TO THE DAMAGED OF THE WALKER OR PELTON CASE. OUR CURRENT ASSESSMENT
IS BASED ON WHAT WE HE HAS CONFESSED TO
WHICH IS SUBSTANTIALL LESS THAN THE DAMAGED HE COULD HAVE
DONE.
KNOWN INTELLIGENCE COMPROMISED BASED ON LONGTREE'S CONFESSIONS
••

(b)(1)
TS/CW)
••
_HE PROVIDE A FLOOR PLAN OF THE EMBASSY IN MOSCOW ••••••••••••••••••••
•• IN ADDITION HE STOLE
EMBASSY PHOTOGRAPHS ••
•••••••••••••••••••••
_HE PROVIDE ASSESSEMENT DATA ••••••••••••••••••••••••• AS WELL AS THE

(b)(1)
(S)
A NUMBER OF FSN WORKING IN THE EMBASSY
-HE ADMITS MAKING A SURRUPTETIOSENTRY INTO THE COMMUNICATION ROOM IN VIENNA
••
-HE ADMITS STEALING ON BURN BAG ••
•••
-HE ADMITS TO BEING TASKED TO IMPLANT LISTENING DEVICES IN THE AMBASSADORS
OFFICES IN MOSCOW AND VIENNA BUT DENIES HAVING DONE SO.

Counterintelligence (CI) is the featured concern in e-mail written by the FBI's man on the NSC staff, David G. Major, since the FBI is responsible for tracking foreign spies in the United States. This January 15, 1987, e-mail, at the urgent request of National Security Adviser Frank Carlucci (FCC), provides an extraordinary TOP SECRET damage assessment of the Lonetree spy case, which concerned the Marine guard at the U.S. embassy in Moscow who worked for the KGB. The deleted lines, especially the ones labeled TS/CW for TOP SECRET/CODEWORD, probably refer to information from electronic intercepts and overhead photography—"sources and methods"—which Lonetree might have compromised. Pelton and Walker refer to National Security Agency turncoat Ronald Pelton and to U.S. Navy warrant officer John Walker, who both were convicted of espionage in separate cases.

WORST CASE DAMAGE LONGTREE COULD HAVE DONE
-HE COULD HAVE •• IN MOSCOW AND VIENNA
-HE HAD THE OPPORTUNITY TO STEAL BURN BAGS CONTAINING STATE DEPARTMENT
CLASSIFED DOCUMENTS ON ALMOST A DAILY BASIS IN MOSCOW AND •••••••••••••
••
-HE PERIODICALLY GUARDED A WAREHOUSE OUTSIDE THE EMBASSY COMPOUND IN MOSCOW
THAT CONTAINED ITEMS PLACED IN THE EMBASSY SECURE AREAS AND HE MAY HAVE
ALLOWED KGB TECHNICAL TEAMS TO PLACE DEVISED IN THESE ITEMS (DESK, CHAIRS, ETC)
-HE WAS TARGET AGAINST ••• AND HE
COULD HAVE FACILITATED A COMPROMISE ••••••••••••••••••••••••••••••••••••••

(b)(1)
(TS/CW)

MEMO FOR FCC FROM DGM, NEED SOONEST TODAY-TOP SECRET

-HE COULD HAVE COMPROMISED THE COMMUNICATIONCENTER ON A REGULAR BASIS.

LONGTREE'S RECRUITMENT
HE WAS NOT BLACKMAILED.IN 9/85 HE MET A 26 ATTRACTIVE FEMALE SOVIET NATIONS WHO
WORKED IN THE CUSTOMS SECTIONS OF THE EMBASSY IN MOSCOW. THIS WAS FACILITATED
BECAUSE THE FEMALE SOVIET NATIONS WERE INVITED TO MARINE PARTIES HELD IN THE
EMBASSY.THEY BEGAN A SECRET SEXUAL RELATIONSSHIP WITH HER IN JANUARY 1986 USING
HER APARTMENT. (A NUMBER OF THE OTHER MARINES KNEW OF THIS BUT DID NOT REPORT
IT,DESPITE THE FACT IT WASA VIOLATION OF REGULATIONS). IN JANUARY 1986 SHE
INTRODUCED HIM TO HERE "UNCLE" IN A SAFEHOUSE. DURING THE SECOND MEETING
WITH THE UNCLE SASHA (EITHER A CO-OPTED OR OFFICER OF THE KGB/SCD) HE WAS
ASKED FOR CLASSIED INFORMATION WHICH LONGTREE PROVIDED. THE FEMALE
PARTICIPATED IN THESE MEETING WITH THE KGB IN MOSCOW.(SHE WAS FIRED BY
THE EMBASSY IN 12/85 FOR POOR WORK PERFORMANCE, AND IS REPORTED TO BE
CURRENTLY WORKINGFOR THE IRISH EMBASSY IN MOSCOW). LONGTREE WAS NOT
BLACKMAILED IN ANY MANNER. WHEN HE WAS TRANSFERED TO VIENNA, SASHA
CONTINUED TO MEET LONGTREE IN VIENNA FROM JUNE 1986 UNTILDECEMBER 14,1986.
THEY HAD NUMBEROUS MEETING DURING WHICH PERIOD LONGTREE ADMITS RECEIVING
$3500.

MOTIVATION
LONGTREE ADMITS TO DOING THIS BECAUSE HE LIKED THE INTRIGUE, WAS FLATTERED
THE KGB WAS INTERESTED IN HIM, AND FOR REVENGE AGAINST THE US BECAUSE OF
INJUSTICES COMMITTED AGAINST THE INDIANS IN THE PAST 100 YEARS(HE IS AN
AMERICAN INDIAN)

TWIST
UNLIKE OTHER CASES WE HAVE SEEN IN THE PAST THE KGB CONTINUED
TO OFFERED LONGTREE THE OPPORTUNITY TO DEFECT OPENLY, WHICH MAY INDICATE
HE HAD KNOWLEDGE OF DOING SOMETHING FOR THE SOVIETS IN MOSCOW THE KGB
WISHED TO PROTECT. HE WAS SCHEDULED TO TRAVEL TO MOSCOW BLACK IN JAN 1987
for further training.

POLICY IMPLICATIONS
-this vindicated our policy OF EXCLUDING SOVIETS FSN WORKING IN THE EMBASSY
IN MOSCOW AND MAY SUGGEST WE DO THE SAME IN OTHER WARSAW PACT COUNTRIES

-THIS PUTS INTO QUESTION THE CI TRAINING GIVEN TO THE MARINE GUARDS
BEING ASSIGNED TO WARSAW PACT COUNTRIES

-this could be the IMPITUS TO BEGIN POLYGRAPHING MARINE GUARDS FOR CI
ISSUES APERIODICALLY WORKING IN WARSAW PACT COUNTRIES.

■■■

VIENNA AND MEXICO APPROVED BY THE PRESIDENT IN JANUARY 1985, should be
put in place as soon as possible(LONGTREE WAS MEET IN KNOWN SOVIET OPERATIONAL
SIGHTS IN VIENNA FROM JUNE-DEC 1986)

Later that day, Carlucci's staff express
their appreciation for Major's instant
response on Lonetree. By 1995,
however, intelligence analysts concluded
that the Lonetree brouhaha was largely
a diversion mounted by the KGB to turn
U.S. attention away from the real
espionage damage being done at the
time by Aldrich Ames.

01/15/87 16:14:44

FROM: NSPWH   --CPUA   TO: NSDGM   --CPUA
To: NSDGM   --CPUA

*** Reply to note of 01/15/87 12:31
NOTE FROM: PAUL W. HANLEY
Subject: MEMO FOR FCC FROM DGM, NEED SOONEST TODAY-TOP SECRET
Thanks, Dave. Very helpful. We're saying nothing except that the
Marines are investigating with a view to prosecution; the State
Dept is assessing the damage.
The plot's going to thicken a lot when we get to the court-martial.
I suspect that if they convict him the Marines may want to shoot
him. In view of Pelton's and Walker's fate, and how much more
damage they did, this may prove contentious. The whole counter-
espionage world will probably get a lot of attention as a result,
which may not be a bad thing. Now's the time to think the implications through.

These two fabulously detailed e-mail messages give what amounts to an insider's history of espionage directed at the United States from 1975 to 1985, in the guise of a passionate argument for polygraphs, the so-called lie detector. First, on December 20, 1985, to a colleague and again on December 23 forwarding the first message on to his superiors, David Major makes the case for polygraphing as a screening mechanism to deter would-be spies. The two deleted sections seem to refer to aspects of cases still considered sensitive a decade or more later; and the first one is especially interesting, since it tells the story of Larry Chin, a CIA employee who beat the polygraph for nearly thirty years. Some obscure references:

```
To: NSWFM    --CPUA

NOTE FROM: David Major                        12/23/85 09:46 ***
Subject: Polygraph and Espionage
BILL these are some specific examples of the reality of espionage and
polygraph that I believe you should know. In addition this is the type
of facts I believe the President should also know and realize the box
he could place us in and the dis-service he would do by stepping away
from the polygraph as screening tool. I would also add the ROBERT SATLER
case, a GDR agent directed to join the NSC because we do not POLY screen.
*** Forwarding note from NSDGM    --CPUA    12/20/85 14:39 ***
To: NSFEG    --CPUA

NOTE FROM: David Major
SUBJECT: Polygraph and Espionage


In this morning's press conferenceLarry Speak's comments have really
hurt us on the issue of implementing NSDD 196 relating to the polygraph.
In essence Larry stated that only people who are suspects in an espionage
case will be given a polygraph. This is 180% in the wrong direction.
Ed has attempted to tilt this in the correct direction that it will be used
for screening.A key element here is we have continually stated that a poly-
graph on its own will not result in adverse personnel action, but one tool
in our counterintelligence and countermeasures arsenal. This position can
only hold true if the simple request to take a polygraph is predicated on
an active investigation. If we only give polygraphs to suspects or potential
suspects then our whole premise of no negative inference resulting from a
polygraph unless independly cooperated will go down the sewer.

Per you request on individual espionage case and the polygraph I would
point out the following about, some of the most significant case:

From 1975-1985 48 individual have been indicted, arrested, and/or
convicted of espionage;of this number only two LARRY CHIN ••••••••
••••••••••••••••••••••••••••••••••••••••••••••••••••••••••••••••••••••
••••••••••••••••••••••••••••••••••••••••••••••••••••••••••••••••••••••
••••••••••••••••••••••••••••••••••••••••••••••••••••••••••••••••••
```

(b)(1)
(5)

Larry Speak[es] is White House press secretary at this time; NSDD 196 is the controversial National Security Decision Directive issued by President Reagan on November 1, 1985, decreeing polygraph tests for all persons with access to sensitive compartmented information (SCI—in other words, beyond SECRET). At the time, Secretary of State George Shultz threatened to resign if forced to take the polygraph, and an uneasy truce ensued as the Reagan administration backed off its government-wide plans.

(b)(1)
(5)

The files of the CIA, NSA, and recently the FBI reveal numerousexamples of individual who were directed by hostile intelligence service to apply of employment in the intelligence community, discovered by the polygraph CI screening process. The reason this is not seen in the publicdomain is that they were not guilty of espionage since they did not gain access to classify informationand thus not prosecutable.

In addition there are numerous examples of agents of hostile country intelligence services being directed away from agencies and assignments who require an espionage polygraph, and into agencies that do not or did not use the polygraph as a screening tool. ••••••••••••••••••••••••••••••••
••
••
••
••
••

(b)(1)
(5)

RUDOLPH HERMAN was an KGBColonel living in New York as an USA citizen from 1968-1980. As a KGB illegal he recruited his son in the KGB, sent him to Georgetown University and directed him to join the intelligence community when he graduated. He was told not to able to the CIA since they used thepolygraph to screen but join the State Department where their was no polygraph.

In another ongoing case a individual was recruited by the KGB who financed the individual education at George Washington University and then was to join the intelligence community. This person graduated and began to apply to the CIA and NSA and discovered the need to take a polygraphtold the KGB. They advised they could not help get thru the polygraph so directedthe individual to join Stateor DOD (prior or DOD polygraph program)

As late as the summer of 1985 the KGB had the opportunity to place an agent of theirs,(very productive agent for over 3 years) into NSA but told the agent they could not train this individual to beat the polygraph

This type of situation is repeated over and over again. Individual who may have been caught by the SCREENING polygraph if it had been in effect

WHITE HOUSE E-MAIL

WILLIAM BELL (Hughes Aircraft-Special Access program 1981) Eugene
Madsen (Pentagon Situation room Navy yeoman with SCI access);
RON PELTON-NSA and KGB agent; WILLIAM KAMLIES-CIA and GRU agent;
ED HOWARD-CIA and KGB agent all volunteered after they left govt
service and thus choice to wait until they left the threat of the polygraph
before they became clandestine agents.

Based on my conversation with PAUL THOMPSON it appears their is some mis-
understanding re the practical aspects of Espionage investigations.This
NSDD was not designed to effect leaks thereforewhat really happens in
espionage cases is relavent to our policy. Unlike leak cases the predication
of the espionage case begins with the knowledge of exactly who is the subject
and it is a matter of proving the case or you know there is a penetration
in an agency but you have no suspects or then learn who it is. Leaks and
espionage are just differert.

12/23/85 13:24:34

FROM: NSWFM   --CPUA
To: NSPBT   --CPUA

NOTE FROM: WILLIAM F. MARTIN
Subject: Polygraph and Espionage
Paul, David makes some very good points here. How often do we do checks
on secretariat personnel? It seems to me that if I were the other side I
would think placing a low level clerk in the secretariat would be ideal. I
mention this because Cathy Millison recently remarked to me that it had been
several years since she had gone through a background check. Obviously this
has also crossed your mind no doubt, but in light of David's analysis that
the KGB targets agencies which did not use polygraph I would be comforted to
know that clearances are current on many of our oldtimers. Any thoughts on
this?
*** Forwarding note from NSDGM   --CPUA

The most secret information in the spook world falls in the area of "intelligence sources and methods," whether they are human agents (HUMINT), electronic intercepts (tapping wires and frequencies), overhead photography, or an "all-source" combination. That's why we don't know the precise subject of these two e-mail notes from October 23, 1986, in which Robert Earl and

Craig Coy comment on an alarming piece of news from the White House Situation Room (WHSR) evening summary (distributed via e-mail). The codeword "Spectre," which is censored from Earl's e-mail and released in Coy's e-mail, refers to sensitive compartmented intelligence on terrorism. We can also guess that the subject probably concerns the Middle East, because

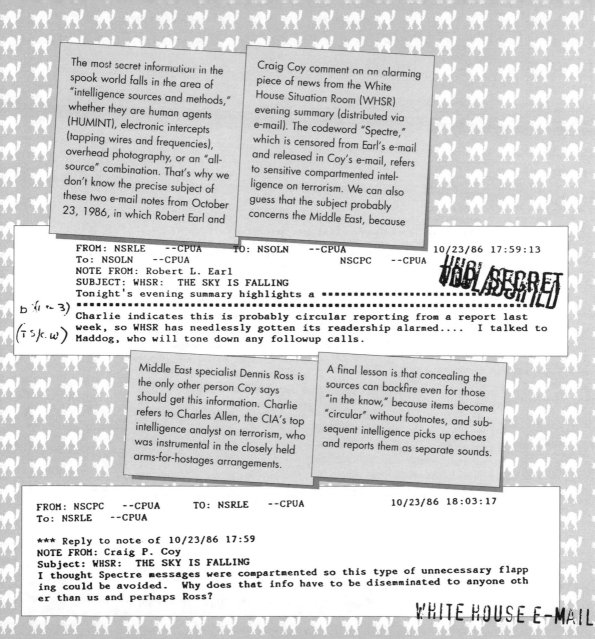

```
FROM: NSRLE   --CPUA    TO: NSOLN   --CPUA        10/23/86 17:59:13
To: NSOLN   --CPUA                 NSCPC   --CPUA
NOTE FROM: Robert L. Earl
SUBJECT: WHSR:  THE SKY IS FALLING
Tonight's evening summary highlights a ••••••••••••••••••••••••••••••••••
••••••••••••••••••••••••••••••••••••••••••••••••••••••••••••••••••••••
Charlie indicates this is probably circular reporting from a report last
week, so WHSR has needlessly gotten its readership alarmed....  I talked to
Maddog, who will tone down any followup calls.
```

b (1 - 3)
(T S)(c.w)

Middle East specialist Dennis Ross is the only other person Coy says should get this information. Charlie refers to Charles Allen, the CIA's top intelligence analyst on terrorism, who was instrumental in the closely held arms-for-hostages arrangements.

A final lesson is that concealing the sources can backfire even for those "in the know," because items become "circular" without footnotes, and subsequent intelligence picks up echoes and reports them as separate sounds.

```
FROM: NSCPC   --CPUA    TO: NSRLE   --CPUA        10/23/86 18:03:17
To: NSRLE   --CPUA

*** Reply to note of 10/23/86 17:59
NOTE FROM: Craig P. Coy
Subject: WHSR:  THE SKY IS FALLING
I thought Spectre messages were compartmented so this type of unnecessary flapp
ing could be avoided.  Why does that info have to be disemminated to anyone oth
er than us and perhaps Ross?
```

WHITE HOUSE E-MAIL

```
                                                    09/18/86  14:08:24

To:  NSOLN      --CPUA

NOTE FROM: Craig P. Coy
SUBJECT: charlie allen
charlie called to say he was on the way over to talk to the lawyers re. the
taps. he is under the impression you want him to not be forthcoming due to the
lack of legal foundation. he will try to deflect their questions but warns you
may have to go to the top to move this one.
```

This chilling e-mail raises all kinds of questions about the power of the White House staff to order extralegal surveillance inside the United States. Counterterrorism staffer Craig Coy warns his boss, Oliver North, on September 18, 1986, that Charlie Allen of the CIA was facing problems with getting permission for wiretaps. The "lawyers" probably refers to the Justice Department section that manages the legal process for getting secret wiretaps for intelligence purposes. Although the government's requests have to be approved by a special federal court in Alexandria, Virginia, they are rarely if ever denied. From the date of the e-mail, we can guess that these taps are intended to monitor the secret visit by Rafsanjani's nephew, Ali Bahrameni, to Washington, as part of the Iran-contra arms-for-hostages negotiations.

For anyone who's ever wondered how the CIA jets its agents around the world, this minutely detailed sequence of e-mail provides more information than has ever before been made public. The White House staff are working

```
To: NSJMP   --CPUA                                          05/19/86 23:00:07

*** Reply to note of 05/19/86 20:51
                                          -SECRET-  UNCLASSIFIED
NOTE FROM: OLIVER NORTH
Subject: IRAN AND TERRORISM
We will endeavor to do it any way you want but we are experiencing significant
logs problems which are considerably eased by the use of a military a/c which
can deliver the people, communications equipment (classified SATCOM, beacons ,
etc.) and still provide a modicum of rest. The present plan includes the A/C
as a part of the OPSEC in that RCM has reason to use such an A/C and we have
little hope of moving Waite to/through Cyprus on a commercial flight. The same
applies to a lesser extent to RCM.
```

as travel agents, calling the CIA and the Pentagon for flight arrangements, putting together one of the most harebrained, high-level diplomatic shuttles ever attempted: The secret mission by former National Security Adviser Robert McFarlane to Tehran in May 1986 to barter arms for the hostages held in Lebanon. The dialogue is between Oliver North and John Poindexter, starting on May 19 with an appeal for a military aircraft (a/c) to take McFarlane (RCM) and the satellite communications (SATCOM) equipment to Iran. Waite refers to Anglican Church representative Terry Waite, who is to provide public cover for any resulting hostage release.

```
FROM: NSJMP   --CPUA     TO: NSOLN   --CPUA                05/20/86 09:27:11
To: NSOLN   --CPUA

*** Reply to note of 05/19/86 23:00
                                          -SECRET-  UNCLASSIFIED
NOTE FROM: JOHN POINDEXTER
Subject: IRAN AND TERRORISM
DOESN'T CIA HAVE AN AIRCRAFT THAT COULD BE USED?  WHAT DOES CASEY USE?
```

WHITE HOUSE E-MAIL

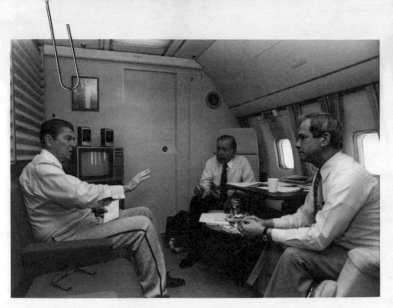

Reagan, Regan & McFarlane on Air Force One 6-21-85

CONUS refers to continental United States. Under the censored line is a reference to St. Lucia Airways, the CIA proprietary owning the 707s and based on that Caribbean island, according to press reports. UNODIR stands for "unless otherwise directed," a classic bureaucratic maneuver.

05/20/86 10:38:12
FROM: NSOLN   --CPUA   TO: NSJMP   --CPUA
To: NSJMP   --CPUA

*** Reply to note of 05/20/86 09:27

NOTE FROM: OLIVER NORTH
Subject: IRAN AND TERRORISM
The CIA has one 737 here in CONUS which does not have the range or speed of a
G-3. There are two proprietary 707s; both of which are based overseas with
•••••••••••••••••••••• neither of which are certified for operations in CONUS.
When Casey travels overseas he usually flies by USAF (89th SAW) A/C. It would
appear that this military a/c thing is in the realm of too hard. UNODIR by
1200 local, I will seek to make other arrangements. North

(b)(1)
(C)

To: NSOLN   --CPUA

```
                                              05/20/86  14:10:03
*** Reply to note of 05/20/86 10:38   --SECRET  UNCLASSIFIED

NOTE FROM: JOHN POINDEXTER
Subject: IRAN AND TERRORISM
IT IS NOT THAT IT IS TOO HARD; I JUST DON'T THINK IT IS A GOOD IDEA. LEAKS AT
THIS POINT COULD BE DISASTROUS. THIS IS DIFFERENT FROM OTHER SECRET MISSIONS
IN THAT ANYBODY THAT KNOWS ANYTHING (OR THINKS THEY KNOW SOMETHING ) CONNECTED
WITH THIS MISSION WILL BE SORELY TEMPTED TO TALK ABOUT IT AFTERWARDS IF IT IS
SUCCESSFUL. LET ME KNOW WHAT YOU WORK OUT.
```

North ultimately turns to his partner in the Project Democracy enterprise, retired Major General Richard Secord, recipient of nearly $70 million of secret, no-bid, noncompetitive government business at North's behest. Secord's codename is Copp.

P/U means pickup; George Cave is the CIA's top Farsi-speaker and Iran expert; Howard Teicher serves on the National Security Council staff with North; and TLV stands for Tel Aviv, the last stop before Tehran.

To: NSJMP   --CPUA

```
*** Reply to note of 05/20/86 14:10
                                              05/20/86  15:37:49

NOTE FROM: OLIVER NORTH          --SECRET UNCLASSIFIED
Subject: IRAN AND TERRORISM
Copp has been told to charter two a/c. The first a/c will p/u Cave Teicher and
the communicators at Dulles, proceed to NY, p/u RCM and deliver all to London.
This a/c will then proceed from London to Cyprus w/ Waite. The second a/c will
meet RCM and party (North will join in London) and proceed to TLV. While this
procedure breaks the chain of knowledge of the first air crew as to RCM's
destination, it also results in more people being brought into the picture. We
are out of vetted aircrews but hope that with the false docs we can at least
keep the second aircrew from learning exactly what is going on. We still have
a major problem with customs/immigration that we would have avoided w/ a
military a/c. We are working hard on solutions, will keep you apprised.
```

WHITE HOUSE E-MAIL

The final itinerary gives all the details, in what reads like a Top Secret TripTik from AAA, complete with codenames like "Goode" (North's phony passport is in the name William P. Goode). The three censored letters just before Frankfurt probably are "COS," meaning the CIA chief of station there. The PRT-250 is a secure communications device.

05/20/86 23:47:34

To: NSJMP   --CPUA

*** Reply to note of 05/20/86 14:10

--UNCLASSIFIED

NOTE FROM: OLIVER NORTH
Subject: IRAN AND TERRORISM
This is further re transportation arrangements for RCM & party: Cave + Teicher + Communicators will depart IAD aboard Private (Democracy INC.) G-3, stops in NYC to p/u RCM. G-3 Proceeds direct to Rhein Main military airfield, cleared thru customs by CIA ■■■■ North & Waite picked up in London by Lear 35 owned by Democracy INC. European subsidiary. Lear 35 drops North at commercial side of Rhein Main, North passes thru customs/immigration as Goode, proceeds to military side to rvs w/ RCM party. Lear 35 proceeds to Larnaca w/ Waite aboard ■■ RCM party on arrival at RM offloads from G-3, transloads to CIA 707 (if available) or to chartered Swiss Challenger a/c for direct flight to Tel Aviv. Still having focal point clearance problems for bringing G-3 into RM w/o customs/immigrations clearance. We are going to have to bring ■■■ Frankfurt into this to work out clearances. Will talk to him tonight via PRT-250 @ approx 0300. Shd have answer shortly thereafter.

NOTE FROM: ROBERT E. LINHARD
SUBJECT: RESPONSE TO GANG OF 6 ON NUCLEAR TESTING

SECRET/SENSITIVE

SVEN, SORRY TO ADD TO YOUR BURDENS, BUT I WILL DROP OFF AN ACTION THAT HAS JUST
COME IN CARRYING MY NAME (1622) WHICH IS DUE NEXT WEDNESDAY.   IT IS A RESPONSE
TO THE GANG OF 6 ON NUCLEAR TESTING.   COULD YOU CONTINUE TO FOLLOW-THRU ON THIS
ONE?

ALONG THE SAME LINES, CIA •••••• CALLED TO TELL ME THAT WE HAVE INDICATIONS
THAT THE SAME GROUP WILL WRITGAIN TO THE PRESIDENT AND THE GORBACHEV NEXT
WEEK ASKING THE PRESIDENT TO ACCEPT THE TESTING MORATORIUM AND ASKING GORBACHEV
TO EXTEND IT UNILATERALLY IF NECESSARY UNTIL THE SUMMIT. ••••••••••••••••••
•• THIS WILL
BE REPORTED AS A ••• ITEM NEXT WEEK.

THIS ARGUES THAT YOU MAY WANT TO TRY TO PUT THE RESPONSE TO BED AS SOON AS
POSSIBLE.   I WILL GIVE JMP A SHORT HEADS UP ON THIS VIA SEPARATE PROFS.

b)(1 + 3)

(S)

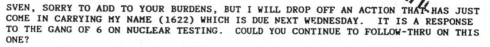

This February 28, 1986, e-mail
tells one of the CIA's success
stories, illustrating how stolen
information can give the president
an advantage in foreign relations.
Career air force officer Robert
Linhard is the NSC staffer tracking
nuclear arms control issues, and he
tells his colleague Sven Kraemer
about an intelligence coup that
will allow the White House to do

a preemptive public relations strike.
"Gang of 6" is White House slang
for what is formally known as the
Five Continent Peace Initiative,
involving Argentina, Mexico, India,
Greece, Sweden, and Tanzania,
pressing both the United States and
the Soviet Union for a total ban on
nuclear testing. Playing to world
opinion, Gorbachev is a step ahead
of Reagan, having announced

a unilateral moratorium on under-
ground testing. The censored portions
of the e-mail probably give the
method used by CIA to pick up the
information that a new Gang of 6
initiative would be coming "next
week," and the three-letter deletion
probably refers to the NID, National
Intelligence Daily.

NOTE FROM: David Major
SUBJECT: ROY GODSON
ROY HAS BEEN AN UNPAID CONSULTANT TO THE NSC ADVISOR AND PFIAB SINCE
1981. HE HOLDS TS/NSC CLEARANCES ANSD HAS ASSISTED A NUMBER OF THE
DIRECTORATES IN THE NSC TO INCLUDE; ARMS CONTROL, PUBLIC DIPLOMACY,
CMS AND US AMONG OTHERS. HE WAS NOT INVOLVED IN THE IRAN/ARMS TERRORIST
ISSUE IN ANYWAY.
HE HAS PROVEN TO BE A VALUABLE AND VERY DISCREAT ASSET TO US. HE DOES
NOT PUBLICIZE IN ANYWAY HE IS A CULSULTANT. HE IS A RECONIZED ACADEMIC
SPECALIST ON SOVIET ACTIVE MEASURES AND INTELLIGENCE POLICY ISSUES WHO
PROVES US A UNIQUE INSIGHT. BOB GATES ALSO FREQUENTLY MEETS WITH ROY ON
INTELLIGENCE ISSUES.
HE PROVIDES A SPECIAL UTILITY TO ME IN ADDITION TO OTHER MEMBERS OF THE NSC
STAFF(AS HE WORKS WITH A NUMBER OF DIRECTORATES THE DETAILS OF HIS INVOLVMENT
WITH THEM IS UNKNOWN TO ME).(1)ACTIVE MEASURES-NEXT TO NO ONE IN US GOVT KNOW
MORE ABOUT AM INCLUDING CIA, DI AND DO SPECALISTS.HE SAVES ME ENERGY AND
RESOURCES IN ANALYSISOF AM AS HE STUDIES THIS COMPLEX AND SENSITIVE AREA
OF ACTIVITY IN THE US AND ALLIED COUNTRIES. HE IS FREQUENTLY CALLED UPON FOR
ADVISE BY INR, USIA, AND CIA, IN ADDITION TO PREPARING REVIEWS OF OUR STAFF
RECOMMENDATIONS. HE SERVES AS OUR ALTERNATE ON THE ACTIVE MEASURES WORKING
GROUP.(2)INTELLIGENCE POLICY ISSUE-ROY HAS NEVER WORKED FOR ANY ONE
INTELL AGENCY YET HE IS A LEADING ACADEMIC STUDENT OF US INTELLIGENCE
POLICY.HE CORRDINATES 25 ACADEMIC IN THE "CONSORTIUM FOR THE STUDY OF
INTELLIGENCE WHICH DOES TWO THINGS (A) TRAIN ACADEMICS THRU OUT THE USA
ON NECESSITY FOR ALL ELEMENTS OF FOREIGN AFFAIRS AND INTELLIGENCE (B)
TRACK LONGRANGE NEEDS OF INTEL COMMUNITY. YOU MAY HAVE SEEN THE 7 VOLUME
SERIES ROY EDITED WHICH CONGRESS AND FORMER SENIOR POLICYMAKERS CONSIDER THE
BEST WORK OF ITS KIND ON INTEL POLICY. SINCE ROY DOES NOT HAVE THE PREJUDIC
OF A SPECIFIC AGENCY CULTURE HE SERVES AS EXCELLENT SOUNDING BOARD ON POLICY
RELATING TO INTEL AND CI ISSUES. I HAVE BEEN ABLE TO TASK ROY TO REVIEW THE
STACK OF MATERIAL THAT COMES IN FROM AGENCIES AND HIGHLIGHTSKEY
POLICY ISSUES ON CI AND INTEL AND PUBLIC DIPLOMACY AREAS.

Proof that information is power comes from this fascinating e-mail about the inside-outside relationship between an erstwhile academic, Professor Roy Godson of Georgetown University, and the intelligence community. Written by the FBI's man on the National Security Council staff on February 2, 1987, this testimonial to Godson's value leads with the fact that he is an *unpaid* consultant.

(However, Godson later testified under oath that he was paid $150–200 per day for his work at the NSC.) Why does David Major think Godson does all this for free? The very last sentence gives the answer: Godson gets access to the government's secrets, and in exchange for giving advice, he builds a career as an intelligence expert. Major makes one mistake, however, in

that within a few months, the news would break that Godson helped steer a $100,000 contribution from Richard Mellon Scaife into Oliver North's offshore gun-buying accounts. PFIAB stands for President's Foreign Intelligence Advisory Board; TS means Top Secret; DI refers to the CIA's Directorate of Intelligence; DO to the Directorate of Operations; INR to the State Department's Bureau of Intelligence and Research; AM to "active measures"; and CI to counterintelligence.

02/12/86 15:46 ***

To: NSRBM   --CPUA   JOHN M. POINDEXTER NSWRP   --CPUA   JOHN M. POINDEXTER
NOTE FROM: Jack Matlock
SUBJECT: Spydust Report

State plans to issue a report on the results of the EPA and CDC on the use of NPPD against Embassy officers in Moscow. Report is to be issued Friday, Feb. 14. Findings are: (1) Lab tests show that NPPD is not a mutagen in mammalian cells, therefore there is no reason to suspect health hazards, particularly when small quantities are involved; and (2) NPPD was not detected in 436 samples taken from apartments and offices of Embassy employees (this represents 20% of the employees, selected on a random basis). Finally, in a follow-up study concentrating on th vehicles of Embassy employees most likely to be targeted, NPPD was found in five of 30 vehicles.

Release to the press will follow a briefing of Embassy employees Friday. The results are, of course, reassuring so far as health hazards are concerned. They also show -- since traces were found in five automobiles -- that the chemical was used as we originally charged.

One question that the study does not answer is whether the Soviets discontinued the use of NPPD after our representations last summer. (The traces found in cars could have antedated our demarche.) We should have an answer to this latersince new cars were brought in in January and they are being monitored to determine whether usage has continued. But for the time being we can neither confirm that the practice stopped or cite clear evidence that it has continued.

These arrangements for notifying Embassy personnel and releasing the results of the study to the public look fine to me. I think State should handle the public aspects. However, you may wish to give the President an advance brief on the findings.

WHITE HOUSE E-MAIL

CHAPTER 11

CENSORS AND SECRETS

One of the original motivations for the founding of the National Security Archive came from two reporters comparing the heavily censored versions of documents on El Salvador human rights issues they had won from the government through the Freedom of Information Act. In one case, *New York Times* reporter Raymond Bonner had the top half, and *Washington Post* reporter Scott Armstrong had the bottom half. Retired foreign service officers working at the State Department as declassification reviewers had, only a few months apart, reached diametrically opposed conclusions as to what was actually sensitive in that particular cable.

In the thousands of declassified documents that cross the archive's transom every year, we see hundreds of examples of this subjectivity of the truly sensitive. We don't complain too much, however. Having two or more versions of the same previously classified document is truly a boon to researchers, because the government's censors very kindly highlight with black lines and blotches the really interesting portions of the document.

The multiplicities of this particular twentieth-century abstract art form boggle the mind. The garden variety form is simply a function of the passage of time, that is, the older the document is, the more likely it is to be released in full, thus allowing the comparison to the previous censored versions. However, in some cases, the securocrats reclassify information that has previously been released in full—something of an attempt to put the toothpaste back in the tube, as it were. For example, the 1987 Iran-contra Congressional hearings featured heavily censored e-mail exhibits that had been printed in full only a few months earlier in the Tower Commission report; a best-selling book apparently unread by the hapless Congressional committees.

The declassified White House e-mail is particularly rich in secrecy variations. For one thing, the e-mail has dribbled out of the government over a lengthy period—from February 1987 (release date of the Tower Commission report) all the way through April 1995 (the last release in our lawsuit). The passage of time alone would have produced multiple versions. But a more important factor relates to the extraordinarily candid language used in the e-mail, which only heightened the anxiety of the censors.

This chapter provides a number of these comparisons, so you may judge for yourself: Were any of the blacked-out portions really dangerous to the United States? I believe you will find that, for the most part, the censors were attempting to black out embarrassment—embarrassment to their bosses, to themselves, to other agencies especially in the intelligence community, or to allies like Israel. It's an old story, this attempt by every administration and every bureaucracy to control the information available to the citizenry, because information is power—power to frame the policy debates and thereby to win them. Richard Nixon was hardly the first, and surely not the last, president to invoke "national security" to cover his sins and shortcomings.

President Reagan & his national security advisers
(Oliver North at far left) in the Oval Office 4-4-85

Weinberger & Reagan in the Situation Room 5-18-87

This January 21, 1987, e-mail deserves pride of place in the Censorship Hall of Fame, proving the almost complete subjectivity of national security secrecy. The same National Security Council staffer, David Van Tassel, declassified both versions—the first on June 6, 1994, and the second on June 15—but somehow thought an almost completely different set of words was sensitive the second time around. Only three lines are missing from both versions. The side-by-side comparison shows that the cuts don't truly protect national security; rather, they disguise a highly embarrassing discussion, led by President Reagan's national security adviser Frank Carlucci, and dominated by Secretary of Defense Caspar ("Cap") Weinberger, about providing arms and other support to Iraq's president Saddam Hussein through third parties, paying off Egypt through debt forgiveness, and wondering whether certain aircraft carrier battle groups ("CVBG") were nuclear-capable. The e-mail's author is William Cockell, a National Security Council staffer who seems to have been serving as something of a notetaker at the discussion, and whose e-mail is designed to keep nonattendees (such as Deputy National Security Adviser Colin Powell) in the loop. When we brought this to Van Tassel's attention, to his great credit he released the document in full. The three lines in the middle are: Cap pointed out that this might be a good time to press Egypt on a nuclear transit. Frank noted that Mubarak had just committed the ultimate folly—he rejected the President's invitation. He speculated that we might be able to move Hussein [of Jordan] into that slot.

WHITE HOUSE E-MAIL

*** Resending note of 01/21/87 11:55
To: NSCNC   --CPUA   Colin L. Powell   NSWHP   --CFUA   Colin L. Powell
NOTE FROM: William A. Cockell
SUBJECT: Iran-Iraq

Frank opened the discussion by reviewing the shopping list of
possible US actions which Dick Murphy had brought over last
evening. He said Dennis Ross would be coordinating with Rick
Armitage so Frank could brief the President today.

Cap felt it clearly was time to drop any pretense of even-handedness.
We should no longer talk about ending the war "with no winners or
losers." Iran is the aggressor in this case; and we should not
only be supportive of Iraq, but should be seen to be supportive.
This is an opportunity to recoup some of our standing in the
region and regain credibility with the Arab states. With regard
to accelerating arrival of the CVBG in the IC, Cap pointed out
that if we are going to do it, we should take action now, since
it will take a while for the battle group to transit. Defense
would not want to put the carrier into the Persian Gulf, but
having it on station in the Northern Arabian Sea made sense.

(b)(1)(s)

This led to a

discussion of the FMS debt restructuring issue. The problem is
basically a political one, Frank observed. If we provide relief for
Egypt and others, the domestic program constituencies will be up in
arms, and the heat from the hill will be intense. Cap commented that
there are sound national security reasons from trying to provide
Egypt some debt relief. Egypt is critical to the Mideast peace
process; and in a contingency, we could well require Egyptian
cooperation in the matter of bases, or other support. Cap said he
intended to raise the FMS debt issue with the President, and urge
him to direct Baker to be more forthcoming. Even if domestic
pressures preclude our doing any more, it would be useful for the
Administration to be seen (by the Egyptians) as at least attempting to
provide greater relief. (Frank asked me to obtain talking points for
the President to use with Cap. I passed the requirement to Steve
Farrar who has provided them to Bob Pearson.) Discussion then
returned to the issue of Murphy's shopping list. Frank continued
to go through the items, and Cap was generally supportive and
reiterated his view that we should not only take action to assist
Iraq but ensure that the assistance is visible.

(b)(1)
(5)

The Iraqis' problem
is not lack of weapons, but one of leadership and morale. We need to
stiffen them up some way. Frank observed that if we are looking
for a symbolic gesture, the sending of a team to discuss their
needs with the Iraqis might be a good approach. Cap agreed, and
the discussion ended on that note.

236

```
*** Resending note of 01/21/87 11:55
To: NSSSG   --CPU.     Colin L. Powell    NSWAP   --CPUA    Colin L. Powell
NOTE FROM: William A. Cockell
SUBJECT: Iran/Iraq
```

Frank opened the discussion by reviewing the shopping list of
possible US actions which Dick Murphy had brought over last
evening. He said Dennis Ross would be coordinating with Rich
Armitage so Frank could brief the President today.
Cap felt it clearly was time to drop any pretense of even-handedness.
We should no longer talk about ending the war "with no winners or
losers." Iran is the aggressor in this case; and we should not
only be supportive of Iraq, but should be seen to be supportive.
This is an opportunity to recoup some of our standing in the
region and regain credibility with the Arab states. With regard
to accelerating arrival of the CVBG in the IO, Cap pointed out
that if we are going to do it, we should take action now, since
it will take a while for the battle group to transit. Defense
would not want to put the carrier into the Persian Gulf, but
having it on station in the Northern Arabian Sea made sense.
Someone asked whether there is a non-nuclear battle group presently
in the Med that could be used for the IO. No one knew whether one
or both of the carriers now in the Med were nuclear.   (b)(1)
                                                                    (s)

Classified by: Multiple Sources
Declassify on: OADR   NSC-000151

                                                                    (b)(1)(s)

transit.

                                           The problem is
basically a political one, Frank observed. If we provide relief for   (b)(1)(s)
                       the domestic program constituencies will be up in
arms, and the heat from the hill will be intense. Cap commented that
there are sound national security reasons from trying to provide

                                                                    (b)(1)(s)

                                           Discussion then
returned to the issue of Murphy's shopping list. Frank continued
to go through the items, and Cap was generally supportive and
reiterated his view that we should not only take action to assist
Iraq but ensure that the assistance is visible. "Even if they
don't need (U.S.) arms, we should make the offer," he felt, to
impress on the Iraqis our bona fides and show the other Arabs as
well that we want to be supportive. Others were not sure that
an arms sale offer would be appropriate, or that it would play well
politically here. There would be perception problems. Some would
suggest it was a ploy by the President to deflect criticism of the
Iran arms deal. An inconclusive discussion ensued about the
legality of providing arms to the Iraqis through third parties,
etc. No one was sure how the law might constrain our authorizing
GCC countries to transfer US equipment to Iraq, e.g. Cap agreed the
arms would be essentially a symbolic gesture. The Iraqis' problem
is not lack of weapons, but one of leadership and morale. We need to
stiffen them up some way. Frank observed that if we are looking
for a symbolic gesture, the sending of a team to discuss their
needs with the Iraqis might be a good approach. Cap agreeed, and
the discussion ended on that note.

WHITE HOUSE E-MAIL

This October 24, 1985, e-mail from Oliver North to Ray Burghardt demonstrates the ludicrous secrecy claims that the Central Intelligence Agency routinely gets away with, thus flouting democratic norms of accountable government. For years, the CIA filed court papers insisting that the two words at the end of the first line of this note, about the release of the kidnapped daughter of President Duarte of El Salvador, would "cause serious damage to the national security" if released, because "it could adversely affect the ability of that source to collect information in that part of the world." But when the full text emerged from a 1994 declassification, it turned out that the two words were "CIA and," as in Oliver North had reconfirmed with CIA and State. The last sentence provides a classic summary of the downside of e-mail—"these damned machines."

```
MSG FROM: NSOLN   --CPUA     TO: NSGFB   --CPUA        10/24/85 18:08:29
To: NSRFB   --CPUA

*** Reply to note of 10/24/85 16:54

NOTE FROM: OLIVER NORTH                        UNCLASSIFIED  (S)  (b)(1) + (b)(:
Subject: Release of Ines Duarte
STOP, STOP, STOP When Ines was released at 1310 EDT I reconfirmed w/ ████████
State existing plans for onward movement of Ines, her father and other family
mbrs as we agreed at last week's BIG. State (Woods and Walker) and I have
talked several times about the content of a PR msg to Duarte and a press
release for Speakes use. The trouble with these damned machines is that people
across the hall from one another don't even talk to each other anymore.
```

The Reagans and the Duartes 10-14-87

These versions of the same Oliver North November 9, 1985, e-mail contain the very helpful highlight provided by the government's censors of a process normally completely hidden from public view—the distribution of intercepted communications gathered by the National Security Agency. Here, Gen. William Odom, the head of NSA, seems to have been attempting to maintain standard NSA electronic surveillance of Iran and Israel, which would have picked up the arms shipments then being arranged by North's confederates. We now know that dozens of top Reagan administration officials got copies of NSA intercept reports on the Iran arms deals in 1985 and 1986, but all chose to look the other way.

```
MSG FROM: NSOLN   --CPUA      TC: NSJMF   --CPUA           11/09/85 13:15:27
To: NSJMF   --CPUA

*** Reply to note of 11/09/85 12:24
                                                          UNCLASSIFIED
                                          -- SECRET --

NOTE FROM: OLIVER NORTH
Subject: RESTRICTED DISTRO OF NSA PRODUCTS
No problem.  Through Charlie Allen (who set up coverage) we have told NSA to
██████████████████████████████████ Who the hell does Odom think he is?
   Y  RESTRICTED DISTRO OF NSA PRODUCTS
```

(b)(1)
(c)

```
To: NSJMP   --CPUA                                        11/09/85 13:15:27

*** Reply to note of 11/09/85 12:24
                                  UNCLASSIFIED
                         -- SECRET --

NOTE FROM: OLIVER NORTH
Subject: RESTRICTED DISTRO OF NSA PRODUCTS
No problem.  Through Charlie Allen (who set up coverage) we have told NSA to
stand down on dedicated coverage and allow normal closed distro for very
sensitive products.  Who the hell does Odom think he is?
```

What a difference a day makes! On August 22, 1994, the National Archives'
declassification officer thought this e-mail (from June 5, 1986) was just SECRET/CODE
WORD, and two lines should be censored. On August 23, the same text rated TOP
SECRET as well as CODE WORD protection, and three central bullet-point paragraphs
needed to be censored because their release would cause "exceptionally grave

06/05/86 12:35 *

To: NSOLN   --CPUA

NOTE FROM: David Wigg
SUBJECT: Memo For Ollie North
Scott Sullivan and I met this A.M. with Alan Gerson and Chuck Cooper of DOJ.
We presented a proposal to work closely with NSC on a very quiet basis to
research ways and means to squeeze off the flow of funds to terrorist organizations in the international financial system (same approach I used for Nic.
trade embargo strategy). They were in enthusiastic agreement and are going to
begin preliminary research immediately. We see a plan going something as follows:

o Justice looks at existing laws both here and abroad (particularly Europe) to
determine legal vehicle(s) needed to monitor/freeze/seize funds flowing to
known terrorists. They will have some preliminary info. in about 10 days.
o NSC/Justice calls in •••   (b)(i
••   (5)
o We then put together a comprehensive gameplan to maximally track financial
flows from Syria, Libya, Iran, etc. through the 400 or so principal banks that   1.3(c)(4
make up the interbank market; to notify and work with European Govs. to fill   F
gaps in our coverage and to cooperate with us in freezing/seizing assets as
appropriate (all on confidential basis)..
o We also would undertake an overt campaign to selectively expose particular conduits without compromising sources/methods.
o The foundation will all be laid without Treas./State/Comm./STR knowledge
and we will go to John with a complete package and plan probably to be
presented by him over breakfast to Shultz with Casey/Meese/Weinberger to back
him up as appropriate. They can then roll the others after going to the Pres.

If it is done right, and the legal work is tight, it should work like the
embargo.

damage" to the national security. From the context—discussions between National Security Council staff and Justice Department lawyers about the finances of international terrorists—it's clear that the core of the censorship relates to the National Security Agency and its capacity to listen in on most international telephone conversations, cables, telegraphs, wire transfers, and the like.

To: NSOLN   --CPUA

NOTE FROM: David Wigg
SUBJECT: Memo For Ollie North
Scott Sullivan and I met this A.M. with Alan Gerson and Chuck Cooper of DOJ. We presented a proposal to work closely with NSC on a very quiet basis to research ways and means to squeeze off the flow of funds to terrorist organizations in the international financial system (same approach I used for Nic. trade embargo strategy). They were in enthusiastic agreement and are going to begin preliminary research immediately. We see a plan going something as follows:

(b)(1)
TS/(cW)
1.3(a)(4)

o We also would undertake an overt campaign to selectively expose particular conduits without compromising sources/methods.
o The foundation will all be laid without Treas./State/Comm./STR knowledge and we will go to John with a complete package and plan probably to be presented by him over breakfast to Shultz with Casey/Meese/Weinberger to back him up as appropriate. They can then roll the others after going to the Pres.

If it is done right, and the legal work is tight, it should work like the embargo.

AUG 3 1994

Partially Declassified/Released on _____
by NARA on the recommendation of the NSC.

F. -1105

WHITE HOUSE E-MAIL

digital

I N T E R O F F I C E   M E M O R A N D U M

Date: 28-Apr-1986 03:53p EDT
From: Scott Sullivan
         SULLIVAN
Dept: DECISION SUPPORT STAFF
Tel No: 6919

TO: See Below

Subject: Smoking Gun?

At my request,

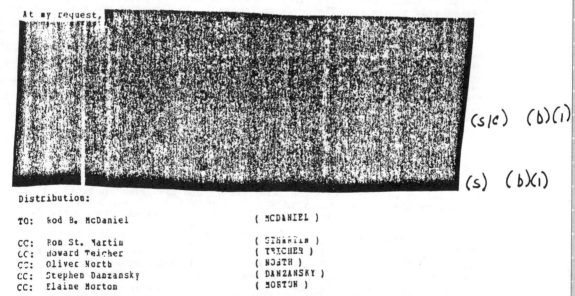

(s/c) (b)(1)

(s) (b)(1)

Distribution:

TO: Rod B. McDaniel   (MCDANIEL)

CC: Ron St. Martin   (STMARTIN)
CC: Howard Teicher   (TEICHER)
CC: Oliver North   (NORTH)
CC: Stephen Danzansky   (DANZANSKY)
CC: Elaine Morton   (MORTON)

     Smoking Gun?

Bibliography

"Administration Appeals Judge's Ruling on Files," *Washington Post*, 18 April, 1993, A-30.

Amended Complaint, Armstrong et al. v. Bush et al., United States District Court for the District of Columbia, C.A. No. 89-142 (Feb. 23, 1989).

"Appeals Court Strikes a Blow for Posterity," *San Francisco Chronicle*, 14 August, 1993.

Armstrong et al. v. Bush et al., 924 F.2d 282 (D.C. Cir. 1991).

Armstrong et al v. Executive Office of the President et al., 1 F.3d 1274 (D.C. Cir. 1993).

BABCOCK, CHARLES R. and OBERDORFER, DON, "Computer Detective Found Crucial Data, Intern's High-Tech Sleuthing Led to Files," *Washington Post*, 28 February 1987, A-10.

BARBER, LIONEL, "Secrets of Irangate 'Stored in Computer,'" *Financial Times*, 17 February 1987, 4.

BETTS, MITCH, "Profs system gave clues in probe of Iran scandal," *Computerworld*, 2 March 1987, 2.

BRETSCHER, CARL, "The President and Judicial Review Under the Records Acts," *George Washington Law Review*, vol. 60, June 1992, 1477-1508.

CARNEY, ELIZABETH NEWLIN, "At the Archives, Controversy's Routine," *National Journal*, 13 March 1993, 628-30.

Complaint for Declaratory and Injunctive Relief, Armstrong et al. v. Reagan et al., United States District Court for the District of Columbia, C.A. No. 89-142 (Jan. 19, 1989).

CORNWELL, RUPERT, "U.S. Electronic Mail at Centre of Latest 'Tapes' Controversy," *The Independent*, 29 April 1992, 10.

ELMER-DEWITT, PHILIP, "Can a System Keep a Secret?; The Iranscam revelation raises thorny issues about privacy," *Time*, 6 April 1987, 68.

ELMER-DEWITT, PHILIP, "Who's Reading Your Screen?," *Time*, 18 January 1993, p. 46.

"E-mail for the Ages," *San Francisco Examiner*, 8 April, 1992, A-16.

"Exclusive: Reading Ollie's E-Mail," *New York Magazine*, June 1994, 20-21.

HALL, STEPHEN D., "What Is a Record? Two Approaches to the Freedom of Information Act's Threshold Requirement," *Brigham Young University Law Review*, vol. 1978, no. 2, 408-435.

"History and the 'Save' Button," editorial, *Washington Post*, 21 August 1993, A-20.

HOUSTON, PAUL, "Clash Over White House Tapes Speeds Toward a Court Ruling," *Los Angeles Times*, 20 May 1992, A-5.

KAPLAN, FRED, "Suit Targets White House Messages," *Boston Globe*, 17 July 1989, 1.

KAPLAN, FRED, "Presidential Erasures Must Get OK, Court Says," *Boston Sunday Globe*, 17 September 1989.

LABATON, STEPHEN, "Protecting History, and the Forgettable, on Disks," *New York Times*, 8 January 1993.

LABATON, STEPHEN, "Angry Judge Says Defiant Bush Plans to Purge Iran-Contra Data," *New York Times*, 15 January 1993, A-1, A-18.

LABATON, STEPHEN, "A Judge Issues Contempt Order in Archives Case," *New York Times*, 22 May 1993.

LARDNER, GEORGE, JR., "White House Barred from Destroying NSC Files," *Washington Post*, 20 January 1989.

LARDNER, GEORGE, JR., "U.S. Archivist to Quit, Run Bush Library," *Washington Post*, 13 February 1993, A-5.

LARDNER, GEORGE, JR., "Justice Dept. Weighs Criminal Investigation of U.S. Archivist," *Washington Post*, 24 February 1993, A-17.

LARDNER, GEORGE, JR., "Archivist Was Sounded Out In December on Library Job," *Washington Post*, 3 March 1993, A-2.

LARDNER, GEORGE, JR., "White House, Archivist

Held in Civil Contempt," *Washington Post,*
22 May 1993, A-3.

LARDNER, GEORGE, JR., "Administration Loses
Ruling on Computer Tapes," *Washington Post,*
9 June 1993, A-17.

LARDNER, GEORGE, JR., "Court Orders Computer
Memos Saved," *Washington Post,* 14 August
1993, A-1, A-8.

LEWIS, NEIL A., "Government Told to Save Messages
Sent by Computer," *New York Times,*
14 August 1993, A-1.

LEWIS, PETER H., "Gore Preaches, and Practices,
the Techno-Gospel," *New York Times,* 17 January
1994, D-1.

LOCY, TONI, "Judge Orders Opening of NSC E-Mail
Records; Agency Ruled Subject to Access
Guidelines," *Washington Post,* 15 February 1995,
A-6.

MCGEE, JIM, "Clinton Tries to Limit Access to NSC
Data," *Washington Post,* 26 March 1994, A-7.

MCGOWAN, CARL, "Presidents and Their Papers,"
Minnesota Law Review, vol. 68 (December 1983),
409-37.

MARKOFF, JOHN, "Computers Challenge Freedom
of Information Act," *New York Times,*
18 June 1989.

MEEKS, BROCK N., "Uncovering the Secret History
of the Cold War; The National Security Archive
Beats the White House," *Wired* December 1993,
48-52.

MILLER, MICHAEL W., "Historians Crusade to
Preserve 'E-Mail,'" *Wall Street Journal,*
31 March 1992, B-1.

O'NEIL, JOHN, "Judge Orders Bush's Computer
Records Preserved," *New York Times,*
7 January 1993, A-15.

O'NEIL, JOHN, "Some Bush White House Tapes
Lost, Archivists Say," *The New York Times,*
14 March 1993.

REID, T. R., "'Security Experts' Should Have Read
Up on the White House Computer,"
Washington Post, 2 March 1987, F-21.

REID, T. R., "Erasing the Myth on Deleting Files
Without a Trace," *Washington Post,* 22
July 1991, F-14.

SCHNEIDERMAN, RON, "Avoiding sins of transmis-
sion: Ethics for the corporate network,"
Computerworld, 13 July 1987, S-9.

SHEEHAN, CATHERINE F., "Opening the
Government's Electronic Mail: Public Access
to National Security Council Records,"
Boston College Law Review, vol. XXXV, no. 5,
September 1994, 1145-1201.

TACKETT, MICHAEL, "Computer Log Tells Iran Tale;
Printouts Give Probers Memos by Key Officials,"
Chicago Tribune, 14 February, 1987, 1.

TACKETT, MICHAEL, "Computer Files May Tell
Scandal Story," *Chicago Tribune,* 5
April 1987, 1.

"The Computer That Kept Secrets," *Newsweek,*
23 February 1987, 20.

WALLICH, PAUL, "Is It History or Just E-mail?"
Scientific American, May 1992, 20.

WILSON, DAVID L., "National Archives Issue
Guide-lines for Preserving Electronic Mail,"
Chronicle of Higher Education, 30 March 1994,
A-26.

YANCEY, MATT, "Bush Officials Ordered to Preserve
Copies of Computer Records," *Washington Post,*
16 January 1993.

YORK, MICHAEL, "Court Bars Destruction of Records,"
Washington Post, 7 January 1993, A-1, A-5.

About the Editor
Acknowledgments

ABOUT THE EDITOR:

Tom Blanton is executive director of the National Security Archive and an active participant from the beginning in the White House e-mail lawsuit. He served as the Archive's first director of Planning and Research beginning in 1986, became deputy director in 1989, and executive director in 1992. Previously, he worked as a journalist, foundation staffer, campaign consultant, and Congressional aide. He co-authored *The Chronology* (New York: Warner Books, 1987) on the Iran-contra affair, and served as a contributing editor to three other books: *Litigation Under the Federal Open Government Laws* (Washington, D.C.: American Civil Liberties Union, 1993); *Eyes on the President* (San Francisco: Chronos Publishing, 1992) on George Bush; and *Atomic Audit* (Washington D.C.: Brookings Institution, forthcoming) on the nuclear arms race. His articles have appeared in the *New York Times*, the *Washington Post*, *Los Angeles Times*, the *Wall Street Journal*, the *Boston Globe*, and other publications. He has been elected or appointed to leadership positions in the American Library Association and the American Society of Access Professionals; he has appeared on national broadcasts ranging from ABC News *Nightline* to CNN's *Crossfire*; and he has done freedom of information missionary work in two dozen foreign countries from Japan to Albania. The son of Rev. Leonard C. Blanton and the late Ruth Simpson Blanton, he is a graduate of Bogalusa (La.) High School and Harvard University, where he was an editor of the *Harvard Crimson* and won the Newcomen Prize in Material History for his honors thesis. He lives in Chevy Chase, Maryland, with his wife, Anne Lewis, and their daughter, Katherine.

ABOUT THE NATIONAL SECURITY ARCHIVE:

Founded in 1985 by Scott Armstrong and a group of journalists and scholars, the Archive is an innovative non-governmental research institute and library based at The George Washington University in Washington, D.C. Over the past ten years, the Archive has become the most prolific and successful non-commercial user of the Freedom of Information Act, and has built what the *Christian Science Monitor* calls "the largest collection of contemporary declassified national security information outside of the U.S. government." The Archive has published over 250,000 pages of declassified documents in books, microfiche and CD-ROM formats described by the *Washington Journalism Review* as "a state-of-the-art index to history."

FOR FURTHER INFORMATION, please e-mail the Archive at nsarchiv@gwis2.circ.gwu.edu, or send snail-mail to the National Security Archive, 2130 H Street N.W., Gelman Library Suite 701, Washington D.C. 20037.

ACKNOWLEDGMENTS

First, I want to thank Scott Armstrong, the founder and first director of the National Security Archive (from 1985 to 1989), who also insisted on filing suit when we found out about the planned destruction of the White House e-mail. Without his vision and drive, the Archive would not exist, nor would the White House e-mail. He well deserves the legal immortality he has earned as lead plaintiff in the e-mail lawsuit(s).

As indicated in the introduction, Eddie Becker served as our early warning system about the e-mail, asking the hard questions at the National Archives in January 1989, alerting us to the impending destruction, and sticking with the lawsuit from then to the present. Without Eddie's inquisitiveness and computer sense, the e-mail would be long gone.

We have had the great good fortune to be represented by a series of extraordinary public interest lawyers during the course of the e-mail case. First, I'd like to thank Kate Martin, then at the Center for National Security Studies and now CNSS's director as well as general counsel of the Archive, who pulled an all-nighter with Eddie Becker and me to write the first legal complaint, affidavits, and Freedom of Information Act requests necessary to get into court to save the e-mail.

Throughout the early phase of the case, the Archive's then-general counsel and now board chair, Joseph Onek, provided acute legal advice as well as significant support from his firm. Sheryl Walter, who served as the Archive's counsel from 1989 until going into government service in 1994, played a vital role in the case for five years, coordinating the plaintiffs and adding her considerable legal wisdom to the fray.

With the e-mail saved, the case turned in early 1989 to sudden-death procedural wrangling, unprecedented interpretations of the records laws in the electronic era, and ground-breaking questions of presidential power. To fight the government on these issues, we signed up the best in the business—the Public Citizen Litigation Group, then headed by Alan Morrison. That outstanding advocate—Katherine A. Meyer of PCLG—won the first few rounds of the case, almost all by knockout.

When Kathy went into private practice, Michael Tankersley of PCLG took up the cause, devoting five years of his life and thousands of hours of extraordinary labor to managing a spectacularly successful legal campaign. Michael wrote dozens of briefs, took piles of depositions, made multiple oral arguments in the district and appeals courts, and watchdogged every issue in the case from the loftiest constitutional question to the tiniest technical preservation matter. Michael and subsequently Lucinda Sikes of PCLG did the hard labor involved in our FOIA claim that produced the documents in this book. Their talented colleagues at PCLG—David Vladeck, Patti Goldman, and Alan Morrison—all pitched in wherever needed and to great effect.

In addition to Scott Armstrong and Eddie Becker, the Archive benefited tremendously from the involvement of several other co-plaintiffs in the case. We owe special thanks to the Center for National Security Studies, then headed by Morton Halperin, who gave early and immediate support to the lawsuit; to then-CNSS researcher Gary Stern; to the American Library Association, especially Anne Heanue and Eileen Cook of the Washington office and then-executive director Thomas Galvin; to the American Historical Association, especially Page Putnam Miller of the National Coordinating Committee for the Promotion of History and former AHA president Samuel Gammon; and to former U.S. Senator Gaylord Nelson, the author of the Presidential Records Act. I would like to thank the visionary philanthropists who underwrote the staff time and other costs the Archive incurred in the e-mail lawsuit, particularly Lance Lindblom and the J. Roderick MacArthur Foundation; William Bondurant and the Mary Reynolds Babcock Foundation; Donald Ross and the Rockefeller Family Fund; Deborah Tuck, Robert Stix and the Ruth Mott Fund; Mary Stake Hawker and the Deer Creek Foundation; Martin Teitel and Roxanne Turnage and the C.S. Fund; Margery Tabankin and Barbra Streisand of the Streisand Foundation; Wade Greene and members of the Rockefeller family; Larry Kirkman and the Benton Foundation; and Arthur Gelb and the New York Times Company Foundation.

I owe a special debt to those funders who kept the Archive alive during the course of the e-mail lawsuit by generously underwriting our other projects. In this regard, I thank the John D. and Catherine T. MacArthur Foundation, especially Ruth Adams, Kennette Benedict, and Kimberly Stanton; the Carnegie Corporation of New York, especially

Frederic Mosher, Jane Wales, and David Speedie III; the Ford Foundation, especially Susan Berresford, Gary Sick, Stan Heginbotham, and Nancy Andrews; the Compton Foundation, especially James Compton and Edith Eddy; the Soros Foundations and the Open Society Institute, especially Aryeh Neier and Anthony Richter; the W. Alton Jones Foundation, especially J. P. Myers and George Perkovich; the Arca Foundation, especially Smith Bagley and Janet Shenk; John Tirman and the Winston Foundation; Harriet Barlow and the HKH Foundation; Mary Estrin, Robert and Marcie Musser, and the General Service Foundation; the Japan Foundation; and Akira Saito and The Yomiuri Shimbun.

Throughout the case, the Archive benefited enormously from the insightful advice and technical guidance, provided pro bono, of David Bearman, head of Archives and Museum Informatics in Pittsburgh, as well as from the impressive network of other electronic archiving experts marshaled by David on our behalf.

Inside the Archive, practically the entire staff contributed to the lawsuit and to this book, and deserve my thanks. I particularly want to thank Peter Kornbluh, who provided very helpful editorial suggestions; Malcolm Byrne, who assumed a far-larger-than-fair share of the organization's management duties while I labored on this book; and Sue Bechtel, who provided support and good cheer at every turn. Also, Robin Rone, Pamela Morgan, and John Martinez enthusiastically took on the significant task of creating the index for this book under severe time pressure, and performed superbly. Lisa Thompson and Margarita Studemeister also deserve credit for their work more than a year ago to convert into digital form the White House lists of e-mail potentially subject to our FOIA requests so that we could select the items that make up this book.

My research assistant, Ian Stevenson, deserves my special thanks. Ian performed every book-related task, large and small, with enthusiasm, speed, and tenacity, while simultaneously preparing for and finishing the Boston Marathon.

Many people in the U.S. government contributed (wittingly or unwittingly) to this book; most would, I'm sure, not appreciate being mentioned here. However, I would like to thank the people who declassified the documents herein, including Nancy Menan, Steve Tilley, and David van Tassel. I would also like to thank Steve Branch and Wendy Sparks at the Ronald Reagan Library in Simi Valley,California, for their responsiveness and assistance in finding the photographs included in this book.

At The New Press, I owe a special debt to Diane Wachtell, whose enthusiasm was contagious and whose insights were too. Never shy, Diane shaped this book and disk from the very moment of the first glimmer of a concept, in the middle of a New Press editorial meeting, when I was just making things up. Thanks also to André Schiffrin, who provided his pontifical blessing to the whole project through periodic encyclicals. Thanks also to Jerome Chou, my phone pal, who gets things done; to Edward Mansour for his meticulous copy editing; to Grace Farrell for grace under fire; and to Hall Smyth and Gordon Whiteside for the spectacular design and arduous layout.

Finally, and most of all, I thank Anne Harmon Lewis, my wife. Daily support and encouragement, helpful critiques, wise perspective—all these she provided and more. Authors always use metaphors of gestation and giving birth to describe the book creation process, but there's nothing like seeing the one you love going through the real thing, to impoverish any such figurative claims on sympathy—especially when our daughter Katie beat this book into the stores with a February arrival. Now, finally, I can invoke the immortal words of Ralph Kramden (or was it Ricky Ricardo?): "Honey, I'm home."

Index